Praise for *Redlined*

"In this compelling journey into the depths of racism, Linda Gartz peels back the onion of America's original sin to a new level in a captivating personal story told through the lives of her Chicago family. Gartz probes the invisible web of oppression that affected both whites and blacks. *Redlining* destroyed the American dream without its victims even knowing it."
—BILL KURTIS, author, Peabody and Emmy Award-winner, news anchor for CBS Television network, and TV host for A&E

"Many watched from afar as Chicago and other major cities underwent rapid racial change in mid-twentieth century America. Linda Gartz lived it . . . with her sharp eye, excellent writing, and unique perspective, she brings this critical and turbulent period to life."
—STEVE FIFFER, coauthor of *Jimmie Lee & James: Two Lives, Two Deaths, and the Movement that Changed America*

"Moving and empathetic, Linda Gartz's memoir illuminates the inner worlds of two generations of white working-class Chicagoans . . . who remained in a struggling black community long after their white neighbors had fled—a deeply humane perspective on [how] economic need, racism, and ideals of duty shaped the lives of urban white Americans in the twentieth century."
—BERYL SATTER, Professor, Department of History, Rutgers University, and author of *Family Properties: Race, Real Estate, and the Exploitation of Black Urban America*

"Gartz's unflinching family memoir offers both intimacy and insight into personal and historical injustices. She traces her parents' marriage . . . as they confronted rapid racial change in 1960s Chicago. She deftly interweaves a story of family striving, domestic resentments, and individual decency with the seismic cultural shifts of America's social and sexual revolutions."
—AMANDA I. SELIGMAN, Chair, Department of History, University of Wisconsin-Milwaukee, and author of *Block by Block: Neighborhoods and Public Policy on Chicago's West Side*

"Fearless and precise in her rendering of the intimate truths of her family, rigorous in her analysis of the banking and housing industries, Gartz has written a book that is impossible to put down. . . . An extraordinary achievement."
—SHARON SOLWITZ, author of *Once, in Lourdes*

"In this remarkable memoir, Linda Gartz [takes] her readers on a journey that is neither sentimental nor nostalgic. Committed to finding the truth at every turn, she tracks not only her own experiences but also the social and cultural changes that reshaped twentieth-century America."
—FRED SHAFER, School of Professional Studies,
Northwestern University

"In *Redlined*, Linda Gartz explores . . . family, self-sacrifice, and opportunity, but also inequality, racism, and revolution. Deftly weaving together a treasure trove of detailed firsthand accounts, she provides an absorbing view into the life of a family unwittingly caught up in both its own domestic struggles and the turbulent social reckonings of the 1960s."
—ANJALI SACHDEVA, author of *All the Names They Used for God*

"Linda Gartz mines a wealth of family letters, diaries, memories, and history to tell a vital American story of immigrant dreams . . . self-reliance, and heartache—ultimately intersecting with what has become the essential national topic, the racism that weaves itself through all our personal and shared histories. Beautifully told and a compelling read."
—JIM GRIMSLEY, author of *How I Shed My Skin*

"With tender and open-eyed concern, Linda Gartz adeptly explores how the human need for recognition and equality is waylaid both by doors slammed against legal access and connection and by the tyrannies of power wielded behind closed doors."
—ANNE CALCAGNO, Professor, School of the Art Institute of
Chicago, and author of *Love Like a Dog*

"Deeply personal yet wide in scope, Gartz's writing seamlessly blends her parents' struggles as landlords on Chicago's West Side with the injustices imposed on African Americans by racist housing policies. *Redlined* is a vivid and historic account of rapid racial change in the community Gartz and I have both called home."
—MARY NELSON, founding president of Bethel New Life and
faculty at Asset Based Community Development Institute
at DePaul University (Chicago)

"Intimate and honest, Gartz's memoir exposes the complex motivations that intertwine the lives of a white couple with their black tenants and renders one of the twentieth century's most troubled eras through the lives of those who lived it."
—SHARON DEBARTOLO CARMACK, MFA, CG, author of *You Can
Write Your Family History* and *Tell it Short: A Guide to
Writing Your Family History in Brief*

Redlined

A MEMOIR OF RACE, CHANGE, AND FRACTURED COMMUNITY IN 1960s CHICAGO

LINDA GARTZ

SHE WRITES PRESS

Published April 3, 2018
Printed in the United States of America
Print ISBN: 978-1-63152-320-5
E-ISBN: 978-1-63152-321-2
Library of Congress Control Number: 2017959873

Interior design by Tabitha Lahr

For information, address:
She Writes Press
1563 Solano Ave #546
Berkeley, CA 94707

She Writes Press is a division of SparkPoint Studio, LLC.

This book is dedicated to my parents, Lillian and Fred, without whose commitment to detail and writing, my book wouldn't exist. Their good hearts and striving, optimistic natures kept them going despite life's hard blows. They were an inspiration to their children.

I also dedicate this book to my husband, Bill, the love of my life for more than five decades. Without his constant devotion and support, this book couldn't possibly have been realized. I love you with all my heart.

And to my sons, Evan and Sam—you have filled my life with love and pride.

Foreword

This is a work of nonfiction. Everything in this book is true to the best of my memory or based on diaries, letters, documents, and photos from my family archives. If I write about the inner thoughts of a person, it is because those thoughts are recorded in a diary or a letter. I create scenes based on what I've read and my intimate knowledge of my family members' or friends' traits and gestures. I have researched any historical events that I cite. Some names have been changed to protect peoples' privacy.

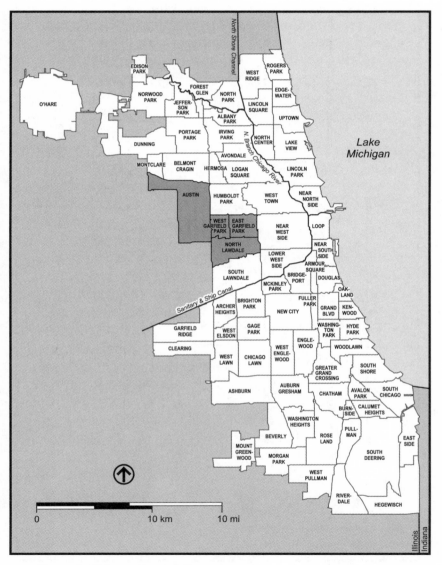

Figure 1: Chicago Community areas
Produced by the University of Wisconsin-Milwaukee, Cartography & GIS Center.

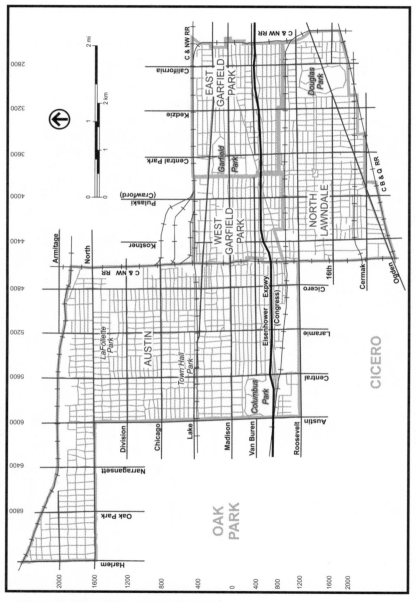

Figure 2: West Side community areas
Produced by the University of Wisconsin-Milwaukee, Cartography & GIS Center.

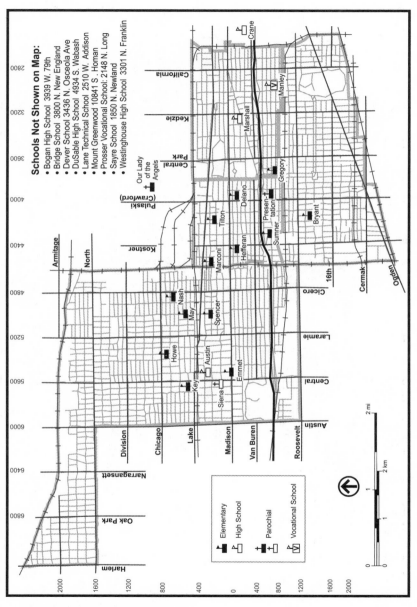

Figure 3: West Side Schools

Produced by the University of Wisconsin-Milwaukee, Cartography & GIS Center.

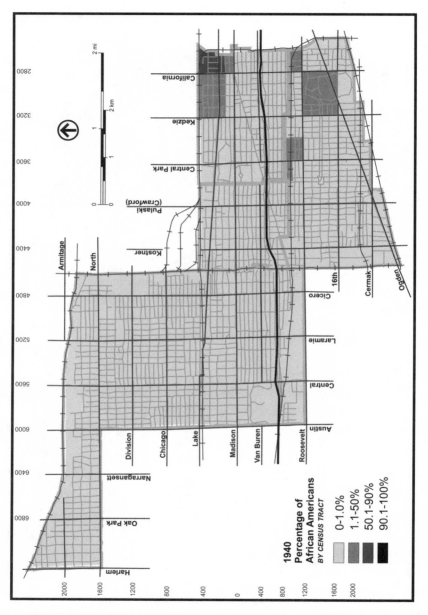

Figure 4a: Racial composition of the West Side, 1940

Produced by the University of Wisconsin-Milwaukee, Cartography & GIS Center.

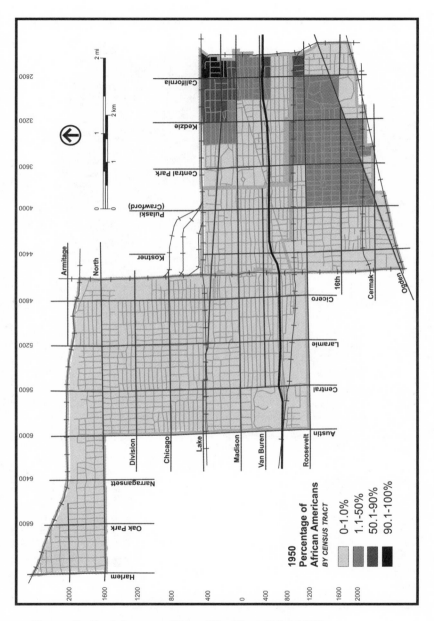

Figure 4b: Racial composition of the West Side, 1950
Produced by the University of Wisconsin-Milwaukee, Cartography & GIS Center.

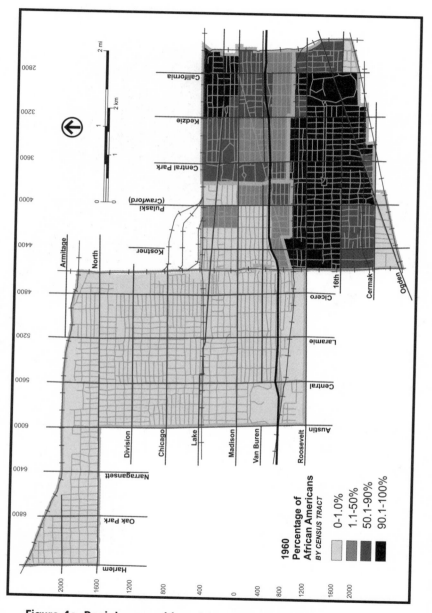

Figure 4c: Racial composition of the West Side, 1960

Produced by the University of Wisconsin-Milwaukee, Cartography & GIS Center.

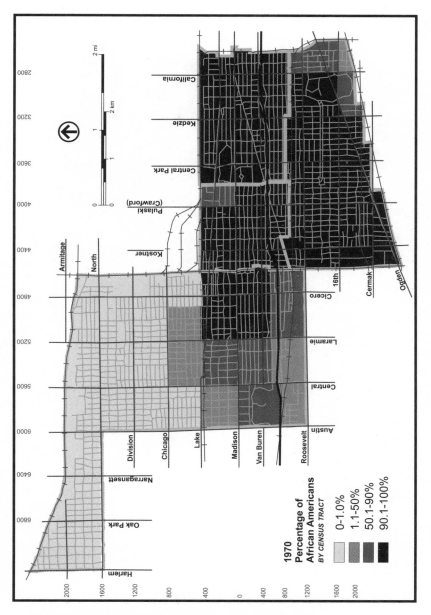

Figure 4d: Racial composition of the West Side, 1970

Produced by the University of Wisconsin-Milwaukee, Cartography & GIS Center.

Contents

PROLOGUE: The Attic

Kaiser Wilhelm II, the ship that brought Lisi Ebner, Dad's mother, to America, September 26, 1911.

On the night of August 14, 1965, my nineteen-year-old brother, Paul, walked toward flames on Chicago's deserted Madison Street. He couldn't reconcile the West Side he'd known since birth with the mayhem unfolding just ahead, where crashing glass and the sucking whoosh of Molotov cocktails played against a smoky red sky. As Paul headed east toward Pulaski Road, a scrum of black men turned a corner and came into view. In moments, they surrounded Paul. One said to him, "What you doin' here, white boy? Don't you know they killin' your kind?"

Nearly thirty years after race riots had wracked our life-long West Garfield Park neighborhood, Mom had died in 1994, just five years after Dad had passed away. Readying our former home for sale, my two brothers and I scoured the house, separating trash from treasure. In the attic, we found our gold.

Standing under naked beams in the dim light, we discovered a large box labeled in my mother's neat printing: "Lil and Fred's Letters and Diaries." I ripped off the packing tape and folded back four cardboard flaps. A misty spray of dust and the odor of old paper wafted up. Peering in, I dug out several small books, the oldest dating to 1927—a diary Mom had started at age ten. Flipping through the pages, I recognized in her youthful handwriting the fledgling swoops and curves of the adult script I knew so well.

Intermixed with Mom's diaries were ten years' worth of Dad's journals. We pulled out bundles of letters, neatly secured with string, each with a label: "Fred's and Lil's Letters, 1949," then "Fred's and Lil's Letters, 1950," and so on throughout Dad's thirteen years of travel. Digging deeper, we found a parchment-wrapped package, bound with pink ribbon tied into a bow, like a present across the decades. On the wrapping, Mom had written: "Greeting Cards Between Fred and Lil, 1942–1949," then another, "1950–1953," and several more multiyear packets. Farther down were Dad's annotated daily calendars from the sixties through the eighties, and Mom's seventeen spiral notebooks, with detailed entries of increasing chaos on the West Side and her rising fury at my father.

We moved on to Grandma Gartz's cedar chest, which had come to be stored in our attic after she and Grandpa had died. It was filled with letters, diaries, documents, and photos spanning the twentieth century. "Listen to this," one of us would call out in astonishment. Then all paused as a line from a letter or journal entry was read. Our ancestors' pack-rat traits, once an object of our head-shaking bemusement, infused our attic labors with amazement and joy. For a solid week we tossed, culled, and pondered what to keep. After filling a Dumpster with the useless and unsentimental, we stored twenty-five bankers' boxes of our treasures in my garage, where their secrets lay silent, like the contents of an ancient, unopened tomb, as I got on with the business of life and family.

For decades, I had puzzled over what had caused the demise of my parents' marriage—Mom's hurtful recriminations against Dad, followed by his wounded retreat, their rift reducing me to tears. And what of the downfall of our community, where Dad's parents had lived for half a century, raised three sons, and bought property, the apogee of the American dream?

At the time of increasing turmoil between my parents, coinciding with the racial upheavals on Chicago's West Side, I had been a teen and a young adult, with no context for the strife in my home or on the streets. But now, a nagging inner voice echoed in my head, luring me like a siren song: *the archives might hold clues, answers.*

I finally gave in, hauled out one box after another, and began reading: my grandfather's 1910 journal of his daring journey from Transylvania to America; diaries from Dad's and Mom's youth, revealing their inner thoughts and passionate courtship; court records and diary entries of my maternal grandmother's psychosis; letters between Dad and Mom during his thirteen years of grueling travel; Mom's diaries of their twenty-year-long effort to maintain quality buildings in a riot-riven landscape and her downward spiral into bitter rage; her vicious attacks on Dad, his parents, and me, a participant in the 1960s sexual revolution.

The archives blazed light onto long-hidden family secrets, but to understand what had happened to our *community*, I needed more, so I devoured everything I could find about racial change in American cities. I learned that our family's fate on Chicago's West Side was entangled with racist mortgage policies and predatory real-estate agents, which together undermined the housing dreams of both blacks and whites.

Within the story of our family's presence on Chicago's West Side throughout most of the twentieth century lies a larger truth that is still playing out today in the segregation that costs Chicagoans billions of dollars each year and grows the homicide rate.[1]

This is also my story—of growing up in a sprawling West Side rooming house filled with wacky tenants and my live-in delusional grandmother; of seeing Mom manage alone while Dad traveled for weeks at a time; of my quest for independence just as America exploded in the social revolutions and racial upheavals of the 1960s and 1970s. But it was my dismay at the unraveling of my parents' marriage that prompted my search for answers in the family archives. These treasures, which had lain in the dark for decades, now illuminated the path that led to domestic collapse, from the ravages that mental illness wreaks upon families to the insidious role parents can play in undermining the marriages of their children.

With the civil rights movement as backdrop and a crumbling marriage in the foreground, this story tries to make sense of the racial transformation of our Chicago West Side community and its impact on our family dynamic, also formed by love, loss, madness, race, rage, and, ultimately, forgiveness.

CHAPTER 1: On the Street
Where We Live

Our street: the 4200 block of Washington Boulevard.

Saturday, June 22, 1963
*Well, the mystery of who bought the Young-Parker
house has been solved. As more or less expected,
the colored moved in today. It somehow gives me a
squeamish feeling to be confronted with the actual
fact of having them on our block. The question is,
what course to follow? How long before no whites
will be renting here anymore?*
—from the diary of Lillian Gartz

For years, the prospect of blacks moving into our West Side Chicago community terrified my parents and our neighbors. They talked about it in the alley, on the sidewalk, after church (in hushed tones), or while stopping for a chat when Mom and I shopped on Madison Street, the West Side's bustling commercial area. I overheard comments like "If the colored come here, the neighborhood will be destroyed" and "Everything we worked for is tied up in our house. If the colored move in, we could lose it all." The adults' conversations made it sound as if they thought an invading force were at the city gates.

We kids picked up on the frightening future should the "colored" come to our area. Each comment we overheard added another boulder to a growing wall of resistance against unknown people. But now that a black family lived just two doors away, the wall had been breached. "What's going to happen?" I asked Dad, who was seated at a card table strewn with notes, writing up reports for his job.

Dad looked up. As usual, he was calm, but his signature smile was absent, his eyes serious. "We can't know yet. Let's just sit tight until we see how they act."

Mom was indecisive, too. She had written further in her diary:

> We have hopes of getting $25,000 if we sell. We should, but will we? The question is, what course to follow? Contemplating renting it out—but what a headache! How long will it be before no whites are renting here anymore?

The new African American family on our block must have been plenty jittery themselves. Although we saw no violence toward them, only four years earlier, thousands of whites, throwing bricks and shouting racial epithets, had converged on the first house sold to blacks in West Garfield Park.

This Saturday night, with our windows open to let in a

breeze, we heard the new kids in their backyard, shooting off popguns at ten thirty. "Why are those kids making all that noise so late at night?" Mom griped, pacing the dining room, poking her head out the back door, unable to concentrate on her bills and financial work. Sure enough, the newcomers were "causing problems."

Mom decided she'd give the neighbors a hint. She let out our two spotted mutts, Buttons and Bows. Bounding into the backyard, the dogs barked at the unusual commotion. Paul yelled across the fences, "Stop annoying the dogs!"

"We ain't botherin' your dogs," a young voice called back.

"Well, it's too late to be making noise. Why don't you go inside?"

The laughter and shouts ceased; the popguns went quiet. A door banged shut. "They went right in," Paul said, holding open the screen door. The dogs leaped into the house in tail-wagging unison.

"They went right in?" Mom asked in disbelief, looking up from the checkbook she was struggling to balance.

"Yeah. I told them that it was too late for noise, and they . . . they just stopped and went inside."

"Oh," said Mom, looking around, as if searching for an answer to this puzzling outcome. "That's a surprise."

"A good sign, too," said Dad, "that they care what their neighbors think."

But local whites stayed on high alert. Our neighbor to the east talked to Mom over the fence about moving. "The colored keep ringing my bell—to see if I'm selling, I suppose," she said, petting her pop-eyed Chihuahua. "I'd just as soon get out before it's too late."

"We're trying to decide what to do, too," said Mom, mopping the sweat trickling down her cheek that hot June day.

Except for a black girl in my class at my local grade school, I didn't know any African Americans—nor did my parents. Prior to the civil rights movement, which had been steadily gaining steam during the spring of 1963, blacks had been virtually invisible in our segregated lives. We saw no blacks on television (except for *Amos 'n' Andy*, which was later decried for its stereotypical portrayal of African Americans). I saw no blacks in magazine or newspaper ads, and no blacks on billboards, unless we drove through a black neighborhood—where I felt as if we'd entered a foreign country.

My childish understanding had been that blacks had their neighborhoods and we had ours, as if it were simply the natural order of the world.

But now a black family lived just two doors away. That "order" was shattered.

CHAPTER 2: Nothing from Nothing Is Nothing

Josef and Lisi Gartz, Dad's parents, wed in
Chicago, October 13, 1911.

West Garfield Park lies five miles due west of downtown Chicago. In 1912, Dad's immigrant father, Josef, had landed his first decent-paying job in this community, at the lunch counter of Joe Nelson's Saloon, serving up free sandwiches with every five-cent schooner of beer. Dad spoke with naked admiration for his parents and their bold decision to strike out from their tiny towns in Transylvania for a country more than five thousand miles distant. Whenever my brothers or I asked Grandpa Gartz why he'd come to America, he answered with the same cryptic remark: "Nothing from nothing is nothing."

Grandpa had seen his widowed mother barely eke out a living, standing in a snow-fed river, beating clothes clean on rocks. He had to leave school after the fourth grade and was eventually apprenticed to become a master carpenter. By age fifteen, he'd seen enough of struggle and poverty. He started saving money for his exodus to the "promised land." Six years later, on Christmas Eve 1910, he boarded a train heading to the Port of Bremen, where he'd catch a ship to America. But he'd been too impatient to wait for the required visa.

At a border stop thirty-five miles outside Vienna, a guard shook Grandpa awake and asked for his papers. A daring scheme entered my grandfather's brain. "One moment, please," he said. "I'll fetch them from my luggage." Instead, he exited the train and climbed the outside ladder to the top of the car, where he lay flat, buffeted for two hours by bitter December winds before the train chugged into Vienna. "I thought I would fly away like a piece of paper," he later wrote to his sweetheart, Lisi Ebner, my future grandmother.

After more close calls with border guards, he arrived in the Port of Bremen, where, on December 31, 1910, he climbed aboard the steamship *Friedrich der Grosse*. I imagine his churning gut and thumping heart, his high elation and jangly hopes, as he made his way to the ship's deck. At age twenty-one, he was embarking on the boldest adventure of his life. From the deck, he gazed down at throngs crowding the dock far below, waving handkerchiefs, bidding farewell to those departing. "They know this is a journey of life and death," he wrote in his diary. "They may never see us again."

On January 11, 1911, his ship docked at New York's Ellis Island. From there he traveled first to Cleveland, Ohio, eventually making his way to Chicago, where he channeled his formidable determination to persuade Lisi Ebner to join him.

They had fallen in love before he'd left. She was a like-minded striver with intelligent, dark eyes and a powerful aspect, her black hair parted down the middle and drawn straight back. In photos from this era, she stands erect and proud, her confident gaze looking to the distance, like a military commander, fully in charge. He had written to her throughout his journey, but he pulled out all the stops in a May 1911 letter:

> *Dearest Love, Precious Sweetheart, Darling Lisi,*
> *If you love me, I hope that you also will come here. . . .*
> *I would greet you with greatest joy and thankfulness,*
> *and take you in my arms. . . . If you don't want*
> *to come, then I also know that you don't love me.*
> *Because if you loved me, you wouldn't do anything*
> *other than come here.*

How could she resist? Lisi left behind her beloved employer of five years and a large, devoted family, arrived in Chicago on October 11, 1911, and married my grandfather two days later. They eventually had three sons: Will, born in 1913; my dad, Fred, in 1914; and Frank, in 1924.

At the time of Dad's birth, in 1914, West Garfield Park was a neighborhood of wooden sidewalks, dirt streets, and butterflies fluttering above open prairies. Just down the street from Joe Nelson's Saloon, near Crawford (now Pulaski) and Madison, Dad admired the Herculean biceps of the local blacksmith as he wielded red-hot horseshoes, beating them with rhythmic clangs. During the 1920s and '30s, hotels, ballrooms, theaters, and the impressive Midwest Athletic Club rose up, increasing the neighborhood's stature and prestige.[2] An L train at Lake Street and Crawford whisked workers to downtown offices. My grandparents' work added to the community's increasing appeal. Shortly after Dad was born, Grandpa began his lifelong career in the janitorial business, at one of the many buildings he and Grandma would care for—pristine, thanks to their flawless upkeep.

Like most new immigrants, Dad's parents put in long hours and saved money, but even in that world, their frugality was obsessive, their work ethic preternatural. Grandpa liked to brag, "When I was young, nobody could work me tired!" Often putting in sixteen- to twenty-hour days, he and Grandma Gartz spent virtually nothing. Their sons wore hand-me-downs from tenants or clothes Grandma made. With his carpentry skills, Grandpa could repair anything, including cast-off furniture he found for their home. They grew vegetables in the summer, canned in the fall, and raised pigeons and rabbits on the back porch for meat. They figured out how to invest in the stock market, then lost $20,000 of savings in the 1929 crash.[3] During the Depression, they started over, saving three-quarters of Grandpa's janitorial salary, eventually buying West Side properties and becoming landlords.

My grandparents' make-do, disciplined lifestyle left an indelible impression on Dad, shaping the future he would one day envision with my mother.

CHAPTER 3: If We Won't Be Happy, Who Will?

Dad and Mom on an early date, fall 1941.

I knew Mom had fallen for Dad early on in their relationship, but I had never known her rarefied emotions, her idealized vision of their future together, until I found her personal diary. Reading her ecstatic entries drew me into her young heart—and the thrill of falling in love.

Mom headed to downtown Chicago on Saturday, May 10, 1941, for a night of dancing at Moose Hall, a castle-like edifice with turrets and thick stone walls at Dearborn and Ontario. In the 1940s, young people flocked to events like this, hoping to meet a partner for the evening—or for life. I can see Mom striding into the brightly lit hall with her signature bouncy step, wearing a fashionable, fitted dress that showed off her fine legs, slim waist, and curvy hips. She surely shone like a beacon: high cheekbones slanting up to lively turquoise eyes; dark, shoulder-length curls framing a creamy-skinned face; red lips so full, they might have seemed pouty if she hadn't radiated so much cheer.

She scanned the room . . . *Could it be? Fred Gartz!* Her heart leaped. She had met him the previous November at another dance. What a grand time they'd had! So why hadn't he ever phoned her for a date? But now—a second chance! He was as good-looking as ever: dark hair, a wave on his crown catching light, taller than she, just enough that she could imagine her head resting on his shoulder. Mom walked right over and greeted him with a megawatt smile.

"Hi, Freddy."

"Lil! Hello. Won't you join us?" He stood up, pulled out a chair, and introduced her to his two brothers and their friends. Within minutes, Mom and Dad were so lost in each other, the dance hall and everyone in it disappeared. Half an hour passed before they heard the music call.

He extended his hand. "Shall we dance?"

"Do you know how to rumba?" she asked, with flirty eyes and smile.

"No, but I'm sure you can teach me."

By the end of the evening, Mom knew she'd found her man. She wrote:

There's no doubt about it; I'm in love with him. He's really the first man I've met that I think I'd like to marry—intelligent, crazy, fun, and we have no end of things to talk about.

Less than two weeks later, Mom wrote:

Tuesday, May 20, 1941, 11:00 p.m.
Quite a thrill awaited me when I came home tonite.
Fred sent me a card from Turkey Run [a state park in
Indiana] reading, "Have substituted hiking and horsing
for the rumba for the time being. This place is grand.
Now, auf wiedersehen." I felt so elated and happy. I
must be in love with the guy & I haven't even gone out
with him. I now have a glimmer of hope he'll phone.

For whatever unexplained reason (insecurity? fear of
rejection?), Dad waited until August 14 to call Mom for a
date, set for the next evening. She wrote, "Finally—I heard
from Fred Gartz. . . . I hope and pray this will lead to more
and frequent dates!"

They started with a German movie, then a stroll through
nearby Lincoln Park Zoo. Caressed by the warm summer
breeze, they walked arm in arm, laughing and exchanging
stories. After a couple mugs of frosty beer at nearby Sieben's
Brewery, they returned to the park. When she got home,
Mom surely tore open her diary:

I think we both knew why we went back [to the
park]. We sat on a bench hearing the lions roar and
quacking of a duck. Oh, it was heavenly! He knows
all the little innuendoes of kissing, and I ain't so bad
m'self, if I do say so. We kissed for about an hour
and a half. Tonight was like a page from a storybook,
and he definitely is the man I want to marry. Dear
God, please let it come true!!

Mom's words opened a door into her twenty-three-year-
old heart, and I peered in, watching my parents' blossoming
love unfold and expand like a pop-up card. I was eager for more,
knowing how lucky I was to meet them as they once were.

The rest of their summer and fall swirled by, Mom recording each date with certainties of her love. They swam at North Avenue Beach, sang German and popular songs to Mom's backup on the piano, crunched through gold and red autumn leaves during a walk or a horseback ride in local forest preserves. At the end of a Lake Michigan pier, they grasped each other's hands, extended their arms, and spun in circles as the wind tangled Mom's hair and waves crashed against the pilings. Dad shouted above nature's din, "It's great to be alive!" and Mom said she couldn't agree more.

1941–42

December 7, 1941: The Japanese bombed Pearl Harbor, plunging America into World War II. But Mom had love, not war, on her mind that holiday season. On New Year's Day, she and Dad went to a then-famous Chicago restaurant, Math Igler's, nicknamed Home of the Singing Waiters. The male servers dressed in lederhosen, suspenders, and green felt hats, each with a jaunty feather spearing from the band; the women wore dirndls, Bavarian folk dresses. After belting out old favorites to the accompaniment of a German band, they returned to waiting tables while music played.

In between bites of food, Mom and Dad danced the night away. As the evening drew to a close, an elderly couple approached them. "Excuse me," the woman said, smiling at my parents. "We always watch the young couples when we go out and pick one that we'd like to be if we were young again. Tonight, we wish we could be the two of you."

Mom told us kids this story often over the years. I always loved hearing it, loved seeing Mom's eyes sparkle, the sweet pride playing across her smile as she shared how their joy radiated, like a star shooting light to all within its orbit.

In the spring of 1942, Dad was hired as a blasting powder blender at the Kingsbury Ordnance Plant, a production factory for war munitions in LaPorte, Indiana. Crafting powders for bullets and bombs was dangerous work, but the job nearly doubled his salary, and he could still date Mom by driving back to Chicago most weekends.

Two months after he started, his personal world blew up. He often spoke about this watershed trial in his life. But when I came upon the letter he'd written to his parents at the time, Dad's own words sharpened his ordeal into focus and drew me into his anguish.

He was testing and mixing some concoction when his boss summoned him. "I have a very painful duty to do, Gartz, but I'll have to let you go."

"What? Why?" Dad was blindsided.

"I don't know. Talk to Personnel."

In Personnel, Dad was shuffled from one man to another, each claiming to know nothing, lying, or making sly comments like, "You know why." Caught in a Kafkaesque nightmare of subterfuge and deceit, he couldn't eat or sleep. "I'm staying here to stand up for the family honor," he wrote his mother.

Non-confrontational by nature, and after a lifetime of skirting conflict with his overbearing mother, Dad had mustered all his courage to stand up to power. After more than a week of runarounds, he finally scored a meeting with the personnel director. For more than an hour, the man interrogated Dad, demanding a complete family history, questioning Dad's loyalty to America, and threatening the entire Gartz family with an FBI investigation. He then moved on to more pointed questions.

"Why do you cross your sevens? And why do you write the letter *F* like a German?" The veil was lifting. "You speak with a strong German accent. Why?"

"A strong German accent? I was born in Chicago! I'm as American as you!" Astonished, Dad realized that under the duress of the accusations he had spoken slowly and deliberately, giving the impression he was struggling with the language. In fact, Dad's parents were ethnic Germans from what is today Romania.

The personnel director was satisfied, but wartime xenophobia trumped logic. The plant refused to reinstate Dad, who returned to Chicago. Within a week after his return, Mom recorded what happened.

> *Fred told me at 2:30 a.m. Sunday, 5-17, really that he loves me. . . . One split second before he did so, I murmured, "Je t'aime," which of course he did not understand. Ever since then we have been happier than ever before in our lives. Fred tells me the nicest things—that he loves me more all the time, that I get sweeter as time goes on, that he's never loved anyone like he has loved me, that he has wanted many things badly in his life, but never anything half so much as he wants me.*
>
> *We have never had an argument since our first date, 8-15-41. So if we won't be happily married, who will?*

In July they lay under a spangled night sky, the music from downtown Grant Park's outdoor concert stirring the warm summer air—and their hearts. Dad gave Mom his Alpha Lambda Xi fraternity pin, telling her that, like the symbol on the pin, she was his guiding star. She in turn gave him her Waller High School ring. When Mom returned home, she wrote: "Tonight might be called the night of his proposal, for he called me 'Mrs. Gartz' and said how good that sounded."

The "Mrs. Gartz" comment was all Mom needed to hear, and she knew. Mom leaped into making wedding plans, and Dad went right along. Fear of rejection had been embedded in his childhood, so he had couched his proposal in an oblique allusion.

———

That summer of 1942, while Mom was writing about her days of bliss, she began a separate handwritten record in a small spiral notebook labeled "Case History." It was as if she didn't want to taint her diary's joyous expressions of love with another, darker reality.

Her mother, my grandma Koroschetz, was losing her mind.

CHAPTER 4: Madness and Marriage

Lil, Mom, and her "Mama," Grandma
Koroschetz, 1922.

1942

Mom began recording her mother's bizarre behavior on August 15, 1942, two months before she and Dad were to be married. In June of that year, my grandma Koroschetz had peered out the kitchen window of their Near North Chicago apartment on a blustery day, demanding, "Who's making those doves fly around out there?"

Mom looked through the glass, caught in her own swirl of confusion. "Mama, that's just the wind blowing some scraps of paper."

"No! Someone's made those doves come here just to

aggravate me!" Grandma K shouted. It was the beginning of a downward slide. Always quick to anger, Grandma K was now not just bad-tempered but also paranoid and delusional.

Mom arranged a vacation that August with her parents at Lake Como, a resort in southern Wisconsin, hoping the country air and peaceful surroundings would soothe her mother's nerves and give her seventy-one-year-old dad a break. When they opened the door to their rustic cottage, a strong smell of gas assaulted them. "They're trying to kill me!" Grandma screamed, backing out, her eyes wild.

"It's okay, Mama," my mother said, running into the darkened room, straightening a burner knob left askew. "Someone just forgot to turn the stove all the way off."

Throughout the trip, Grandma K either remained locked in a morose silence or went on the attack. If Mom or her father attempted conversation, Grandma shook with a fierce anger and yelled, "Keep your big mouth shut!" or, "You'd be better off with plaster in your mouth!" When Mom was silent, her mother accused her of "hiding something."

"She told Papa to get out of her sight," Mom wrote. "She said to me, 'You do nothing but make trouble!'"

Page after page, Mom documented her mother's paranoid thoughts and behavior, but one scene captures it best.

At two in the morning, the darkness blazed to light in their cottage. Grandma ripped off the covers from her sleeping husband and glared down at him, screeching, in her drawn-out Austrian accent, "You cr-r-r-rook, you!" He lay blinking and astonished.

"You've hidden my pills in your bed!" she screamed, eyes blazing. "Get up! Get up! I want them. You're both cr-r-r-rooks!" Mom and her father finally were able to calm her, but Mom's dread and confusion wouldn't let her sleep.

After fourteen days of living with Grandma K's frenzied accusations, Mom broke down. Wracked with sobs, she choked out to her mother, "You have made these the most miserable two weeks of my life."

1927–37

Mom was bound to her mother by a paradox: "My mother was so good to me," she told us kids, but just as often remarked, "I was afraid of my mother." It wasn't until I came upon Mom's youthful diaries, which she began at the age of ten, in 1927, that I came to understand the provenance of her loyalty—and fear.

Grandma K *was* good to her daughter. A graduate of a prestigious Viennese dressmaking school, Grandma often worked an entire weekend to create a gloriously detailed blouse or layered skirt for Lillian, her only child. Mom was the only girl in the neighborhood who had matching outfits for herself and her dolls. For birthdays, Christmas, and graduation, Mom's parents showered Mom with the most beautiful gifts they could afford. She was the center of their world. At times my mother wrote, "I sure do love her."

But Mom's diary entries also reveal swift and harsh punishments. Grandma K smacked Mom in the face, hit her on the head, or gave her a "good licking" for "not following the rules" or "being fresh." Mom accepted consequences that logically followed disobedience, but Grandma K's irrational anger gave my mother every reason to be "afraid of Mama."

Any minor misstep—placing cream precariously in the icebox, mixing Thanksgiving stuffing in the "wrong" way, smiling in a manner her mother didn't like—triggered Grandma into a full-blown rage, raining blows on Mom and calling her "ass," "animal," "streetwalker," and "whore."

Over the years, Mom wrote with deepening frustration about Grandma K's explosions—like the time Mom mistakenly tossed out a scrap of fabric she found on the floor, intended as a pocket for a suit Grandma was making. Mom apologized and confessed her error.

Grandma K raced at Mom, screaming, "You ungrateful wretch! You lazy hussy! Now that I've finished *your* suit, you don't give two cents for how much I have to work!" Eyes alight with fury, she yanked Mom's hair and smacked her about the head, hurling insults and blows. "Selfish ingrate! Careless, useless girl!" Mom vainly tried holding back tears.

"She reminds me of the sea," Mom wrote afterward. "First she's calm, and suddenly, without warning, she's so wrathful and furious you hardly believe she's the same person."

Over the years, Mom's parents had tried multiple ways to earn a living, modeling a striving work ethic and frugality. They saved their money and bought a two-flat. Grandma K started a dressmaking business; Grandpa K founded a small machine shop, skipping dinner and working late into the night. They even opened a delicatessen, but each entrepreneurial venture failed. Still, Grandma's occasional seamstress work, their rental income, and the salary Grandpa earned as a talented tool and die maker gave them a decent life.

Then the stock market collapsed in October 1929, plunging America into the Great Depression, devastating my grandparents' income. The Depression hit manufacturing and machinists, like my grandfather, the hardest. Chicago lost 50 percent of its manufacturing jobs between 1929 and 1933. My grandpa K was one of half a million people in the city without work.

In the spring of 1932, when Grandpa K was already sixty-one years old, my fifteen-year-old mom wrote, "The Depression is getting worse. Papa has had no work since before Christmas." Hoping to garner some extra income, her parents divided their flat in two, planning to rent out the back bedroom, kitchen, and bathroom, hot water included, but renters were rare.

By April the family's finances were so desperate, they had to apply for food assistance. "Nothing fresh," Mom wrote with dismay at the contents. "Rotten coffee, dried prunes, raisins, canned peaches, beans, split peas, etc. Five cans of tomatoes." Later that summer, Grandpa K found temporary machinist work, making about forty-five cents an hour[4] the few times he was called in.

One of those calls ended in calamity. On January 19, 1934, a punch press crushed two of Grandpa's fingers. Mom's knees buckled. Her face turned white. "Papa lost two fingers when he was twenty-two, and now these two. Goodbye, guitar."

At the time of the accident, Mom was entering her senior year in high school. Her father couldn't work, rental income was hard to come by, and the bank began harassing the family for missed mortgage payments. "Why don't you pull your daughter out of school and send her to work?" one bank representative suggested.

"Oh, no!" Mom's parents were united. "Our daughter has to finish high school."

Mom graduated from Waller High School in January 1935 at age seventeen, the highest-achieving girl in her class. After a dogged search for a job, she landed a typist position at Sears Roebuck, earning a raise after just a few months for her "excellent work." She became the family breadwinner, giving 75 percent of her wages to her parents.

It wasn't enough.

Foreclosure and eviction notices began arriving at my grandparents' house, but Grandma K declared, "These aren't for us," and scrawled, "Return to Sender" on every one—because the family last name had been misspelled.

Arriving home from work on March 3, 1937, Mom came upon a devastating scene. Her mother sat on a chair in front of their house, head buried in her hands, Grandpa K's arm around her shoulders. Tables, chairs, lamps, dishes, clothes—everything they owned—lay piled on the sidewalk, as neighbors gawked and whispered.

Mom surely was overcome with guilt and despair. "My parents were so good to me" was true, but Mom's fear of Grandma K would prove to be as potent as her love.

CHAPTER 5: Resistance and Devotion

Gartz Family: Lisi, Josef, Frank "Ebner," Will, and Fred (Dad), 1926.

D ad's family fared far better than Mom's during the Depression, despite the loss of all their savings in the 1929 crash. Dispirited, but possessed with entrenched optimism, resilience, and hope, Dad's parents committed to starting over with more determination than ever. The janitor for up to sixty-five apartment units in West Garfield Park, Grandpa Gartz worked around the clock. Grandma helped manage the tenants, kept track of their finances, and did all the "women's" work. With a free apartment thrown in, my grandparents saved an astounding three-quarters of Grandpa's $200-per-month salary.

West Garfield Park was just coming into its own when Dad was born in 1914, a year after his older brother, Will. Forced to share attention at the tender age of twelve months, Will preserved his status through obsessive obedience. Dad, sensitive and whimsical, quickly learned he could never be as rule-bound as his older brother, so he carved out his own niche in the family by doing whatever came into his head. It was an approach that didn't sit well with a young immigrant mother determined to raise "good boys." Grandma Gartz, reared with nineteenth-century, small-town, Germanic values, punished both her boys physically for "bad behavior." More prone to boyish shenanigans, Dad endured the pain and humiliation more often. When they misbehaved, Grandma G whacked their bare bottoms with a heavy, wet clothesline or made them kneel on hard peas. Will got into line pretty quickly, but Dad resisted however he could.

Early in my childhood, Dad shared with me the rancor he felt toward his mother: how she took the side of the tenant children over his; how she slapped his face—back and forth, back and forth—when he tried to explain his side of an altercation; how, when he was five years old, she threatened to kill him with a two-by-four—after she found out he and a neighbor girl had played the age-old game "I'll show you mine if you show me yours." Teeth clacking in fear, he admitted his moral turpitude and took his whipping.

The stories of his mother's harsh punishments tormented my young heart. I sobbed myself to sleep, thinking of the injustices he suffered, wishing *I* could be his mother. *I'd* be fair—and treat him with kindness! But Dad figured out the means to get around his mom's demand for control.

When she made him wear a dress to keep him grounded, he defiantly wore it outside to play baseball with the guys, figuring fun was worth a few jeers. I was captivated by his gleeful recollection at outwitting his mother. He would forever figure out how to maneuver around whoever tried to deny him happiness. He'd make his own fun.

Dad mightily resisted his mother's attempts to control him, but he could never, not in his lifetime, escape her scorn. He couldn't free himself from her disdain at his ideas and interests, the way she would grab a cherished possession from his hands. A magic "glue" that made smoke rise from pinched fingers? "Foolishness!" she declared, and threw it into the blazing furnace. He protected his treasures by climbing to the top of the church belfry and hiding them in a dark corner.

She succeeded only in driving his behavior underground, in fostering a fear of rejection and the thrill of "getting away" with something.

In my parents' attic, when I dug through the box labeled "Fred and Lil's Journals," I came upon two of Dad's diaries from his youth. One started in 1933, when Dad was eighteen; the second continued through most of 1935. He made almost daily entries.

Standing in the dim light, I fingered the embossed green cover of the first, gingerly turned yellowing but still-sturdy pages, and touched the words. Dad's voice and personality emerged—like a ghost rising from its crypt, as if his spirit hovered beside me, whispering secrets no one else had ever heard.

His youthful life unspooled off the pages like an old film, whisking me back to his everyday world, where I saw familiar traits manifested in his younger self: a poetic soul, a love of science and nature, a fascination with guns, a simultaneous pursuit of fun and devotion to work that tapped his boundless energy—and always, an abiding secrecy.

Fearful that his parents might find his diaries, Dad devised a simple code.[5] With a little analysis, I deciphered it, though it would have been incomprehensible to his time-pressed, foreign-born parents. Entries like kissing girls, making off with some high-school chemistry equipment, or quarrels with Grandma and Grandpa Gartz were encoded.

Despite his mother's harsh treatment, the family was close. My grandparents set aside Sundays to spend time together with their boys, whether by enjoying the simple pleasure of chatting on a bumpy streetcar ride, lounging at the beach, or savoring a picnic in nearby Garfield Park. Dad admired his parents' grit, ambition, unrelenting work ethic, and determination to send their sons to college. Dad and Will pitched in with work, helping the family survive the Depression.

After school and all day on Saturdays, Dad threw himself into chores until suppertime, squeezing in homework afterward. At various times, he cleaned the house, washed down the pantry, or scrubbed floors. He showed vacant apartments to potential renters, dusted hallways, cooked dinner, painted, sorted and repaired screens. He ran errands; washed dishes, laundry, and windows; chopped wood; and paid his father's janitor union dues.

In the winter, he rolled wheelbarrows of coal, shoveled it into voracious furnaces, removed the unburned "clinkers," and disposed of ashes. He and Will helped his dad shovel snow from the front and back porches of multiunit apartment buildings and their surrounding sidewalks, sometimes until two in the morning, then started up again four hours later. On Saturdays, Dad worked all day on chores, from nine to five.

But no matter how exhausting his schedule of school and household duties was, Dad never missed a chance for fun. The center of his social life was Bethel Evangelical Lutheran Church, where his best friends in the active youth group rode horseback in the summer, jostled and found romance on hayrides in the fall and sleigh rides in the winter. He practiced weekly with the choir, sang at Sunday morning services, and performed in operettas held across the street in Tilton Elementary School's auditorium. Movies, sledding, Ping-Pong, basketball, fencing, swimming, biking, baseball, reading, parties—he did it all.

He had a romantic love interest at Bethel, but he hadn't met anyone he wanted to marry—until he fell in love with Mom.

1942

After the Lake Como trip with her parents, Mom wrote little about her mother. She was juggling her demanding job as executive secretary to the president of the Bayer Company and pulling together every detail of her wedding. She commissioned a creamy satin wedding dress for herself and three bridesmaid outfits made from fuchsia and plum velveteen, the skirts overlaid with net. Typical of Mom's life philosophy, they combined beauty and practicality. The festive net was removable so that the skirt could also be suitable for daytime wear.

She decided on a bride's bouquet of fat white mums, chose the reception hall, ordered dinner for thirty and a jukebox for music, and typed up a ten-page, minute-by-minute script to direct every participant in the ceremony. But Mom had no mother with whom to share her joy. The morose and erratic behavior she had recorded during the Lake Como trip continued into the fall. Whenever Mom tried to share her excitement about the wedding plans, Grandma K waved her away. "Why do I want to hear about that?"

Dad and Mom wed, November 8, 1942.

Grandma hadn't expressed any dislike for my dad, but was it mere coincidence that her irascible and combative personality transformed into insanity just as Mom was about to be married? Or did the loss of her treasured child to marriage trigger such a transformation in her fragile mind?

On November 8, 1942, Grandpa K walked his daughter, glowing in her shimmery bridal gown, down the aisle of Bethel Church and gave her hand to my dad. Standing at the altar, bathed in the golden November light streaming through Bethel's soaring stained-glass windows, they made their vows, then exited down the church steps, ducking under a hail of flying rice. In the photos, they radiate hope and happiness, posing arm in arm on the church steps. Even Grandma K is smiling, perhaps caught up in the spirit of the many well-wishers.

After what both agreed was a perfect reception at the Central Plaza Hotel at Central and Lake Streets, my parents drove to the small basement apartment they had rented two blocks east of the church for their first night together. Lifting Mom into his arms, Dad looked down into her smiling, eager face and carried her across the threshold to begin what they were certain would be an ideal life together.

CHAPTER 6: Death

Mom and her "Papa," 1937.

WWII Army Air Corps navigator 1st Lt. Frank Ebner Gartz, 1944.

1943–45

Among the treasures found in my parents' attic was my grandma Gartz's cedar chest, moved from my grandparents' house to ours after my grandparents died. In the chest, Dad's mother had saved passports, postcards, love letters between her and Grandpa, scribbled notes, and letters from Romania. But my most exciting find was a plastic bag stuffed with nearly three hundred letters written to and from my dad's kid brother, Frank Ebner Gartz, during his World War II service from 1943 to 1945. An electric rush prickled my skin. For the first time, I'd meet not only my uncle as a young man but also my parents as newlyweds and my grandparents in their regular, work-a-day world, and I'd see firsthand Chicago's West Side home front during the war.

Two months after my parents' wedding, eighteen-year-old Ebner (everyone in the family called him by his middle name, pronounced "ABE-ner") reported to the local military draft board on January 23, 1943, and shipped out that same day for basic training. The letters between him and his family and friends flew back and forth as he crisscrossed the country for two years, training for the Army Air Corps. By the spring of 1944, he had passed the grueling exams to graduate as a navigator for the B-17 heavy bomber.

While Dad's family fretted over Ebner's safety, Mom and her mother faced the imminent death of Grandpa K from throat cancer. A lifetime smoker, he had inhaled each unfiltered Camel until it burned his fingertips, then inserted a toothpick into the glowing nub to suck out the last puffs of nicotine.

By the summer of 1943, Grandpa had wasted away to a skin-wrapped skeleton, nursed at home through his final days by Grandma K. Her losses had been steadily mounting: their home, foreclosed in the Depression; her only child, married and moved out; and now her husband, terminally ill.

Grandpa K died on September 17, 1943, plunging my bereft grandmother again into a black hole of delusions, each loss sinking her deeper into a dark place. She claimed Mom had killed her beloved "Papa" by giving him poisoned Coke. Despite this absurd accusation, Mom invited Grandma K to move in with her and Dad—a mere ten months after their wedding. Dad went along, undoubtedly to assuage Mom's anxiety over her despondent mother, who now slept on the couch a few feet outside the newlyweds' bedroom in their cramped three-room apartment. I'm sure he thought it would be a short-lived arrangement.

He was wrong.

Eight months passed before Grandma K rented her own place, about seven miles away. Even then, she often stayed overnight, bedding down on their flowered sofa. My parents' lives became entangled in Grandma K's precarious mental state, as they simultaneously worried about Ebner's destiny in flak-ripped skies.

Ebner was assigned to the Second Bomb Group in Italy, where he flew twenty bombing missions from January through May 8, 1945, when the war in Europe ended. But he didn't return to Chicago. At twenty-one, he had landed a coveted job, navigating to destinations surrounding the Mediterranean and transporting VIPs—generals and congressmen—who were arriving to rebuild Europe.

Throughout his service, his most faithful correspondent had been his mother. I was dumbfounded by what I read. Instead of the cold, judgmental woman I knew and Dad had described, Grandma Gartz emerged as a loving, devoted, and worried mom. In her prayer-filled letters, she exhorted Ebner to care for his health, inquired into his studies, and often wrote about his at-home girlfriend, Cookie, whom Grandma cherished: "I like nothing better than you and Cookie spend the life together," she wrote in her broken English.

But Dad's mom held no fondness for my mother. In one of Grandma's letters, written just months after my parents married, I discovered her blatant animus toward Mom: "Your Cookie is 1,000 times Lil. Lil is only for herself." For the first time, I learned that Grandma Gartz had disliked Mom from the get-go. Her antipathy would taint our family life for decades to come.

On October 17, ten days after it had been written, a letter arrived from Italy that stopped my grandmother's heart. Her beloved youngest son was "seriously ill . . . with infantile paralysis [polio infecting the spinal cord]."

In a panic, every family member sent out a flurry of encouraging words to Ebner. A few weeks later, all their letters were returned with a bold *DECEASED* stamped in red across each envelope. Ebner had been dead for five days before the family even knew he was sick. A letter of condolence from Ebner's commanding major confirmed Ebner had died at 10:15 p.m. on October 12, 1945.

Grandma G had lost not only her son but also the treasured girl she was certain he would marry, stuck instead with my "only-for-herself" mom as her daughter-in-law.

Ebner had been Dad's best friend. Kind, sweet, funny, and adored by all, Ebner was the one son who could have brought together all the family's disparate personalities. Like a stone to everyone's hearts, the ripples of his death eroded the shoreline of our lives, deepening Grandma G's ill will toward my mother and disdain toward my father.

For the two grandmas, one mourning a son, the other a husband, grief was a rope, entangling the entire family, strangling and choking off love. As Ebner lay dying in an iron lung thousands of miles away, my parents conceived a baby, which Ebner had written he longed for.

CHAPTER 7: Shock

Fred and Lil with Grandma K in my
parents' Keeler Avenue apartment.

1946

Half a year after learning of Ebner's death, and six months
pregnant, Mom was feted by forty-six coworkers and friends
at her farewell party in April of 1946. For nine years, she
had devoted her formidable organizational skills and driven
work ethic to serve as executive secretary to the president of
the Bayer Company. With Mom's departure, her boss had to
hire two women to do the work she had done singlehandedly,
a fact which Mom spoke of proudly, but which I see as sad
and prescient. She would forever do more than was expected,
gaining no recompense in return.

At the end of my mother's last day at the Bayer Company, Mom and Dad returned to their apartment to find Grandma K sitting silent and morose on their flowered sofa. "I'm very tired," was all she said.

"What's the trouble?" Mom asked.

"I walked all the way from my house to downtown." It was a distance of eight miles.

"Why on earth would you take such a long walk?"

"Somebody told me to."

Two months later, frantic about her mother's increasingly unstable behavior, Mom typed up a twenty-five-page report for the psychiatrist entitled, "Case History of Mrs. Louise Koroschetz, April 13, 1946 to June 18, 1946." Until I dug through the archives, I had never seen this report and had heard only snippets of Grandma K's bizarre behavior from this time. Mom had told me only, "I cried buckets of tears over my mother."

Just as a playwright presents characters on a play's opening page, Mom listed the various people mentioned in the case history, followed by the role of each in the unfolding saga. Her words reveal a troubling drama, featuring a woman with an unraveling mind—in an era when treatment for mental illness was mired in the Dark Ages.

Mom's meticulous records drew me into her anguished helplessness with each of Grandma K's heart-stopping delusions, exposing my grandmother's fractured sense of reality, as if she viewed life through a broken mirror. Mom entered scores of examples in vivid detail. A sampling: Grandma believed people spied on her, that the landlord purposely didn't repair a banging pipe in the bathroom so he could track when she was home, that the tenants one floor down burgled her apartment. She locked up her radio in a cabinet, fearing that Peeping Toms used it as a magical device to leer at her as she undressed. Dead Grandpa K spoke to her. With delight, she told my parents about an amusing speech she had made to the president, who had laughed good-naturedly.

Leaning over her back-porch railing, Grandma K screeched at the women in the apartment below: "Why are you running a whorehouse here? You're all WHORES!" She spoke in absurd riddles, about double-talk and signs and motions people made. Mom wrote:

> When she gets into one of these spells, her eyes get a rather wild look, and she will start raising her voice louder and louder, and then she pounds her fist on the table to emphasize a statement: "I'm an American! The red, white, and blue must fly all over the world!"

The case history left me breathless with the impact of Grandma's mental illness on both my parents. In the last few months of Mom's pregnancy, they had no time or peace to relish the upcoming arrival of their first child, no privacy— only unending strife, worry, and aggravation. Dad was still grieving for his brother but had to draw upon his emotional reserves to support Mom.

⎯⎯⎯⎯

"Lee-lee-an! Lee-lee-an!" My grandmother stood on the front steps of her apartment building late one June night, crying out my mother's name in a drawn-out Austrian accent as the summer breeze nibbled at her nightgown. Her landlady called my parents. Groggy and frightened, they drove the seven miles to pick up Grandma K.

When they arrived, they found her sitting on the front steps still in her nightclothes and slippers, clutching her purse, her eyes unfocused and bewildered. "Mama, come home with us," said Mom gently, helping her shaky mother to stand, leading her to the car.

On the ride back to my parents' place, Grandma held her purse close to her mouth, mumbling, "False alarm! False alarm!"

"What are you doing, Mama?"

"This is a microphone. I can hear better what they're saying to me."

Over the next two days, my mother created the case history with its twenty-five pages of Grandma's irrational behaviors. After reading through Mom's document and meeting Grandma K on June 19, the psychiatrist prescribed electro-convulsive therapy (ECT), also known as shock treatment.

ECT was a recent breakthrough in treating psychoses and mood disorders in the 1940s. It was used for the first time on a human subject in Italy on April 15, 1938, and seemed to cure the patient of his hallucinations. Enthusiastically embraced in the United States, shock treatment was to be administered to my grandmother, just six years after its introduction into this country.

Following Grandma's ECT treatments, Mom was distraught with what she saw. Grandma K didn't speak a word, and she had no memory—not of her recent meals, nor any of Mom's previous visits. The psychiatrist brushed aside my mother's fear. "She's nicely confused," he said.

Over the next two weeks, Grandma's disorientation slowly dissipated until, by July 14, she was discharged from the hospital. "She seemed very normal," Mom wrote. "We took her to Lincoln Park on a picnic. The psychiatrist performed a miracle on Mama, and we can really feel grateful."

I sensed Mom's desperate and futile hope in those words. It was an era when few effective treatments existed for mental illness, when the very diagnosis was shameful and misunderstood. Families grasped at any straw that might hold them steady in the storms of insanity, so Mom eagerly believed this respite from her mother's outbursts meant she was cured.

The only real miracle in their lives occurred just three days after Grandma K returned to my parents' apartment.

On July 17, Mom gave birth to Paul Ebner Gartz, his middle name in honor of Dad's dead brother.

Grandma Gartz's response to the usually joyous news of a first grandchild was grim: "Don't have children. They'll only be used as cannon fodder."

CHAPTER 8: The Best-Laid Plans

Mom with baby Paul, summer 1946.

1946–49

My parents' three-room flat was now tighter than ever, with Grandma K often sleeping overnight and the baby's crib squeezed in. Mom didn't write much the following few years, but photos show me that Grandma K was a constant presence in their lives—even on vacations. In one 1947 picture, she's lying on a cot, reading the newspaper, outside two tents, camping with the young family in Wisconsin. Although Grandma K was capable of fending for herself, even working as a seamstress at a downtown women's clothing store, my parents had virtually no family time without her.

An exception was a June 1948 driving trip to America's

West, which Mom, Dad, and two-year-old Paul took with Dad's parents and brother, Will. Grandma K rented her own place, but Mom invited her to stay in her and Dad's more pleasant apartment while they were away. Upon their return, the neighbors reported that Grandma K had repeatedly lambasted my parents for trying to starve her to death—despite the fact they had given her money to buy food at the A&P grocery store across the street.

But soon a happy surprise offset their anxiety. While traveling, Mom had become pregnant with a second child, me. Their one-bedroom apartment was too small for the growing family *and* Grandma K. It was time for a major change. In December of 1948, Mom and Dad closed on their first home—a two-flat at 4222 West Washington Boulevard in Dad's lifelong neighborhood of West Garfield Park, a block away from where Will and Grandma and Grandpa Gartz lived.

Just in time to undermine my parents' excitement over their new home and the anticipation of a second baby, Grandma K again careened into insanity, hurling outlandish accusations at Mom and Dad or staying in bed all day, arising only for meals. After reading Mom's case studies, I detect in the timing of my grandmother's downward spirals a pattern, which my mother apparently never grasped—or at least, certainly never acknowledged.

Each of Grandma K's mental breakdowns coincided with my parents' most joyous occasions. Grandma K was belligerent and delusional just before their wedding, before Paul's birth, and now, again, the month before I was born. It's impossible to know whether Grandma K had some control over her mentally ill brain, although in many diary entries I see how deftly she played the guilt card against both my parents when it suited her.

The timing of my grandmother's serious meltdowns shows me that whenever Mom's attention might be distracted from her mother, Grandma K turned sullen and confrontational, delusional and paranoid, forcing Mom to divert her focus away from her own family happiness and cater to her mother. Did Grandma give in to her psychosis at these times, drawing Mom tightly into an orbit with Grandma at the center?

Dad hated argument, so I'm sure he hid his frustration at the volatile disruption his mother-in-law injected into their lives. His childhood had taught him not to fight openly with his powerful mother, knowing he could never win. In Mom, he had found and married another strong-willed woman, and he would have had little luck convincing her Grandma K's psychotic presence was undermining their marriage and family life.

Mom called an ambulance on February 20, 1949, to transport her mother to Cook County Psychopathic Hospital, where two doctors evaluated Grandma K. They testified in Cook County Court on February 28, three weeks before I was born.

> We find that the said Louise Koroschetz is mentally ill and is a fit person to be sent to a state hospital for the mentally ill . . . that her disease is . . . psychosis. . . . We would respectfully recommend that she be sent to some public or private hospital or asylum for the mentally ill.

Grandma's symptoms certainly fit the diagnosis of psychosis: depression, anxiety, suspiciousness, delusions, hallucinations, ongoing unusual thoughts and beliefs. Medication would be the first line of treatment today, but effective psychotropic drugs were nonexistent at the time. Mom was caught in a quandary, both psychological and fixed in the real world.

Mom had always feared her mother's wrath, yet she also had absorbed Grandma K's devotion to her as the only child.

This potent combination of fear and love bound Mom to Grandma K even more tightly than the bonds of her ardor or concern for Dad. Swept up in the desperation her mother's illness wrought, and within weeks of giving birth, I'm sure Mom had little capacity or energy for self-examination.

In the outside world, perhaps she had seen the stark, gruesome photos of neglected patients in psychiatric hospitals featured in a 1946 *Life* magazine photo essay.[6] She often talked about the movie *The Snake Pit* (nominated for Best Picture at the 1949 Academy Awards), which depicted staff at mental institutions as cruel and incompetent.

Maybe those portrayals, combined with the fear and love she felt toward Grandma K, prompted her to ignore the doctors' advice. Just two weeks after my birth on March 23, 1949, Mom had her mother discharged so she could move with us into our new home on Chicago's West Side.

Our two-flat at 4222 West Washington Boulevard.

The two-flat at 4222 West Washington Boulevard was a fixer-upper for sure, but the bones were beautiful—leaded-glass windows facing the front, classic chunks of greystone lending weight and grandeur, a relief of vines and a carved birdbath decorating the concrete pinnacle. My parents envisioned a bright flower garden and space for the kids to romp in the compact backyard.

A single family occupied the first floor. On the second floor, a seventy-year-old woman held the lease and rented out two of the four bedrooms. Subletting was against building code, but for many it was an easy way to make ends meet. If Chicago building department inspectors snooped around, a show of cash usually made them go away.

My parents decided the second-floor apartment was best for us, but they didn't ask any of the existing three tenants to leave. Our family just moved right in with them. "How could you share your living space with a bunch of strangers?" I asked my mom years later, incredulous at this setup.

"It never occurred to me that it was odd," Mom said. "Seemed like the most natural thing in the world." The arrangement bemused me: my parents, newborn me, three-year-old Paul, and off-balance Grandma K would share the intimacies of their already-complicated family life with three people they had never met before. Mom's childhood diaries held the answer for me: renting out half their apartment in the 1930s was how Mom's parents had survived the Depression.

The flats in the building were known as shotgun apartments because of their long and narrow design. If you thought to do such a thing, you could pull the trigger of a gun in the kitchen at the back end, and the bullet would fly straight through the dining room, hallway, living room, and out the front window.

Each of the three live-in tenants on the second floor occupied one of three bedrooms: two on either side of the long hallway connecting the dining and living rooms, and one that overlooked the front porch. My parents took the back bedroom, just off the kitchen and across from the only bathroom, which would be used by six adults and Paul. Snugly tucked into a corner of my parents' room, my crib stretched along one wall to the doorway.

Grandma K and Paul, then almost three, slept in the "dining room," Paul on a cot and Grandma K on a low bed that nestled perfectly into the twelve-by-six-foot alcove on the room's west side. Dad rigged up a clothesline spanning her space so she could pull across a sheet, providing her with a modicum of privacy. A built-in, oak-trimmed china cabinet held her clothes and sundries.

Overflowing with ideas for their new home, Dad pictured spending weekends and evenings together with Mom in domestic unity—painting, stripping woodwork, building shelves—to create the lovely home they both envisioned. But it didn't work out that way.

Instead, Dad lost his job.

Mom, baby Linda, Paul, Dad: April 1949.

It's unclear why Hotpoint Refrigeration Company let Dad go that summer of 1949, but it threw my parents into a tailspin. Painful memories of her family's possessions strewn across the sidewalk outside the Koroschetz home came flooding back to

Mom. Would her family again be put out on the street? They would lose their down payment, as well as the $1500 they had already spent on a new furnace. They had set aside Mom's entire secretarial salary for four years; all their savings were tied up in this house. Dad searched the entire summer in vain for a decent-paying job, each day tightening the knot of fear strangling their hearts.

Relief came in August 1949, when Dad was offered a position with the National Board of Fire Underwriters, the NBFU. The starting salary was good, around $3600 a year, but there was one huge drawback: travel—and lots of it.

The National Board's Chicago office sent engineers throughout its territory, comprising Texas, Louisiana, Oklahoma, Missouri, Minnesota, Ohio, Indiana, Michigan, Kansas, Iowa, and Wisconsin. Their job was to document a city's preparedness for fighting fires and natural disasters. Winter was set aside for the lengthiest trips, to faraway, warm-weather states where, in January, fire hydrants could spout water (to test that the pressure was adequate to fight multiple fires at once), and the men could trudge across miles of city streets on outdoor inspections without freezing. Dad would be gone for up to seven weeks at a time during Chicago's harshest months.

Of course, he and Mom would have discussed the pros and cons of working for the NBFU, but really, they had no choice. He needed a job—pronto. Surely their great love, optimism, and steady confidence in the future could weather anything.

Dad didn't know it, but Mom had formed an opinion about such a job eight years prior, when she dated a peripatetic salesman. She made what looms to me as an ironic and prescient entry into her diary. "I have always vowed never to wed a traveling man," she had written. "Life would be just too lonesome." Now she found herself facing just what she had dreaded.

Mom wrote Dad a letter dated October 5, 1949, when he was on an early NBFU trip to Ashtabula, Ohio. She reminded him of their dire finances: they were down to their last dollar, $159 in debt to his parents as well as to their children's accounts, and had to meet monthly mortgage payments. She went on:

> I do hope you are taking advantage of your spare
> time and studying all you can about your job because
> this is such a wonderful opportunity. Please do all
> you can to excel at this job. Don't take it for granted.

My parents were on the cusp of a new life. The excitement of owning their first home, a bulwark against financial insecurity, was now offset by anxiety of the unknown: their impending long separations.

But at the same time, another momentous and historic event was occurring on a national scale, one that wasn't even a flicker in their imaginations. As Dad began his travels in 1949, a mass migration of African Americans, escaping from the oppression and systematic cruelties of the Jim Crow South, was well underway to northern cities.

CHAPTER 9: Redlined

A NEGRO FAMILY JUST ARRIVED IN CHICAGO FROM THE RURAL SOUTH

The Negro in Chicago: A Study of Race Relations and a Race Riot by The Chicago Commission on Race Relations, Photo-about 1919.

1950s

Like most major cities in twentieth-century America, Chicago was rigidly segregated. African Americans were clustered primarily in Chicago's Near West Side and in the South Side's Black Belt, a strip of land that stretched from about Twenty-Eighth to Seventieth Street in 1940 and inexorably expanded as blacks flocked to the city.

Chicago's black population had been burgeoning in these two neighborhoods ever since the beginning of the Great

Migration, when vast numbers of southern blacks moved to northern states and California, starting near the end of World War I and gaining steam in a second wave after World War II. In the 1940s and '50s, three million blacks fled north[7] from the daily degradations and abuses of the Jim Crow South. Hundreds of thousands headed to Chicago, where the black population nearly tripled from almost 278,000 in 1940 to more than 812,600 in 1960.[8]

Like my parents, many whites remained unaware that this massive population shift was underway—or the reasons behind it. They just knew they didn't want African Americans moving into their white neighborhoods.

Most whites were certain that blacks brought decay and dilapidation into every community they entered. When I was young, we sometimes drove through African American neighborhoods, on our way elsewhere, and witnessed blight firsthand: sagging porches and dirty windows; no grass, only twisting weeds in dusty front yards; ill-clad little children playing in the street with no evidence of nearby adults.

A ferocious white backlash erupted when blacks moved into an all-white area.

In July of 1953, a black couple purchased a home in all-white South Deering, on Chicago's South Side. For months, white crowds protested and rioted, hurling bricks, shooting off pistols, and attacking and injuring black passers-by. One of the picketers proclaimed to a CBS reporter that she didn't want blacks in her community because "every place they've taken over, they've turned into a slum."[9]

Whites were certain blacks would devastate their communities—and alongside that, would destroy whites' greatest investment: the value of their homes. In her epic book about the Great Migration, Isabel Wilkerson writes:

> *It was an article of faith among many people in Chicago and other big cities that the arrival of colored people in an all-white neighborhood automatically*

lowered property values. That economic fear
was helping propel the violent defense of white
neighborhoods.
    The fears were not unfounded, but often not for
the reasons white residents were led to believe.[10]

Years later, I learned that the real culprits behind the
decrepitude and the lowering value of white homes were the
policies of the federal government, in alliance with the real-estate and mortgage sectors. In the 1930s, the newly created
Home Owners' Loan Corporation (HOLC), along with the
Federal Housing Administration and other government agen-
cies, began ranking communities to assess their creditworthi-
ness, from A (green), the highest, through D (red), the lowest.[11]

    "If a neighborhood had black residents, it was marked
as D, or red, no matter what their social class or how small
a percentage of the population they made up. These neighborhoods' properties were appraised as worthless or likely to
decline in value. In short, D areas were 'redlined' or marked
as locations in which no loans should be made for either purchasing or upgrading properties."[12]

    The FHA supported these biases. It relied on color-coded
maps to determine "the present and likely future location of
African Americans and used them to determine which neighborhoods would be denied mortgage insurance."[13] FHA
insurance was typically denied to buildings in these redlined
areas. Without mortgage availability, whites couldn't sell
their homes, except to blockbusters, unscrupulous real-estate
agents who used race-baiting to scare whites into selling fast
and cheap for cash. The blockbusters then sold the property
to African Americans at sometimes two to three times the
value of the building. Homes to blacks in the redlined areas
were usually sold "on contract," meaning the deed to the
property remained with the seller, who could repossess the
home after even one missed payment.

White families like ours didn't consider the rampant employment discrimination that reduced blacks' incomes, meaning most could afford only older properties, already in disrepair when purchased. Little money remained for upkeep.[14] With the husband and wife often both working to pay off their contract, and no loans available, neither the time nor the money existed for repairs.

Then there was the insidious role segregation itself played in the decay whites observed. The thirty thousand African Americans arriving in Chicago each year during the 1950s[15] were forced into the limited housing stock of strictly delineated black neighborhoods in the Black Belt and Near West Side. Toilets broke. Closets were turned into makeshift kitchens. With so many people crammed into inadequate housing, buildings and community infrastructure crumbled under the strain.

But most whites never made the connection. White homeowners judged what they observed, placing blame for run-down homes and lowered property values in racially changed neighborhoods squarely on the new residents. Consequently, white homeowners believed they had a strong economic incentive to keep blacks out.

CHAPTER 10: Civil Rights

1963

Before the first black family moved onto our block in June of 1963, the civil rights movement had dominated the news for several years. Just as I was entering my teens, I saw the effects of the racist Jim Crow laws that denied blacks the freedom promised to them a century earlier.

On TV, I watched black teens, along with some white sympathizers, staging sit-ins at whites-only lunch counters. White boys with ducktail haircuts taunted them. In my neighborhood, boys who swore and smoked and rolled cigarette packs in their short sleeves sported those cuts. They were guys who acted tough and postured, ready for a fight. They were boys I avoided. I saw this same kind of teen on my television, spattering the black kids sitting at the counter with eggs, or grinning while they poured a drink over their heads. My stomach roiled at their cruelty. I'd witnessed local mean kids dumping water on a mentally challenged boy, and I had screamed, "Leave him alone!" They only laughed and told me to mind my own business. I hated them.

I heard the name *Martin Luther King* over and over. As a Lutheran, I knew Martin Luther as the man who had confronted the Catholic Church over its unjust practices back in the 1500s. I was confused when I first heard the name.

Martin Luther was a sixteenth-century German monk. *Why did a black man have that name?*

At my all-white Lutheran high school, some teachers talked about King in a way that helped me overcome my confusion. Luther had challenged the Catholic Church's misuse of power in the sixteenth century. One said that today's Martin Luther challenged whites' misuse of power over African Americans in segregated southern states. Blacks were forced to acquiesce to whites in every aspect of life. Jim Crow laws denied them entry into swimming pools, amusement parks, and taxpayer-funded public universities. In many southern cities, blacks weren't even allowed to use the public library. I gained some understanding, but I don't recall much class time spent talking about the civil rights movement—and it all seemed so far away.

I was nearing the end of my freshman year of high school on May 2, 1963, when more than one thousand African American students marched into downtown Birmingham, Alabama. I couldn't reconcile the images of these protesting teens with the fear my family and our neighbors had felt toward blacks. The black kids in Birmingham were about my age; they looked and dressed a lot like me. The girls mostly wore dresses, and their hair was carefully coiffed. The boys sported slacks and button shirts. The teens sang and chanted, "Freedom! Freedom! Freedom!" Even after being arrested, they kept singing through the bars of the paddy wagon—and from their jail cells, where they were stuffed like upright sardines.

Watching TV with my parents, I was flummoxed by competing feelings. On the one hand, I'd never seen protests before, people defying the police. Was that even okay? On the other, I was gripped with horror by the way these well-dressed, singing kids were mistreated. "Why are those kids being arrested?" I asked my parents. "They didn't do anything bad."

My conservative dad said, "When the police say to disperse, they're supposed to disperse. These protests are illegal." He was against anyone disobeying the police.

Mom agreed. "We'll have total anarchy if laws aren't obeyed."

Mom and Dad were wedded to the status quo. Their immigrant parents had raised them—and they in turn had raised their children—to respect authority. But what about those kids who just wanted to sit at a lunch counter? The black people who were made to move to the back of the bus? I imagined myself in their place—the burn of injustice consuming me. But my parents' reverence for law and order made sense to teenaged me, too. How could we have a society that didn't obey the police? I didn't understand what was at stake.

The next day, I watched a news report showing hundreds of black youths gathered in downtown Birmingham. What happened next made me dizzy: Birmingham firemen turned their fire hoses full force on the young demonstrators! The blast of water drove scores of blacks against fences and rolled them along the ground. I thought of firemen as protectors, but in Birmingham, they were on the attack!

Snarling German shepherds surrounded the protestors. I threw my hands over my eyes when the dogs lunged. Teens were dragged away, their shredded pants exposing lacerated and bloodied flesh. Demonstrators lay helpless and injured on the ground, but the police still beat them with batons. I imagined the searing pain of those sticks cracking my bones, my skull.

"Dad, they're sending dogs after them!" I cried out. "Remember how you told me the Indians were mistreated by the white man? The Trail of Tears? These police are so . . . so mean!"

"The colored are expecting too much, too fast. You can't just change society in such a short time."

That opinion was common among whites we knew. Years later, I read King's response to the familiar refrain of "Wait."

For years now, I have heard the word "Wait!" This
"Wait" has almost always meant "Never." It is easy
for those who have never felt the stinging facts of
segregation to say, "Wait." But when you have seen
vicious mobs lynch your mothers and fathers at will
and drown your sisters and brothers at whim . . .
there comes a time when your cup of endurance runs
over, and men are no longer willing to be plunged
into an abyss of injustice. . . . [16]

By the age of fourteen, I'd heard Dad talk about lynching as our family sat tightly packed at the kitchen table, the
steam from our chicken and vegetable soup clouding the air.
"In the South," Dad said, "if a colored man looks wrong at a
white woman, a white mob'll just string him up. No trial. No
questions. Just vigilantes doing what they want. They set the
Negro on a horse, place a noose around his neck, throw the
rope over a tree and tie it tight. Then they smack the horse on
the rear. When the horse takes off, the man dangles from his
neck till he's dead. A mob's a frightening thing."

The image terrified me, but I had no real knowledge of
the torture, humiliation, and lack of basic freedom blacks
had endured at the hands of white people. Except for the
lynching explanation, I don't recall my parents ever talking
about the unfairness in the South. I had never even heard the
term *Jim Crow*. To me, it seemed as if the civil rights movement had just exploded out of nowhere. It was happening in
the South, where black kids couldn't sit at a lunch counter
or go to school with white kids. *That doesn't happen here*, I
thought. My understanding was that we didn't want blacks
in our neighborhood to protect our property. So when Dad
said, "Wait," it made sense to me. How could the status quo
just change overnight?

Were most whites as ignorant as our family was? Years
later, I came to see how myopic "Wait!" was, as if blacks had
been seeking freedom and equality for just a few months rather

than the one hundred years since they were supposedly freed from the cutting chains of slavery. They were still bound, this time by Jim Crow manacles.

But neighborhood whites like my parents weren't thinking about equality for African Americans. They were focused on their own fear—that they would lose their greatest investment, the value of their homes.

CHAPTER 11: Flipped

Linda, 1962 Tilton graduate, with
her 8th grade teacher, Miss Kelleher.

1959–63

On August 1, 1959, four years before the first black family
moved onto our block, a house deeper into West Garfield Park
than blacks had lived prior was sold to an African American
family—on Jackson Boulevard, a couple blocks south and
west of our home.[17]

Before the black family moved in, a mob of more than
one thousand outraged whites, some throwing stones and
bricks, gathered outside the building. The Chicago Police

Department dispatched hundreds of officers to the scene, arresting more than two dozen people. For several weeks, police kept a visible presence in the area, an unusually robust response to white intimidation of blacks integrating a Chicago neighborhood.

I don't recall any discussion about what would have been big news in our community, probably because we had been traveling on a five-week family car trip to the southern and western United States.

One year later, the 1960 census showed that the percentage of African Americans in West Garfield Park had jumped from just about .25 percent in 1950 to 16 percent.[18] In 1960, most blacks lived south of Madison Street, which evolved into a de facto Mason-Dixon line: blacks to the south, whites to the north.

Children would breach the border.

A crisis had been fomenting in black neighborhood schools. The burgeoning population trapped in Chicago's black segregated neighborhoods had created dilapidated buildings, damaged community infrastructure, and strained local schools to the snapping point. In February of 1961, "Willing Willie," the pseudonym of a columnist for the *Garfieldian,* our local West Side newspaper, visited an eighteen-unit apartment building just a few blocks south and east of us. "At the building, Willing Willie observed 'an amazing number of children hopping around in the mud.'"[19] Willing Willie estimated forty to fifty families were living there instead of the expected eighteen. The columnist probably used the technique of counting the multiple name tags on the mailboxes for each apartment, as was highlighted in another *Garfieldian* article.[20]

The abundance of children in black neighborhoods so jammed local schools that pupils often sat two to a desk, sharing the limited number of outdated textbooks; gymnasiums and closets were transformed into classrooms. Unable to accommodate hundreds of extra children, many black neighborhood schools started split-shifts; pupils went to school either morning or afternoon, leaving many unattended for hours while their parents worked.

Just before I entered eighth grade at Tilton Elementary in 1961, CPS had built two new schools in our community to alleviate the pressure of an exploding student population in West Garfield Park. In the fall of 1961, I watched the two co-presidents of my eighth-grade class smiling broadly as each held up a shovelful of gray dirt. Cameras snapped, documenting the ground-breaking for Marconi School, six blocks northwest of us. Hefferan, two blocks south of Madison, opened in September of the same year, but by December of 1961, Hefferan already held double the students for which it had been built.[21]

Other school boundary changes profoundly influenced my, and my classmates', high-school choices. At one time, our home had been in Austin High School's district. Austin, where my father had graduated, was about fourteen blocks west, located in its eponymous community. Two years prior to my graduation from Tilton, Austin was 99.84 percent white.[22] Our home had been redistricted to high schools in East Garfield Park, where the population in 1960 was 60 percent black,[23] and undoubtedly higher by 1962. My two choices were Lucy Flower, a girls' vocational school, known to have tough female gangs, or Marshall, already overcrowded and also notorious for gangs. Dad slapped his left hand with his right for emphasis and shouted, "They expect us to send a young white girl into that dangerous, colored neighborhood? She could be raped!"

The word rang and reverberated in my brain. My gut went queasy. I was about as sexually naive as any thirteen-year-old girl could be. I knew about sex, and I knew that *rape* meant forced sex. For years, my mother had been lecturing me to preserve my virginity for marriage. Would I be a whore, as Mom and Grandma K called girls who had sex before marriage, if I were raped? I hadn't even kissed a boy yet!

I didn't express these thoughts out loud. I was skittish of talking about sex—or rape. I just knew I didn't want to go to those high schools. I had absorbed my mom and dad's fear, an emotion I'd rarely seen in my stoic, forbearing parents.

They were not alone in their panic. Virtually every white parent Mom spoke with in our neighborhood wanted a transfer to Austin. Whites felt beleaguered, that *they* were the victims. Most had no understanding of the cramped and overcrowded conditions in the housing and schools in all-black neighborhoods. They just knew that once blacks moved into their communities, their property, the prideful symbol of their American success, was in jeopardy.

Most of our community was blue-collar: plumbers, printers, factory workers, some police officers and firemen. Dad straddled two worlds. With his chemical-engineering degree from the Illinois Institute of Technology (IIT), he was among a minority in the neighborhood who had finished college. But his blue-collar upbringing, the son of immigrants who had worked as janitors, was just as important to his self-image. He had the interests of an educated man—science, poetry, literature, history—but I feel certain he wanted to replicate his janitor-parents' success with rental property. It meant he held down a full-time job as an engineer with the National Board and did all the manual labor required for our two-flat. Perhaps by doing so, he would show that he could work as physically hard as his parents had—and could finally win his mother's respect. Hiring outside workers for anything he was able to do himself (which was almost everything) would have been shameful in his—and his parents'—eyes.

The whites in most changing communities, usually working-class, felt that they had sacrificed, scrimped, and saved to own their homes, as had my parents. They had played by the rules, kept "their noses to the grindstone," as Dad liked to say, and now their life savings, in the form of their homes, were threatened when blacks moved in. But it was more than that. When whites fled, they lost their community, where they'd attended church, sent their kids to school, and built a web of close friendships.

Of course, blacks had suffered from overt racism, attacks on their homes, overcrowded schools, and the inadequate education of their children. My parents and other whites didn't understand that the racist mortgage laws, originally intended to give preference to whites, had turned around to bite them, and they felt victimized.

Many bristled at being called "racists" by the elite, wealthy people whose Chicago neighborhoods or suburban communities would never have to face integration. Blacks were priced out of those homes.[24]

At the time of the school boundaries change, white parents couldn't understand why their children were being forced into dangerous communities when a safer school, Austin, was just as accessible. It was an attitude my own mother expressed. "Parents met with the alderman," Mom told Dad. "He's adamant. No transfers! So many nice white families are leaving. I think they're trying to drive us out, just to accommodate the colored."

A few months before my Tilton graduation, Mom invited one of the school's teachers for coffee at our house during the lunch hour, so I was home as well. Leaning against the sink, holding the cup before her lips, the steam clouding her glasses, Mom's voice was high and tense as she set the cup down without taking a sip. "We just don't know what to do. I'm scared to death to send her to Marshall in that bad area."

"Have you thought about Luther North?" the teacher asked. "It's a small, Lutheran high school, up near Central and Irving Park."

"I've heard of it," Mom said, running her finger around the cup's rim, "but, no, it hadn't occurred to me." She looked past him, at nothing in particular, lost in thought for a moment, and I knew the mechanics of her mind were churning. That afternoon, Mom was on the phone to Luther High School North (LHN). Registration was still open for the fall, but the tuition would be a financial strain. "Only $560 per year," Mom wrote sardonically in her diary. Because Mom saved all her income-tax filings, I could look up what Dad earned at the time. LHN tuition was about 8 percent of his salary.

From Mom's comments, I knew it was a lot of money, an expense they hadn't planned for. My older brother, Paul, exceptionally talented in math and science, attended Lane Technical High School, a kind of CPS magnet school that accepted only boys who passed an entrance exam. No such school existed for girls. After a brief discussion, my parents decided I should go to LHN, that my safety was their top priority. I felt cherished that my frugal parents would spend such a huge sum just for me, even as guilt tweaked my conscience for taking an unfair share of the family budget.

Within the week, Mom took me to register at Luther High School North.

LHN was far—seven miles northwest, requiring two bus rides—a minimum of forty-five minutes each way on the best of days. I didn't care about the long commute or going to a school where I knew no one. I wouldn't have known anyone at Marshall either. Most of my classmates' families had moved far away from the West Side or found apartments further west, in Austin High School's district.

I was jittery, like any thirteen-year-old would be, anticipating high school for the first time, but I was open to the adventure. Dad had always encouraged his kids to try new experiences. My parents and Dad's family had modeled *selbstständigkeit* (self-reliance) and the need to carry on, preferably with optimism. How could I complain about anything when my parents were making such a great financial sacrifice?

CHAPTER 12: Blockbusters

1962–63

After I graduated from eighth grade in the summer of 1962, CPS made a decision that turned the flow of whites out of our community into a flood.

Hoping to alleviate overcrowding, CPS reconfigured boundary lines for four West Side grade schools. From kindergarten through eighth grade, my older brother and I had walked down our alley the one block to Tilton. It was "our" school. But starting in the fall of 1962, all the kids who lived west of Keeler, including my eight-year-old brother, Billy, had to walk six blocks to the recently built Marconi School, which also drew students from south of Madison. Ever since the house on Jackson had been sold to African Americans in 1959 (and whites had rioted), that area of West Garfield Park had seen a steady increase in its black population.

Not everyone was unhappy about the change. In our neighborhood were plenty of blockbusters—those unprincipled real-estate agents who preyed on racial fears. Whites panicked if they thought blacks were moving into the area, thinking it was better to be among the first to sell before prices plummeted.

When the school districts changed, blockbusters couldn't have wished for a better scenario. Starting in the fall of 1962, waves of black kids crossed Madison Street to walk to Tilton or Marconi, down streets with all-white residents. The block-busters didn't have to hire an African American woman to walk up and down the nearby sidewalks with a baby carriage, a common tactic they'd used in some white neighborhoods, to frighten whites into believing the neighborhood was "turn-ing"—the modified boundaries did it for them.

But the blockbusters didn't stop there. That fall, panic peddling began in earnest. We found flyers with large print in our front hallway warning: "GET OUT BEFORE IT'S TOO LATE!" Other neighbors told of phone calls late at night. The caller just said, "They're coming," and then hung up. "They're trying to scare us," Mom said, staring at the phone receiver for several seconds before placing it back on the cradle. She turned to Dad and me. "But what if the col-ored start buying on our block?"

Dad said, "We have the right to live with the people we want to live with!" But unlike many white West Siders, Mom and Dad never joined neighborhood groups that, with-out saying so directly, worked to keep the community white. My parents were too busy working in their never-ending rooming house to have time for (or even awareness of) such organizations.

They tried writing classified-ad copy for their vacant apartments to encourage white applicants: "Do you feel you're being forced out of your community? Do you want to live with people like yourself?" However, the newspaper rep-resentative said that the newspaper's policy wouldn't allow an ad that seemed discriminatory.

Dad was incensed. "It's my property! I have a right to choose who lives here!"

My parents felt adrift in a gale that blew in without warning, with no port in sight.

Rumors and gossip of race-based attacks, especially at Marconi, exacerbated white fears. We heard that a group of black kids at Marconi had doused a white kid with gasoline and set him alight. Neighbors didn't check the source of these rumors; they simply left. Tension between the races became so fraught that police were positioned outside of the school to separate the black and white kids, sending each group home down different streets.

As the school year neared its end in May of 1963, the world watched, along with me, as peaceful black protestors were clubbed, hosed, and attacked by dogs in Birmingham, Alabama.

A few weeks later, on June 9, my parents and I attended my good friend's Tilton graduation ceremony. It was the first June graduating class after the attendance lines had been moved. I had never seen so many black kids on stage in the nine years I'd attended Tilton graduations. What did it mean? Our block, and nearby blocks north of Madison, were still all white, but the Parker house two doors down was for sale, and the adults were nervous. My parents openly said, "Do you think they'd break the neighborhood?" I knew what that meant. Selling to blacks was a betrayal, destroying everyone's property values.

Yet right here in my former grade school, I could see evidence that blacks had already arrived, but I didn't give it much more thought. At fourteen, I was sad that I'd be losing another neighborhood friend, the girl who was graduating. She and her family would soon be moving two miles west, to the suburb of Oak Park.

That evening, Mom wrote in her diary, "What a change from Linda's graduation last June! Seemed like more colored than white."

She was right. My 1962 graduating class of seventy-four included four African Americans, 5 percent of the total. Just one year later, out of sixty-seven graduates, thirty-nine, 58 percent, were black—more than a 1,000 percent increase.

Two days after my friend's graduation, I was studying for freshman final exams at the dining-room table, when the television distracted me with yet another confrontation between blacks and whites. The TV anchor said President Kennedy had sent the deputy attorney general to Alabama to force segregationist governor George Wallace to allow African American students entry into the University of Alabama. I stared at the screen. I now saw two different sets of authority facing off: a governor with hundreds of Alabama state troopers against soldiers federalized by President Kennedy.[25]

I didn't understand at the time how Wallace had tried to use the Constitution to back racism. Calling on the Tenth Amendment, which gives power not delegated to the federal government to the states, he decried the "oppression of the rights, privileges, and sovereignty of this state," and the "illegal usurpation of power by the Central Government."

Wallace put on a show for his constituents, but he'd known from the start that a federal order trumped his authority, and he would have to allow the black students to register.[26]

That same evening, June 11, 1963, Kennedy spoke on national television, making an impassioned plea to white Americans to treat black citizens as equals.

The next day, on June 12, 1963, in a vicious rejoinder to Kennedy's call for fairness, thirty-seven-year-old Medgar Evers, Mississippi's NAACP field secretary, was shot in the back with a high-powered rifle as he walked from his car to his home. He died an hour later. Again, mass black protests, followed by mass arrests, were broadcast on TV around the world. I later learned that neighbors had heard Evers's children screaming, "Daddy! Daddy! Daddy!"[27] I thought of my own father. What would I do without *my* daddy?

The killer was Byron De La Beckwith, a white supremacist and Klansman. He was released after two trials ended in hung juries. (It took thirty-one years to finally convict De La Beckwith for the murder, in 1994.)[28] Race, now inextricably bound with violence and death, became America's daily news fare that summer and into the fall. Everything in our lives suddenly revolved around race. The civil rights movement filled our television screens and dominated newspaper headlines. Pundits and reporters headed south to document vicious confrontations over civil rights and segregation, while my family and I faced a new racial reality in our own backyard.

Ten days after Evers's murder, the first black family moved onto our block. By August, three more African American families joined them, meaning two-thirds of the homes had black owners, not counting the multiunit apartment building on the corner. "Unbelievably fast," Mom commented. I overheard my parents talking about what they should do, but they made no plans. I'm sure I met the new black family, but I don't remember much. I spent my summer doing chores and traveling miles to Foster Avenue Beach, far north, where my Luther North friends hung out.

My parents and all the neighbors had spoken so fearfully of blacks moving into the neighborhood, but when it became reality, nothing had actually changed—except that we had African American families living on our block! Our new neighbors were friendly and respectful. My parents were friendly and respectful in turn. No violence ensued.

After months of seeing vicious beatings, dog attacks, and confrontations over black youths sitting peacefully at lunch counters or students trying to register at a public university, it was comforting to be in my home neighborhood, where blacks and whites lived peacefully on the same block. But integration was short-lived.

A homeowner of the era, questioning what the correspondents of our local paper, the *Garfieldian*, meant by "integration," wrote to the editor: "From your words, one can only conclude that for you it is the time between when the first Negro family moves in and the last white family moves out."[29] Based on home sales that summer, it appeared that our block was headed down that same path.

CHAPTER 13: A New Start

Linda and Peggy, October 1962. Caricature of Linda's Dad behind them.

1962–63

In the fall of 1962, Dad's job at the National Board of Fire Underwriters was terminated, and he received ninety days of full salary as severance. After a couple months of searching, he was hired as a loss-control engineer at Fireman's Fund Insurance Company. Dad drove throughout his Chicago territory, inspecting bars, bathhouses, hunting-goods stores, motels—any business insured by Fireman's Fund. He chatted up the owners before inspection, not just because they would be more receptive to his recommended changes, but because he loved conversation and interaction. "Every man has his story," he often told us.

He might suggest thick metal fire doors to keep blazes contained or accordion-pulled grates over windows to prevent theft. The secretaries competed to type up Dad's cassette tape–recorded reports, eager for a good yarn. He opened one report on a South Side motel with: "This is a place where the beds never have a chance to get cold."

"You gotta hear this one," said the transcriber passing around the tape.

At the same time Dad was enjoying his newfound freedom at Fireman's Fund, I was discovering a new life at Luther High School North, seven miles from our home and a world away from the West Side. Learning to navigate the shoals of adolescence, I was in a school with a homogeneous population, made up of kids from German and Swedish backgrounds. They had names like Strauss, Radtke, Diener, Faust, Schroeder, and Nelson.

I met my best high-school friend, Peggy, sitting next to me in homeroom, on the first day of school at Luther North. Peggy was very blonde with pure blue eyes, perfect skin, and beautiful, long fingernails. I bit mine. I began the conversation with this pretty girl sitting next to me by openly complimenting her nails, a feature I'd never have. She jumped right in with a funny rejoinder, "My mother sometimes strokes my nails."

"Wow, that's nutty!" I exclaimed. Instantly we were talking and laughing nonstop, and we continued chatting until the bell rang—and between every class for the whole day. Magically, our schedules were identical!

Our personalities melded seamlessly, even though our child-hoods had been markedly different. Peggy's mom read *Seventeen* magazine to know what was "in" for the new school year. I had never heard of *Seventeen* magazine, and Mom had no time to read the women's magazines that piled up month after month. Peggy and her mom shopped for new school clothes in August, just when they'd be the most expensive. Mom and I shopped for some of my fall wardrobe when the winter clothes went on sale in February, purchasing each item one size larger. Grandma Gartz also passed on to me hand-me-downs from tenants. Some of the items were at least acceptable to my untrained eye, so I wore them.

Frugal and practical, Mom had bought Paul a winter coat with two sets of buttonholes. After he outgrew it, she switched the buttons to the left (girls') side when I was ready for it in about third grade, then back to the boys' side for my younger brother. We were middle class but spent money sparingly. My parents' mantra, "Save for a rainy day," meant they could afford LHN tuition.

Peggy, like most Luther North students, came from a middle-class family, too. Her dad was an accountant, and her mother worked part-time at a movie theater, spending most of her income on Peggy's clothes. Sometimes when I went to Peggy's apartment after school, her mother had surprised her with two or three new outfits laid out on her bed! Always dressed stylishly and more adept at negotiating the high-school social scene, Peggy became my adolescent guide and consultant.

She was aware of a high-school hierarchy. I had been unaware of any such hierarchy at Tilton, where I'd had the modest goal of being a good student, and like-minded strivers were my friends. We Tiltonites worked together on the school newspaper and volunteered during recess or in the front office. That seemed cool to me. Kids hung out with like-minded other students, tough kids with tough kids, science geeks with science geeks. I was friendly with all, but I didn't discern that one group was more desirable than another.

Peggy had gone to a school where she felt left out of the popular crowd, and she wanted to find a way in at Luther North. I was definitely not the ticket into the cool crowd, but we had become best friends anyway. I've come to realize a great truth of Peggy's soul. She'd put aside her dearest adolescent desire (at least what she thought it was) for real friendship. But she would have to shepherd me along—and I was in great need of shepherding. I just hadn't realized it until I met Peggy. She must have seen a glimmer of potential.

She insisted we go to football games, where I quickly learned the sartorial expectations. I met her at the field for the first game on a Saturday dressed in a sweatshirt and velveteen pants, onto which Mom had sewn satin fall leaves. She exclaimed, "Gartz! You can't wear an outfit like that to a football game!"

"Oh." Pause. "I thought the fall leaves looked nice. I mean . . . it *is* fall, right?" Chagrined, I found more casual pants for the next game. Raised by parents with zero interest in sports (a complete waste of time, in their minds), attending a football game never would have even occurred to me, if not for Peggy.

Above all, she and I never ran out of things to talk about—which boys we liked, whether we could ever make cheerleader (we never did), or who was in the popular crowd—and how the heck did one achieve that pinnacle of high-school success? She regaled me with advice on improving my appearance. "Gartz! You have to do something with your hair."

I had no idea how to create a stylish coif. Peggy told me I needed rollers to set my hair, and she demonstrated. I bought a plastic bag of large rollers and a card of bobby pins. Each night, I struggled with manual gymnastics, holding a roller in place with some fingers while using others to wrap hair around the prickly cylinder, wisps flying out, finally securing it in place with a bobby pin, my arms growing numb in the process.

I seldom had seen Mom set her hair. She had a natural curl she just brushed into place. About every two months, she went to the beauty parlor for a permanent and a haircut and came home looking like a stranger.

She wore slacks and a simple top every day, clothes easy to work in. But the few times we went out as a family, like for Mother's Day or birthdays, she always looked classy. As a young woman, Mom dressed with great élan. Photos show her wearing fabulous clothes with impeccably matched costume jewelry, hair perfect for the times. Yet she never passed on a sense of style to me. Shopping had to be accomplished as speedily as possible, a chore she squeezed in between her other duties.

———

Despite my attention to Peggy's expert clothing and social advice, I also had a rebellious streak, picked up from Dad, to not kowtow to fashion. "Fashion," he used to spit out. "Changing styles every year. That's just a ruse to get people to dump perfectly good clothes and spend money they don't have!"

Just around the time I started high school, Dad had bought me a raccoon coat (one of those 1920s fads) at a Salvation Army store for five dollars. I cut the tail off an old Davy Crockett hat and had a matching outfit, which I wore to school. Peggy advised against the coat ("It looks ridiculous!"). But a lot of kids thought it was hilarious, in a fun sort of way. At lunchtime, I'd find some students traipsing around the halls in my coat, like the Pevensie kids in *The Lion, the Witch, and the Wardrobe.*

The laughter was mostly good-natured. They had never seen such a coat, bristling with thick brown-and-black fur and wide, capacious sleeves and shoulders.

More than once a kid mocked me, asking "Where'd you get that big animal on your back?" or baring teeth, growling, hands pawing at me like claws. My face flushed hot, but my innards went steely. *My dad bought me this coat! I don't care what you think.* For many mornings, after I'd eaten the soft-boiled egg and grapefruit Dad had prepared for me, I was pleased at his happy smile when he watched me draw my arms through the thick, heavy sleeves and let the full heft of the coat settle on my shoulders. I kissed him goodbye and walked half a block to the bus stop.

I defiantly wore the fur coat every day for at least a week, until any negative comments died down. Only then did I return to my more typical teen coat, which I'd left hanging in my closet until I was certain I had been unbowed by the comments. I wanted to fit in, to absorb Peggy's adolescent wisdom, but I wouldn't succumb to intimidation and abandon a sense of self just to please others.

Peggy and I walked and gossiped together between classes, worked stage crew for the thespians, and wondered if all that guys really wanted from a girl was to make out. We had in common the same sort of thirteen-year-old naiveté when it came to any aspect of sexual matters. We went to parties and had crushes on various boys, but neither of us had a clue as to how to attract them. We admitted to each other that we used our pillows to practice kissing. We were filled with sexual longings we couldn't identify. I felt a sucking deep in my belly drawing down into a place I couldn't name, sometimes catching my breath short. But Peg and I felt certain (based on our mothers' admonitions) that going all the way was for trampy girls who thought sex was the only way to get a guy.

Peggy's parents rented the second floor of a two-flat brick building in a modest and pleasant neighborhood on Keeler near Montrose, five miles directly north of our home at Keeler and Washington. We walked up carpeted stairs to her door, which opened into her living room, taking off our shoes before stepping on the pale-gold carpet to enter into the thoughtfully decorated two-bedroom apartment. No dogs or cats were allowed. Unlike our house, which overflowed with a menagerie of animals that came and went, Peggy was permitted only a small blue-green parakeet in a cage.

Mom and Dad had spent years of personal labor to beautify our home, but we lived with a different mindset. Our house was our business. I just accepted that I grew up with tenants living in bedrooms down the hall, who came and went in our apartment at will and who shared our washroom. Second-floor roomers and basement tenants rang the bell and walked through our flat to pay rent or use our phone, dropping ten cents per call in a coffee cup Mom had set nearby. Mom's office was the dining room, where the table was covered in the sorted piles of her bookkeeping, insurance policies to read, bills to pay, and magazines she might speedily flip through once every two months in search of articles to clip (like "How to Make Old Furniture New Again" or miscellaneous homemaker advice).

Some project was always underway. A tiny sampling: Dad plastered, painted, built shelving, stripped woodwork, and hung wallpaper. Mom taught me to pull out a root-bound fern from its pot, lay a clay shard over the hole of a slightly bigger pot, insert the plant, pour fresh soil around the perimeter, and tamp it down. As we got older, we kids were taught (and expected) to prep and paint the back porch, fences, screens, and storm windows; cut grass; rake leaves—to lend a hand to all maintenance. I recall nothing labeled "boys'" or "girls'" work.

Mom refinished lamps, picture frames, and, most memorably, a Victorian oak desk, its varnish blackened by the passing of time. Dad had purchased it for a song at some secondhand shop. "I've always wanted my own desk," Mom said, inspecting it longingly, opening the drop front, revealing upright file-folder slots and drawers for office paraphernalia. She frowned and looked at Dad. "But when would I ever find the time to work on it?" We could all see the beauty beneath the blackened surface, but the elaborate filigrees, spindles, and raised relief carvings presaged hours of tedious labor. Mom took it on.

That desk squatted on newspapers in our dining room for months, as Mom devoted a little time each day to its renewal. She painstakingly stripped off the sticky black finish, sanded and wiped the wood with a tack cloth to remove vestiges of wood dust—until it stood naked and pale like a freshly scrubbed country gal, ready to be dolled up for a dance. When mom brushed on fruitwood stain, the colorless oak leaped to life; its grain emerged, zigzagging in broad swaths or swirling around the delicate details. After two coats of varnish, it was the belle of the ball. Dad snapped photos. We kids oohed and aahed at its glorious transformation.

I often thought of Mom's months of commitment whenever I saw her working at the desk, a daily reminder of the power of perseverance.

Peggy's apartment was a mere fifteen-minute bus ride east of LHN, so I often spent the night at her house if we stayed after school to practice baton routines, memorize songs for a musical, or write German conversations. She and I were the same size, so I could wear one of her oh-so-cute outfits to classes the next day, thrilled with how fashionable I looked.

During my years at Luther North, the racial change in West Garfield Park continued until it was nearly complete. Returning home to the West Side from Peggy's, I walked two blocks from her house to Pulaski, where I boarded a southbound bus, watching the neighborhoods grow progressively poorer as we bumped along: more currency exchanges with giant yellow signs, more trash in the streets, more bars on the corner, more paint-starved houses, more wan and worried faces. The ethnicity of the people changed, too, first to Hispanic, then Hispanic and black, and finally all black several blocks north of my street, Washington, where Dad always waited at the bus stop to walk me home after dark.

CHAPTER 14: The Long Goodbyes

Dad sleeping on train to Ft. Worth, Texas, January 24, 1956.

1950–51

At the start of 1950, Dad was settling into a watershed period of his life: a new house, a new baby, and a new job traveling to never-visited states. Taken together, these life-altering changes were probably his inspiration to start a diary on January 1, 1950, the beginning of the twentieth century's second half. He could look back someday and recall his thoughts and experiences as they occurred—not through the distorting lens of foggy memory. He had no idea what insights, joy, and sadness his diary entries would bring to me so many decades later.

Dad's diary and the letters between him and Mom during his travels create for me a rising scrim on the set and

74

drama of our lives. The diary entries are a direct link to Dad's internal thoughts. The letters expose their raw loneliness and longing for one another, Dad's arduous life on the road, and Mom's exhaustive accounts of managing alone at home.

Besides taking care of tenants, the building, and family finances, Mom also worked part-time as a bookkeeper. All of this was on top of what was considered a woman's job— keeping house in an era when every dinner was made from scratch, every dish was washed and dried by hand, laundry was squeezed one piece at a time through the washing machine wringer, and clothes were hung on a line to dry outside during the summer or in the damp basement during the winter. The mostly cotton clothes of the period demanded hours of weekly ironing.

None of these chores, not even caring for little children, appealed to her. "I never liked women's work," Mom often said. "It's so repetitive. I like men's work—projects where you can see progress." Mom became increasingly dependent on live-in Grandma K for housework and daily childcare, but her presence came with an emotional cost.

If my parents had wanted a crystal ball to see what future challenges lay in store, they needed only to look at the events during the first week of January of 1950. On New Year's Day, Grandma K had a paranoid breakdown, raising her fist to attack Mom and stopped only by Dad's calming intervention. The next day, one of the roomers in our own flat lolled drunk in his bedroom, soaking the sheets and mattress with a profuse nosebleed. This had all occurred just before Dad had to leave for a week in Ohio. Then he'd be home for less than two weeks before his next trip.

The whole family clustered around the front door on January 22, waiting for Dad's NBFU colleague to pick him up for the long drive to Austin, Texas. I was ten months old and Paul was three—both too young to comprehend how long a twenty-one-day absence would be. But Mom would feel it acutely. Dad's coworker pulled his Studebaker up to the curb as our family exchanged hugs and kisses and "I'll miss you. I love you."

Dad pushed open the outer glass door and walked down the concrete steps into the cold, gray Chicago day. Smiling, Dad waved back at us from inside the car, but a hollow must have settled under his ribs.

Their first evening in Austin, the men sat around an outdoor table at a local tavern, drinking beer in eighty-degree weather, gentle breezes caressing their winter-worn cheeks. Dad wrote to Mom:

> I can hardly believe we're here to work. It's like a vacation paid for. I give thanks to God every day for the blessing of this job. I know it's not easy for you sometimes to take care of everything, and I sure want you to know that I think of it and appreciate . . . what a good soldier you are. Few women, very few indeed, can compare with you. I miss you and the kiddies so much.

It wasn't long before any notion that he was on a paid vacation was knocked out of Dad's head. The temperature dropped to fifty degrees the day after the engineers' arrival, and the work became a relentless grind. Wistful longings fill my parents' letters to each other. From Dad: "I love you so much. I miss snuggling up to you. I'm tired of sleeping alone and getting no kiss good night."

From Mom:

> Home is not the same without you. Paul needs his daddy. On cold nights, I take Paul close; I'm not used to sleeping alone. Poor you, with no one to snuggle. I feel like I'm a widow and the kids are "orfinks." You're gone so long. We miss you so much.

Dad got back to Chicago on February 10. He was home for three weeks before leaving for Beaumont, Texas, on March 1, and returning a month later. Our lives became a frantic rhythm of Dad's travel for up to three or four weeks at a time, sometimes longer. When home, he wrote up reports at the office during the day. Every weekend and evening, well past midnight, he stripped woodwork, painted, scrubbed, and varnished.

As 1950 went by, Dad traveled to Ohio, Minnesota, and Pennsylvania. I stood at the back door, calling for him, "Daddy! Daddy! Daddy!" My one-year-old self couldn't comprehend his disappearance. I lifted the lid of the pink wicker clothes hamper in our bathroom, hoping to find him there. When we heard the bell ring upon his return, I ran to greet him on my clumsy toddler legs, stumbling with my heavy cloth diaper dragging me down. I pushed myself off the floor with both hands to race to the front hallway. Looking way up, I saw his smiling face, framed by the door window, arriving like a big present.

When Dad's travels were close enough to Chicago, he came home for weekends, scrunching himself into a coach seat on a Friday overnight train and settling his wide hat over his eyes. Jostled by the rocking and endless clickety-clack of iron wheels rolling over rails, he slept only fitfully, arriving home to nonstop work on the house. He hadn't known he'd be traveling six months of the year when he'd committed to renovate the two-flat, but he'd do it all anyway.

After two sixteen-hour days of physical work, he rode a Sunday night train back to the target city, arriving bleary-eyed on Monday morning. Images of wood and walls and paint were replaced with mind-blurring city maps, numbers, and calculations—no slowdown allowed. His father's boast, "When I was younger, no one could work me tired"; his mother's refrain, "*Sei Selbstständig!*" ("Be self-sufficient!")— each surely played like an admonishment in his subconscious. Working through exhaustion was expected.

A lifelong achiever, Mom drove herself, too. During the day, she dove into remodeling projects. It was nine thirty or later, after putting Paul and me to bed, racing through our prayers with the speed of an auctioneer, before she could start on the business of the building—noting every expense on her neatly laid-out lined green ledger sheets, paying bills, balancing the checkbook, organizing her figures year-round in anticipation of income-tax season.

By September of 1950, after Dad's first year of travel, Mom's nerves were frayed. "Lil is crabby for some unknown reason," Dad wrote. "As usual, I didn't participate in lengthening an argument, which irked her to no end and she began to cry."

I was eighteen months old at the time of this scene, probably sleeping peacefully in my crib. I only learned of these early conflicts, which they hid masterfully from us kids, through Dad's diary and their letters.

Dad's words "crabby for some unknown reason" tell me that he apparently didn't discern that Mom was becoming ever more resentful of his traveling job, which, just twelve months earlier, she had extolled as "a wonderful opportunity," encouraging him to do all he could "to excel" at the work.

But neither had the skills to resolve their differences. Dad had learned early in childhood to skirt conflict with his overbearing mother—better to say nothing than to fan the embers of acrimony. Mom, raised by a volatile and combative mother, was tenacious and wanted a fight. When Dad wouldn't participate, she cried in frustration. What did Dad do then? Did he attempt to hold her close and kiss her? If so, did she turn away with more accusations or try to talk?

They couldn't get down to the essence of the problem, which was that the strain of living apart for weeks at a time was taking its toll on their marriage. Because of Mom's overachieving competence, Dad never questioned that, even without his presence half the year, she could handle it all: manage the building along with the quirks and stress of three tenants living with our family in the same apartment, and another tenant in the first-floor flat; care for two little children; handle all the financial details of which he had little, if any, understanding. Of course, Mom pushed herself, too—taking on the additional work of sanding, painting, and varnishing.

It is little wonder that she began depending increasingly on Grandma K for help, either oblivious to, or ignoring, the tension and dangers that Grandma K brought into the household. Mom seemed unaware that Dad's strategic interventions prevented Grandma K from seriously hurting his wife.

They didn't have Oprah or Doctor Phil or the now-ubiquitous concept of couple's therapy or thousands of magazine articles to shed light on conflict resolution. They were both stuck with their own past experiences and personalities, and no guidance.

At the end of 1950, we moved down to the first floor, but again, my parents rented out two of the three bedrooms to get ahead of their debt. Mom and Dad took the back bedroom, just off the kitchen, and tucked my crib along one wall. Paul and Grandma K slept in the dining room, through which the roomers walked to get to the only bathroom, a couple steps from my parents' bedroom, where Mom would sleep alone when Dad traveled.

Dad's plan was to transform the second-floor flat into two separate spaces. He hired a carpenter to build walls in the front two-thirds of the second-floor apartment, creating a total of five furnished "sleeping rooms," each to be rented to a single man, all sharing one bathroom, European pension–style. No women were allowed, as that would be unseemly.

Dad would install a locked door between the sleeping rooms and the second floor's back end, which would be remodeled into a furnished one-bedroom apartment. After these conversions, only the basement wouldn't be generating income and adding to the family's financial security.

Dad's vision was to keep the back two-thirds of the basement for his workshop, furnace, and coal room. At the front end, he'd create three furnished, studio-like apartments with a kitchen on one side and a living room/bedroom with a sofa bed on the other. As with the roomers, the three basement tenants would share a single bathroom down the hall. The rent for each would be fifteen dollars per week. If all were occupied, my parents would gross about $2,300 a year. Combined with the rent from the five second-floor rooms and back apartment, Dad's NBFU salary would be more than doubled. But a loan of about $6,000–$7,000, almost 50 percent of the building's initial cost, was needed to finance the construction.

One problem niggled at Dad's plan. Chicago building code disallowed creating residential units in any space two feet or more below grade, and our basement was two feet below grade. He met with a contractor, Krenwinkle, on New Year's Day of 1951, while Mom lay in bed, nursing a hangover. The contractor brushed aside the building code issue. "We'll just fix it," he said. In 1950s Chicago, the common wisdom was that only a fool would let a little thing like a proper permit get in the way of construction. Everyone knew building inspectors had their hands out.

Dad was scheduled to leave for Oklahoma City the next day, and he wanted the work to get started while he was gone. But coming to an agreement with the contractor without Mom's explicit approval was a strategic error. A rigid rule follower, Mom was adamantly opposed to proceeding without a permit.

After kissing Mom, Paul, and me goodbye on January 2, Dad walked out the door into a pouring rain, the neighborhood enveloped in a veil of gloom. Puddles reflecting a leaden sky hugged the curbs. Unable to hail a cab, he took two buses to Union Station, and climbed onto a train jammed with post-holiday travelers. Dad slept a scant four hours before starting work the next day.

On January 5, a special delivery letter arrived for him from Mom. After two opening paragraphs of niceties, she got to the point: "This basement deal has me all upset." She laid out her objections: "I don't want to invest $6,000 without a permit. If he can't get a permit, we shouldn't work with Krenwinkle. What do you think?"

Dad fumed to his diary. "That's just great. Here I am, eight hundred miles away, and she says, 'What do you think?' When I'm gone, she goes behind my back and cancels all my actions." He called her long-distance, and they talked for twenty minutes. His stomach sank at the cost of the phone call: eight dollars—half a day's pay!

Letters flew back and forth, one arriving every two days via airmail. Back in Chicago, the contractor told Mom that she was "unnecessarily concerned." Mom was not mollified, worried the project could be shut down and they'd lose their four years of savings for the down payment, and besides: "I'm hesitant about adding more tasks to my list and having no one at hand to help half the time. This place is so much more work than you realize." She included a multipage rundown of all the chores she had completed during his absence.

Dad wrote calm, reasonable letters in response to Mom's, but he vented to his diary. "After all the work and preparation and approved loan, she does this. What's wrong with her intelligence anyway?" He reassured her that the apartments would be no work: "Once construction is complete, they'll bring in forty-five dollars per week for no time on your end." Mom argued persuasively that such thinking was a pipe dream.

The idea of no work was delusional on Dad's part. Advertising and showing the apartments, cleaning the bathroom weekly, resolving tenant conflicts, keeping up with repairs, tidying up after a tenant left, collecting and recording the rent, performing additional income-tax work, and more: all of these were Mom's responsibilities.

Despite the conflict, they still had tender words for each other. Dad wrote:

> *Dear Lil,*
> *Here it is the beginning of the fourth week that I'm away from home, and it seems like ten years since I've been with you. . . . Eating in restaurants and sleeping alone is not all it's cracked up to be. I miss you and the kiddies so much. . . . I love you. I love you. I love you. Give Paul and Linda a big hug and a squeeze for me and consider yourself thoroughly kissed and loved.*
> *All my love,*
> *Fred*

And crossing in the mail, from Mom:

> *Dear Fred,*
> *Your January trip always seems the very longest in the whole year. I can't wait till you come back. These next three weeks will seem like forever.*
> *Love,*
> *Lil*

By the time Dad returned home, he had been gone for six full weeks, from January 20 to the second week of March—the worst part of the winter.

CHAPTER 15: Travelin' Man

Mom and Dad in happy times, Caruso's restaurant, June 1958.

1951–52

Somehow Dad persuaded Mom to move ahead with the basement apartments in the winter of 1951. I have no idea how he pulled this off, given the strong arguments Mom made against the plan. I believe she didn't want him morose and angry with her—because she still loved him. I know this from photos of the era: the flirtatious looks they gave each other; the broad, happy smiles of a couple in love.

Even as a toddler, I knew my parents were in love. I saw it from my crib, tucked into the corner of my parents' bedroom. One morning, I pushed up from sleep to stand, my hands gripping the back of the crib. My parents were sitting on the edge of their double bed, naked from the waist up, both in their underpants. Mom's dark, curly hair was rumpled. With an adult understanding, I now know they probably had been quietly making love just before they heard me stir. They were smiling up at me when whimsical Dad initiated a simple real-life metaphor to entertain me. He pressed one of Mom's nipples and said, "Bing bong!" He then looked to me with an impish grin. I jumped up and down, squealing in delight.

Mom pressed Dad's nipple. "Bing bong," she repeated in a singsongy voice. Leaping up and down even more frenetically, I screamed out, "More! More!" Mom threw back her head, laughing at my reaction. Back and forth it went, until they probably had to move on with their day. I'm sure they never imagined such a young child would remember the scene. I think I recall it vividly because, even in that brief moment, their joy with each other, and with their little girl, enveloped me in the secure sense that I was in a loving home and had nothing to fear.

When Krenwinkle showed up with the agreement to remodel the basement, Mom studied it for half an hour. Surely with a lump in her throat and a deep sigh, she added her signature to Dad's. But a new crisis was taking hold. That very afternoon, strep throat raced through the family, requiring multiple doctor home visits to administer penicillin shots. Panic undoubtedly edged Dad's gut. He was leaving for Shreveport, Louisiana, the next day.

On the morning of March 6, 1951, Dad kissed Mom's hot, flushed face farewell, promising that his parents or his brother, Will, who all lived together within a block, would take care of shoveling coal into the furnace until she was better. Despite their proximity, Dad's parents offered little help or support to my mother as she struggled to manage without her husband. Grandma Gartz's response to any complaints Mom made of her burdens was patronizing and predictable: "I made it. You will, too."

Until I found Grandma Gartz's World War II letter to Ebner, I couldn't understand her cold and distant attitude to us, but her cruel words exposed her animosity toward Mom, right from the get-go. Grudgingly, Dad's parents agreed to take on the furnace while everyone in the house burned with fever.

In his letters from Shreveport, Dad exhorted Mom: "Don't do anything that's not necessary. Hire out the wash and ironing. Don't burn the candle at both ends. Go to bed by ten thirty. When I get home, I'll help with the shopping."

Dad's absence not only wore on Mom but also stressed out us children, especially Paul. He began acting out, defying my parents' requests, or yelling at them to "Shut up!" Mom's response, borne out of frustration and well learned at the hands of her "Mama," Grandma K, was to give him a "good licking" as she called it, again and again.

"He's an emotional child," Dad wrote to Mom, "and can only be reached through emotion." But Mom was on the home front alone, and not inclined to listen to advice from several hundred miles away.

I was simply born into the new order of things. Even as a toddler, I never expected my mother to entertain me, perhaps another reason why the "bing bong" game was so memorable. I invented imaginary friends with exotic names—Boozlebottom, Kukulook, and Zirah—who took me on adventures to magical lands. I recall Mom as a whirling blur, zipping through the house, moving from one project to the next, seldom able to give me her full attention beyond the basics of good mothering. When I was sick, she laid me on the dining-room couch and sat beside me, dipping a cloth over and over into cool alcohol-water, wiping my hot skin to bring down my fever. I never felt ignored or unloved by Mom, but I realize now, as a mother myself, that she had little time to truly get to know or understand me the way Dad would, despite his absences.

After more than a year of traveling, Dad realized that his coworkers liked to spend most evenings hanging out at bars, drinking the night away, which Dad found both boring and a waste of money. Instead, he preferred to pass the time by himself.

He wrote poetry, hooked rugs, and took up needlework. In Texas, Dad bought two little red felt vests, one for Paul and one for me. On the back of each he sewed our names, and on the front he embroidered western scenes—cacti, horses, split-rail fences, cowboy hats, and lassos. I wore the vest every day after he gave it to me, galloping on horseback through imaginary high chaparral, a landscape I picked up from TV westerns. On one trip around this time, he purchased a large embroidery pattern of Psalm 23 as a gift for Mom. Every Sunday while he was away from home, sometimes until one in the morning, he cross-stitched the words and flowery decorations.

When Dad arrived home on May 4, Mom greeted him in a foul mood. "I'm shouldering all the responsibilities for this remodel alone!" she cried out, breaking down into sobs. They talked into the night. But no matter what reassuring words Dad could offer, they were stuck with a $7,500 loan and needed to finish and rent those basement apartments to pay it off. Mom's bitterness continued for days after his return. He took note:

Poor gal is still all down in the mouth. She's resentful
against the building, the basement apartments, and
me for wanting them. I know it's a lot of work, but
it will be nice when they're done. I just keep quiet
and let her talk. No point in trying to reason with her
when she's in this frame of mind.

Unable to change the reality, Dad let Mom blow off steam. Yet when I read his words, I also sense that he believed Mom would eventually just snap out of it, that he didn't truly comprehend the intense stress she suffered. Mom's goal-oriented nature meant she took on much more work than necessary, but she had argued vehemently against the basement remodel and had agreed only to please Dad—and now she was left holding the proverbial bag. Perhaps Dad believed he just had to weather Mom's "moods" and all would be fine.

It was a serious miscalculation.

CHAPTER 16: Wanna Trade Places?

1952

Despite my father's efforts to come home every possible weekend, Mom was cracking under the strain of his long absences. In June, the whole family went out for dinner to celebrate Grandpa Gartz's sixty-fourth birthday. Dad looked at Mom across the table and saw a wife hardly recognizable from the ebullient, cheerful woman he had married. Her face was drawn and exhausted, with an unhealthy pallor. She had lost weight.

Back at home, all the inner turmoil Dad had seen in Mom's face poured out in her bitter words: "I'm sick of all your traveling." Knowing Dad, he must have tried to console her, but Mom was having none of it. "You're not part of the family!" she spat out. "You're never here. I really don't see why all the wives of the National Board engineers don't just get a divorce. They certainly have the grounds for it! None of them have any husbands!"

Dad wrote no condemnation of Mom in his diary, other than to record her words and note them as "spiteful." He said nothing in return. A counterargument would have only increased my mother's ire. I feel for Mom's predicament, but I also understand Dad's hurt and bewilderment at her vindictive reproach against his work for the National Board, when she had wholeheartedly supported the position. Hadn't she

written him, "Do all you can to excel at this job"? Hadn't she
called the NBFU offer a "wonderful opportunity"? Weren't
his travels supporting the family? Didn't he come home every
possible weekend to be with the family and work to exhaustion on the house?

Except for a couple of mentions in Dad's earliest letters
about seeking work without travel, none of Dad's or Mom's
letters, or Dad's diary, reveal that Mom was pressuring him
to look for a different position. Instead, she made lists of projects for him to start "at seven o'clock, right after dinner,"
allowing him no time to think, much less start a job search.

It's clear from the letters and diary that Dad's travel
was undermining my parents' relationship, so why didn't
they make a no-traveling job their highest priority? Dad's
diary reveals the most plausible answer. He recorded multiple incidents involving his mother-in-law, but an event he
wrote down in detail on July 4, 1952, when I was three, is
an exemplar.

Dad was in the basement when he heard Grandma K's hysterical voice piercing through the kitchen floorboards. He dashed
up the gangway steps, around the porch, up the back stairs,
and into the kitchen where he saw Grandma shouting, jab-
bing her finger at Mom, whose face was folding, on the cusp
of tears. The refrigerator door stood agape. "Who took my
pills? Who? I put them in the icebox, and now they're gone."

Grandma glared at Dad, her eyes "fierce with hate and
anger." She screeched, "You! You took them. *You* are to
blame. There is always something missing whenever you set
foot into this house. We have peace when you're gone!"

Dad spoke levelly. "Please don't scream in my house."

"Your house? Your house?" Grandma shouted, her
anger electrifying the air. "This is not *your* house. It's mine
and Lillian's. We worked for it. Not you!"

That says it all. In Grandma K's warped mind, with Dad gone for weeks at a time, *he* was the interloper in the household.

Paul yelled at Grandma K, "Keep quiet!"

"Leave Mommy alone!" I cried out, my hands over my ears at all the screaming.

They searched the icebox, finally finding the pills in the vegetable bin. "You put them there," Grandma screamed at Dad, "so you can put me in the crazy house again!"

As her mother's agitation and accusations escalated, Mom stood by helplessly, sobbing. She recognized that Grandma K was exhibiting "all the symptoms of 1946 & '49, when she was confined to a mental hospital in each case," Dad wrote.

Dad knew he had to take control and calm his mother-in-law before she spiraled into a total frenzy, so he embraced her. "Look, we don't want you in any hospital," Dad said. "We want you here." It was a strategic gesture on Dad's part. I know nothing could have been further from his true feelings. She pulled away and shuffled to the living room, where she stared out the window at passing cars.

A vicious cycle had evolved—a perfect catch-22. Dad's long absences and the work of the rooming house made Mom reliant on her mother for childcare and housework. Mom's insistence that her psychotic mother live with us made home an unwelcome place for Dad. Until I read Dad's diaries and Mom's accounts of incidents like this one, I hadn't realized— whether I'd suppressed the memories or was simply too young to remember—the toxic effect Grandma K's presence had on our family life. I now believe Dad probably would have sought a Chicago-based job if he hadn't been subjected to Grandma K's diatribes at home.

The day after Grandma's attack against Dad, he drove the family up to Lake Geneva, Wisconsin, for a day of swimming and splashing in its cool waters. He spent all day Sunday on house projects. At around ten o'clock at night, he grabbed a cab to the Greyhound bus depot, then tossed and turned on another miserable overnight ride back to Detroit.

Less than a week after Grandma K's attack on Dad, he received from Mom what he described in his diary as a "nasty letter." I found the letter among their correspondence. In it, Mom made no comment of Grandma K's cruel and delusional accusation against Dad—that he was an unwelcome intruder in his own home. Mom didn't acknowledge his calming intervention, as she stood by helplessly and her little children shouted in distress. Among other details, she wrote:

> *My life while you are gone is equivalent to seven days per week of one of your weekends. You will never know or understand the hectic weekdays trying to get things done. No wonder you like your job—just pack up and go and forget the house.*
> *Love,*
> *Lil*
> *P.S. Wanna trade places for a couple months?*

In a rare rejoinder, Dad defended himself in a return letter.

> *Dear Lil,*
> *I don't think that I have ever failed to recognize or appreciate the excessive amount of responsibility, work, and worry that has, because of my work being away from home, chick, and child, been so unceremoniously heaped upon your shoulders. . . .*
> *I wonder if you would care to "trade places for a couple months?" I wonder if you would care to be several hundreds of miles from home and loved ones, knowing that one or more are sick and there isn't a damned thing you can do for them.*
> *All you'll have to do is wait till the survey is over or till the weekend comes so that you can snatch a*

few moments of normal life together with your family,
even though all of that time is gladly spent on home
activities, only to arrive back in the field Monday
morning, so tired from a lack of a good night's sleep
that you can't get a decent breath of air till after
you've had a night's sleep.

I'm not looking for sympathy. It's just a little
reminder that the hardships of life and livelihood
manifest themselves in many forms and are not all
one-sided. A trade in places can probably take place
with the coming vacation. You and your mother can
go someplace for a couple of weeks, and I'll take
care of the house and kids. Enclosed are my last two
salary checks. I won't need them.
Love,
Fred

Mom had plenty of reason to be frustrated at her predicament. Unlike the persistent image of a 1950s housewife, engaged solely in domestic duties, she had a full-time job, managing all the family and business financial details as well as eleven tenants, two living just down the hall, with the bathroom they all shared just steps away from her bedroom door. All of this with her husband gone half the year. Her work nearly doubled the family income. She was a woman ahead of her time, in a society that provided no support for such a dual role.

But what has struck me most in reading the letters and diaries from this era was Mom's sad inability to recognize Dad's efforts in containing her mother's madness. Mom's relentless and bitter complaints must have pained him even as he strove to demonstrate his devotion to hearth, home, and loved ones.

CHAPTER 17: Tenth Anniversary

Mom with ten mums from Dad for their 10th Anniversary, November 8, 1952.

1952

Among Dad's greatest priorities and joys was planning and executing our yearly vacation, ensuring we'd have at least one week when we could hang out together, day and night, as a family. Our annual destination was Devil's Lake State Park in Wisconsin. Grandma K never joined us. She could manage by herself for a week (she was self-reliant in daily living, which is why my mother so often depended on her for childcare, housekeeping, and cooking), and Dad probably insisted they have at least a few days of family time without her. On August 16, 1952, we headed north.

After a six-hour car ride on 1950s highways, we arrived at a cabin in the woods with bunk beds and an outside hand pump. As soon as we settled in, Paul ran to try out the pump, pressing his arm up and down on the lever at a feverish speed, his face set with determination to pump as fast and hard as possible. He seemed fascinated that his own muscles could make water gush forth. At three, I was too puny to even budge the handle, but I wanted to see where the water came from. I stuck my head under the spout while Paul, in his enthusiasm, didn't miss a pumping beat. He brought the handle full force smack on the bony ridge beside my right eye. Blinded by blood, I ran screaming toward the cabin. Dad flew out the door and scooped me into his arms, Mom right behind him, both of their faces grimaced in fear.

"What happened?" Dad shouted.

"Paul pumped my head," I sobbed.

"I didn't do it on purpose!" Paul yelled. "She's stupid! Just stuck her head under the handle while I was pumping!"

"For God's sake!" said Dad. "You have to watch what you're doing!"

Dad cradled me in his lap, pressing ice from the cooler against the bloody cut. "Do you think she needs stitches?" asked Mom as she dabbed Mercurochrome on the open wound.

I wriggled and screamed, "No! No!" I was panicked at the idea of a needle poking through my throbbing skin. Mom and Dad decided I'd be okay, and within half an hour I was running around again with Paul, a large Band-Aid covering my swollen and bruised temple. A scar still reminds me of the accident, but that's not what I took away from our trip. Walking through the woods, roasting hot dogs and marsh-mallows over crackling campfires Dad taught us to build, climbing towering bluffs, swimming in the warm lake, lis-tening to Mom read *Adventures of Huckleberry Finn* around the fire's dying embers, peering at a night sky blasted with stars—those remembrances will stay with me forever. But having Mom and Dad all to ourselves was the best memory of all.

⁓

During the weeks spanning late October through early November of 1952, Dad's destination was Kansas City, Kansas. Waking at five in the morning on November 1, Dad added the final touches to city maps for the day's first four hours. He set aside the rest of the morning to create a special tenth-anniversary gift for Mom.

He arrived at the local library just as it opened, pulled out a chair at the large wooden refectory table, and sat in the enveloping silence to compose a poem, calling up recollections of their wedding day. After working and reworking his draft, he copied the poem line by line with a fountain pen onto a sheet of crisp parchment paper. Back at the hotel, he preordered ten mums, one for each year they'd been married.

Early Saturday morning, November 8, he rode the train home, prepared to surprise Mom for their anniversary with his poem, the mums, and a special evening he had planned. They'd eat dinner at a cozy German restaurant, Old Heidelberg, followed by the movie *Ivanhoe*. The finale for this perfectly planned celebration would be drinks at a favorite haunt from their dating days, Don the Beachcomber's, in downtown Chicago. Wouldn't his careful planning show Mom how much he loved her? That he appreciated her weeks alone, handling all the details of family life? That despite their separations, their love was still strong? That he *was* still part of the family?

Dad arrived to a sullen November sky, hoping to find his wife in sunny spirits, rather than morose and angry. After entering the front door and setting down his suitcase, he called out, "Hello! I'm home!" Mom came dashing to the living room to greet him, throwing her arms around his neck, kissing his cheeks and mouth over and over.

She took him by the hand, leading him into the dining room. "Oh, thank you, Fred. The mums arrived, and they're just beautiful." Mom saved the little card that came attached to the mums. Decorated with a spray of tiny blue forget-me-nots at the bottom and printed with "On Our Anniversary" at the top, it reads:

> *To the dearest little wife and best friend anyone*
> *could ever hope for.*
> *Love, Fred*

A mini-album of black-and-white photographs taken on that day show Mom and Dad posing separately and together in our backyard. Her bouquet of ten robust mums held before her, Mom's smile and eyes are lively. She's dressed in a light, wide-collared wool coat with her dark curls swept off her face and lipstick brightening her mouth. Dad wears a suit jacket and tie, and a broad grin. They are ready for a perfect anniversary.

That afternoon, Grandma K came down with a fever, but Dr. Peterson couldn't get to the house until after eight o'clock at night. One of the tenants offered to babysit for Paul and me, but for whatever confluence of reasons, my parents decided against going out, abandoning their plans. Dad wrote in his diary simply this: "When Dr. Peterson came, he said that Lil's mother had another strep throat. We stayed home."

Dad doesn't write about Mom's reaction, so I can only speculate. Deep down, Mom's paradoxical feelings of fear and love toward her mother would have squirmed and churned in her gut and electrified her subconscious. If Mom went out, would her mother call her a "selfish ingrate," as she had in the past?

How can I leave my mother home sick? She was so good to me! Mom likely thought.

The first hours of strep—consisting of a hot fever and a raw throat—aren't pleasant, but they're tolerable for a few hours, and a penicillin shot works fast. Another mother might have said, "It's your anniversary. Please go out and have fun," but not Grandma K. Of course, Mom's mother couldn't impose a strep throat onto herself, but it was another joyful occasion ruined by my grandmother.

Dad would have left the decision up to Mom. He knew that if he urged her to go out, she would have been distracted and worried, unable to enjoy herself. Did she apologize to Dad—or just expect him to understand?

She surely noticed his crestfallen face: his eyes first grave, watching, waiting; then, when Mom said they shouldn't go out, he would have turned away, his lips set into a tight line; and Mom would have read the disappointment in his slumped shoulders, his silent stoicism. Perhaps she also thought she saw blame, and she would have stored away a painful reprimand. Dad would not have made any overt accusations, but still, maybe Mom felt that Dad faulted both her mother *and* her for ruining the evening. How unfair! What was she to do with her mother feverish—and needing her?

The only thing for Dad to do after Dr. Peterson left was to give Mom his poem honoring their ten years of marriage.

To My Wife, Lillian, on Our Tenth Wedding Anniversary November 8, 1952

The first four stanzas recall funny and poignant details of their wedding day. It ends like this:

> *Though we've gone through much together,*
> *In sunshine and in stormy weather,*
> *Our spirits still are strong.*
> *Paul and Linda helped our travel*
> *Although to try these to unravel*
> *Calls more for patience, less of thong.*
>
> *And so ten years we've had each other*
> *As wife and husband, father, mother,*

And sweethearts from the start.
You've meant the world and all that's in it
And if I'd twice more to begin it
You'd still be my sweetheart.

For years afterward, they often brought out the poem to share with us kids. I loved to hear it, loved to see how proud of their love they were. Dad gave a modest shrug and a pleased smile. I liked seeing Mom, basking in the devotion of his words; how by reading it to us kids, they honored their marriage. Surely my emotional mom cried after reading Dad's words that night in 1952; surely they made love.

It had to be moments like these that kept the spark alive, and why, as a child, I never discerned my mother's unhappiness lurking beneath the unfailing cooperation and teamwork I witnessed when Dad was home.

If I take away anything from what I discovered in the letters and diaries, it's that their inability to talk openly and non-judgmentally about the issues they faced was the greatest threat to their relationship.

I know they never even considered seeing a therapist or a marriage counselor at that time. I recall them referring to people who did such things as "weak." Self-reliant people should solve their own problems. But I understand now that, without counseling, an open discussion between them would have been impossible.

The years ahead would bring new worries, undermining my parents' happiness further as racist housing policies and city neglect chipped away at our neighborhood, where they had staked their marital and financial future.

CHAPTER 18: A Vision of Decline

Grandma K with Dad, Mom, Linda, Paul, and Billy in our living room, 1954.

1953

For more than three years, my parents had used every waking hour to make a success of their rooming house, the combination of excessive toil and Dad's travel tearing at their love, unraveling their relationship thread by thread. In May of 1953, a full decade before the first black family would move onto our block, Mom heard what would have been disturbing news for a white homeowner at the time.

My parents rented one space in their two-car garage to

a Mr. Birchler, who was about to move out of state. Mom
wrote to Dad about Birchler's comments:

> *He told me that at 14th and Pulaski, where he now
> works at the A&P, the people are mostly all colored,
> whereas three years ago, they were mostly all white.
> He figures the same for this neighborhood within
> five years.*
>
> *I think we should be cautious about spending
> too much on improving our building. I, of course, do
> believe in upkeep, but not too much otherwise.*

Pulaski and 14th, where Birchler worked, was about two miles
south of our home, in North Lawndale. Birchler's comments
appear spot on. The 1950 census reported that North Lawndale
was nearly 87 percent white.[30] Now, in 1953, Birchler noted
that the residents were mostly black. The influx of African
Americans in such close proximity surely alarmed my mother.

On a 1940 HOLC (Home Owners' Loan Corporation)
map of West Garfield Park, where Dad and his family still
lived and worked, their community was marked yellow,
"definitely declining," according to the color code. Redlined
areas started just a few blocks north of our street and continued east toward and around Garfield Park itself. On the map
key, red is marked "hazardous," and HOLC described this
swath of red as "threatened with Negro encroachment."[31]
It's highly unlikely that Mom and Dad would have bought a
home in an area about which such a damning assessment had
been made almost ten years before their purchase.

My parents were undoubtedly clueless about the racist
policy of redlining an area when blacks arrived, but they
knew the outcome. If even one African American moved
into West Garfield Park, property values would plummet for
whites who wanted to sell, threatening the money, sweat,

and marital harmony my parents had sacrificed in creating and maintaining our rooming house. They weren't alone in their fear—or in their ignorance of redlining.

After a white mob had persecuted a new black neighbor, a white woman wrote the following defense of the antagonists, specifically calling out North Lawndale, the area Bircher referenced.

> *[The protestors] have seen what happens to so-called changing neighborhoods. A case in point is North Lawndale. It was a nice-looking section of Chicago. . . . Drive through it now and . . . [you'll] really see blight. It is the mess a neighborhood gets into once it has changed that people object to.*[32]

Another white Chicagoan wrote that he moved his family out of a transitioning neighborhood because of "fear and filth."[33]

The ruinous result of denying, or limiting, mortgages and loans in redlined areas, of real-estate agents who sold houses to African Americans on contract at inflated and barely affordable prices, of the stereotyping and prejudice that crammed black families into burgeoning segregated neighborhoods—was infrastructure breakdown. Whites, blindly or willfully unaware of how these causes all worked together, blamed the victims, African Americans, while simultaneously feeling victimized themselves.

From whites' point of view, families like ours had sacrificed and saved for years so they could own their own home. After working hard and doubling up (as my parents did with several roomers and Grandma K), they had finally made it, but now the rules were changing. For many whites, "it must have felt like bait and switch."[34] They were going to lose everything: community, friends, and the value of their home, which meant much more to them than just a place to live: it was the American dream achieved.

Of course, African American couples had the same dream. They, too, scrimped and saved to buy homes in good neighborhoods. They, too, wanted to own property, wanted their children to attend uncrowded schools. But while whites could live wherever they chose, blacks were vilified and terrorized out of white areas. They were denied mortgages and therefore the ability to build wealth from homeownership—as white families could. (Today, on average, white households have sixteen times the wealth of black households.)[35]

Forced to buy their homes through "contract purchases," many blacks lost their entire investment when they missed a payment for any reason. Whites were laser-focused on the loss of their property values and the ruin they expected would follow when blacks moved into their communities. But the racist lending system, intended to protect white housing privilege, was about to sabotage it.

I discovered that less than four years after my parents had invested so much money, sweat equity, and marital sacrifice into the two-flat, Mom was already worried about their financial future in the neighborhood. She had learned from a departing tenant that the community directly south of our home was now populated mostly by African Americans. Perhaps their treadmill lives allowed only a fleeting contemplation of where they were headed before they were back to putting one foot in front of the other. Even the imminent arrival of another baby seemed to generate little discussion, at least not in their correspondence.

In January of 1953, Dad climbed aboard the Texas Chief southbound train in Chicago, heading for Houston, Texas. By the time he returned home in late February, he and Mom had been separated for thirty-five days. They were so desperate to be in each other's arms again, they gave in to their passion and made love on the bathroom toilet seat, leaving Mom's diaphragm in the bedroom.

Why the bathroom? Probably so they could lock the door against Grandma K and the kids. The result was a third baby, an unplanned love child. Dad related this anecdote to my younger brother, Billy, many years later. Billy has always been proud of his provenance.

During the months from early March to November, neither Mom nor Dad made any mention of the pregnancy in their letters. Mom wrote not one word about feeling ill. She didn't insist that, with a third child, Dad needed to find a job in Chicago, or that their hectic, separated lives would have to change. There was no comment about the financial strain on the family or the added time and effort a new baby would demand.

"Mommy, why is your tummy getting so big?" I asked one day.

"I'm making a baby, and you're going to be a big sister," Mom told me, gently circling her hand around her expanded belly under the loose maternity dress. "I'll need your help to change the baby's diapers and give the baby a bottle." I envisioned the fun I'd have feeding a real living doll—not one I had to just pretend to feed and change.

Dad waited until a week before the baby was due to inform his boss about the imminent birth and tell him that he couldn't travel for a while. Dad doesn't explain his reticence on the subject, but I think it may have been to allow his superiors, who had no empathy for family life, minimal maneuvering room to possibly replace him if he couldn't leave town on their schedule.

"Well . . . I suppose we'll have to go along with you on that one," was his boss's unenthusiastic response.

I stayed with family friends when Dad drove Mom to Garfield Park Hospital. She gave birth to my brother on November 12, and, as was typical of the era, stayed in the hospital for several days. When Mom and Dad arrived to pick me up, Mom carried a pale-blue bundle in her arms and laid it on the couch. "Here's your new little brother, Billy," she said, pulling away layers until the baby's puffy red face, scrunched-up eyes, and shuddering little body appeared. This baby didn't look anything like the baby dolls I'd played with. He was all twitchy! His eyes stayed tightly shut, and his head moved in random movements. And there was more that was strange. "What's that on his leg?" I asked Mom, pointing to something hard and white.

Mom's voice cracked a bit. "That's a cast," she said, gently running her hand down Billy's encased leg. Her eyes glistened. "My poor little baby has a twisted foot. The cast will help fix it." Billy was born with a clubfoot, his right foot turning inwards at the ankle, a common birth defect, easily correctable in the 1950s. Doctors turned the foot outward in stages, casting each rotation to hold the new alignment, replacing the cast often as the leg grew. Within three months, his foot was in the right position.

Mom was instructed to massage the leg twice daily. By this time, Billy looked to me like a real baby. His eyes were open more, and he smiled at us all. I could tickle him or make funny faces, or imitate his gurgling and cooing noises—and he'd laugh. I couldn't wait to help with the massage.

Mom laid Billy onto a waterproof pad she had placed atop the white chenille bedspread on the double bed; she then spread cream onto his newly straightened foot and leg, and showed me how to rub and turn the leg to keep it in alignment. We cooed and smiled into Billy's happy little face, squeezing and rubbing, singing him songs. An easy baby, he was a tonic for my mother, adding sparkles of delight to her life's stress and slog.

In late January, Mom and I sat in Tilton Elementary

School's yawning assembly hall, surrounded by other moms with children spilling across their laps or crawling over the wooden seats, waiting to register for half-day kindergarten. I would begin two months before my fifth birthday, and I felt very grown-up, going to school like Paul. Starting midyear was common in many Chicago schools at the time, allowing what would otherwise have been an enormous class in the fall to be broken into two sections.

My kindergarten class photo shows no African American kids. Chicago schools were de facto segregated because attendance-area boundaries were determined by neighborhoods. But in the Jim Crow South, forced segregation was the rule of law at that time. Living in a child's world, I couldn't have known that just three and a half months after I began kindergarten, the U.S. Supreme Court unanimously decreed that the "separate but equal" doctrine, underpinning southern school-segregation laws, was unconstitutional.

Mom had little time to contemplate the historic significance of *Brown v. Board of Education*. It was probably more important to her that my entry into Tilton meant she would have a break from managing three children all day, now that both Paul and I were in school. The worst of the remodeling was over, but not the stress of eleven tenants, two still renting bedrooms in our own flat.

At around midnight of the same day I began school, Mom wrote Dad a ten-page letter, filling him in on her latest woes. Never one to let weariness interfere with duty, she often relinquished sleep to update Dad on the home front. It must have felt good to unload her frustrations in every letter.

"I was not able to get to bed one single night before twelve thirty, one, one thirty, or two, and then get up by eight. It has been just miserable being so far behind in everything," Mom explained. She ended with: "No break at all— never reading, never having time to read to the children or even sit down and talk to them or Mama."

Dad offered several possible remedies to her grievances

in his February 9 response. First he suggested that when he was home on a weekend, once or twice a month, he would relieve her of all childcare and housekeeping duties, so she could "devote undivided time to keeping up-to-date" on income-tax preparation throughout the year, so as not to be overburdened at the last minute. He added:

> It's high time you GOT SOME HELP for cleaning day. We are not so impoverished that you should do all that yourself. . . . It's not the cost I'm worried about, it's YOU YOU YOU. Please, Lil, let's do something about it while you still can enjoy all those little moments which mean so much to you; moments with some reading, the children, and whatever else you want. These are times I feel utterly helpless and useless in not being able to give more of myself to you.

In Mom's ten-page letter, she had included this comment after her exhaustive list of completed chores: "As your mother so aptly puts it, 'No use in complaining.'"

The remark was classic Grandma Gartz. Even though they lived only a half block east at this time, my grandparents seemed content to watch their daughter-in-law twist in the wind during Dad's lengthy travels. Mom had written to Dad, "As you know, your mother seems determined not to do anything for us or let Pop or Will either. . . . She's always belittling me."

Dad was in solid agreement with Mom on his family's condescending attitudes. Throughout his life, Dad had experienced firsthand his mother's controlling and belittling nature. Will was in the thrall of their mother, and easily controlled by her, while Dad resisted. But still, Dad valued family, and he could never fully withdraw from her psychological grasp.

Grandma G's disdain for my mother probably arose from jealousy, recognizing that Mom was at least as competent and hardworking (the latter being the pinnacle of life values). Perhaps, like many mothers-in-law, she was in competition with her son's wife. I believe she put Mom down so she could feel superior.

One winter, when Dad was gone for six weeks, a defective load of coal was delivered to our two-flat, and Mom awoke in the middle of the night, shivering in a freezing house. To check the furnace, she exited the back door to a blast of frigid air, walked down the stairs and around the house, and descended into a dark gangway, where she entered the basement and tried to relight the bad fuel.

Grandpa had spent the previous thirty years working with furnaces, but he didn't come to her rescue. Mom dropped by her in-laws' house one day during the crisis. "That furnace is driving me crazy," she said. "I have to dig out that bad coal and replace it over and over. I go back upstairs covered in coal dust."

I know the dismissive, disdainful look that would have settled on Grandma's face, the wave of her large, veined hand as if shooing a fly. "You're young yet!" she admonished. "That work is nothing! At your age, no work should be too dirty or low."

Mom concluded her letter to Dad with the implication that he was on a vacation: "So enjoy yourself, dear. There's work when you get home. I feel like an army that's just holding on until help comes."

***

Four and a half years earlier, Mom had been able to rely on Grandma K as a comrade-in-arms, but by the time Billy was born, Grandma K was sixty-seven years old and declining mentally and physically. She hadn't spun out of control prior to Billy's birth, as she had before Paul's and mine, but her behavior had grown unsettling in new ways. She wore the same dress for days at a time, refused to bathe, complained of pains in her legs, and fainted.

My parents never used the term *mental illness* or discussed Grandma's condition with us. The subject was taboo—and shameful. Neighborhood kids sometimes taunted me, "Your grandma's crazy! She was in the nuthouse."

How they found out, I don't know. Had Mom mentioned it to a neighbor, and the osmosis of gossip spread it around? A hot wave of shame washed over me, and I wasn't even sure why, so I just screamed, "You're a liar!"

But I knew things weren't right. I never doubted Mom was in control of the household and us kids, and I never saw my parents fight openly. But she couldn't control Grandma. If she tried persuasion, such as "Mama, let me wash your hair. It will feel so good," Grandma lashed out at her, "Mind your own business!" or screamed non-sequitur epithets: "Streetwalker! Whore." I could see in Mom's eyes a hesitancy in dealing with her mother that I never observed in her interactions with tenants, Dad, or us kids.

I understand now that, just as she had been as a child, she was still afraid of her mother.

CHAPTER 19: Barbara

Linda and Barbara play dress-up, 1961.

1956–62

Oblivious to the family drama, I lived happily in a child's world. West Garfield Park in the 1950s was like a small town, where we knew our neighbors and shopkeepers and could walk to nearby Madison Street, our business district, to purchase whatever we needed. For a kid, it was a place of freedom and adventure. The children played in the back alley, where we pitched balls, ran races, and exchanged gossip. ("Boys pay Rita a nickel to show them her underpants!"

we passed on in scandalized whispers.) We shimmied up gutters, hauling ourselves onto garage roofs burning with sun-baked, melting tar. From our perch, we copped a bird's-eye view into unshaded windows at unguarded couples, prompting giggles and whispers, and dared each other to leap from one roof to the next.

One day in 1956, at age seven, I was bouncing a rubber ball against my garage door, attempting tricks: catching it under my leg or spinning around to grab the ball before it hit the ground. I was determined to master these acrobatics, doing each over and over as if preparing for the Olympics. At some point, I glanced west and saw a new girl exit the gate three houses down. She walked toward me, her eyes flitting around, shy and hesitant. There weren't many girls my age on the block.

"Hi!" I said, tossing the ball lightly in the air and catching it. "My name's Linda. What's yours?"

"Barbara," she said in a lilting southern accent, the *r* softened to *Bah-bra*.

"Wanna bounce a ball with me?"

Barbara had gentle, olive-green eyes and wispy brown hair framing a soft, cherubic face. Light freckles dusted her creamy skin. I bounced the ball down to the ground and caught it over and over as we talked, forgetting my practice. I learned Barbara Hendrix's parents had eloped before finishing high school, then left Mississippi with Barbara and her brother for Chicago, where her dad hoped to find better-paying work. He landed a good job in an engineering department at Western Electric, where he would remain for thirty years.

Mrs. Hendrix was a stay-at-home mom and housewife, but once her children were older, she, too, got a job at Western Electric, testing rocket capacitors. A house-keeping perfectionist, Barb's mom kept every surface of their first-floor flat gleaming and shiny. Her family's crisply starched and freshly ironed clothes, folded like a display in a department store, looked as if they could stand on their own. Some kids in the neighborhood called Barb and her brother hillbillies, but we never did. My parents admired the Hendrixes, with their hardworking, clean, child-centered lives. They in no way fit the stereotype, held in our community, of the "slovenly hillbilly."

We were the perfect friends for each other at that stage of our lives, soaring together into imaginary worlds of pretending at an age that would stun a twenty-first-century girl into humiliation. At eleven, we still played dress-up, taking turns being "prince" or "princess," donning flowery, flowing dresses or velveteen waistcoats and shirts with wide, lacy cuffs Dad had picked up at a Salvation Army store.

Who started each foray into fantasy, I can't say, but we were simpatico to each other's ideas. We were best friends, before that concept became cheapened by a universal acronym, BFF, tossed indiscriminately into texts and greeting cards. We told each other family secrets and knew they were safe; we lay next to each other on sleepovers and talked late into the night, our parents repeatedly threatening to separate us if we didn't "stop talking and go to sleep!"

Barb and her family adored their fellow-Mississippian Elvis Presley, whom my parents viewed as vulgar. When I passed on this judgment to Barb, she laughed at me, especially when she caught me trying to emulate Elvis's moves. Without Barb, I might have kept my parents' parochial views of music, at least for a few more years. Instead, Barbara and I would try dancing the jitterbug to the irresistible beat of "Hound Dog" or "Jailhouse Rock."

We each had different strengths, and I don't recall any competition between us. I was a better student, but I think Barb was smarter. She had what we call today "EQ"—a genius for emotional intelligence—and would say just the right words to make someone feel good. Mom often told her, "Barbara, you are a master diplomat."

On our front sidewalk, we jumped rope or danced self-choreographed routines while belting out songs we'd learned watching the Saturday night television show *Your Hit Parade*. Barb and I stabbed each other's fingers with thick sewing needles, pressed the open wounds together, and declared eternal loyalty to one another as blood sisters, then bound the ritual by solemnly burying a cigar box of personal treasures beneath our crabby neighbor's lilac bush. We rode our bikes under the flickering sun and shade cast by L tracks, unable to talk above the screeching metal wheels and wheezing brakes of elevated trains whisking commuters to downtown Chicago. When we found a loading dock at a nearby factory, we were certain it was a stage, and then and there planned a huge production with song and dance. Since we weren't the likes of Mickey Rooney and Judy Garland in *Babes in Arms*, our grand fantasy never came to fruition.

Unlike many neighborhood kids, we were expected to touch base with our moms off and on, but they didn't keep tabs on us every minute of the day. If Mom sent me to the grocery store, I'd stop by Barb's to bring her along for company. "I can't go until I clean the kitchen," she might say, so I'd pick up the broom and start sweeping or wiping counters until we were done. When I returned home more than an hour later, Mom would say, "For heaven's sake! What took you so long?"

"I had to get Barb."

A simple jaunt to the local library, four blocks distant, turned into a journey of exploratory pleasures as we walked past neighborhood icons on Madison Street, the West Side's vibrant business district. We ogled and giggled at the rocket-shaped breasts of mannequins in Three Sisters dress shop. At high-end Madigan's Department Store, we rode elevators operated by ladies wearing white gloves and fine wool suits. They sat on small, round, black-lacquered benches and asked, "What floor, puh-lease?" We got off at women's clothing and lingerie, where we clucked over the ridiculous prices of expensive outfits and surreptitiously held bras up to our chests.

Leaving Madigan's, we walked past the Marbro theater, promising each other that we'd go together the next Saturday. The Marbro was an expansive movie palace, its interior walls draped in red velvet, its wide, winding, white marble staircase bordered by thick brass railings. On Saturdays, gaggles of children ascended to the balcony, jabbering, joking, poking, and spilling popcorn behind them like Hansel's breadcrumbs. For twenty-five cents, we could watch a double feature, preceded by cartoons starring Daffy Duck, Bugs Bunny, Elmer Fudd, or Sylvester and Tweety Bird. Parents thought nothing of sending their young children alone to the movies.

Barb and I skipped farther east along Madison Street, past Kresge's five-and-dime, where we gawked at unattainable treasures in the toy aisle or posed with our cheeks pressed together in the photo booth. Giggling at our likenesses, we continued toward Pulaski Road, where we turned south for the final block to the library. Inside, we pulled book after book off the shelves, sharing our thoughts about them, trying to decide. Our quietest whispers elicited a scolding "shhhhh" from the stern, eyebrow-raised librarians.

At the high, oak check-out desk, we stretched up our arms to hand our chosen books and library cards to the librarian. After placing one book at a time under a huge, glowing machine, she pressed a button. *Karumpf.* An eerie green light bathed each book and card, documenting the loan. *Kachunk.* She stamped the due date onto a slip of paper glued to the inside back cover. I wished I could do that.

Our selections tucked under our arms, we walked the half mile back home and plopped down side by side on the grass, opened our books, and drifted off on more adventures.

CHAPTER 20: Thief, Robber, Crook

Mom reads to us kids (and puppy, Buttons) around our campfire at Devil's Lake State Park, 1956.

1954–56

When my parents felt they had saved enough of a financial cushion, they moved the tenants from the two hallway bedrooms out of our flat and into vacant sleeping rooms on the second floor. Paul and I, who had slept on cots in the dining room with Grandma K in her nearby alcove, would share the west bedroom. We joined hands on the big brass double bed Dad had bought for five dollars at the Salvation Army. Bouncing up and down in gleeful brio, we shouted over and over, "We have our own room! We have our own room!" Paul was eight, and I was nearly five.

For the previous five years, my parents had been sleeping, first with my crib, now with Billy's, crammed along one wall of the small, dark bedroom off the kitchen. That bedroom was more suitable for Grandma K, a single person. Dad wanted the now-free bedroom across from Paul's and mine so he and Mom could have more space and be closer to their children.

But Grandma insisted on the biggest, brightest room so she could look out the window onto Washington Boulevard. Mom ignored Dad's wishes and acquiesced to her mother, perhaps to avoid a psychotic episode. A short while later, in February of 1954, Mom told Dad, "I want you to make an extra effort to be openly friendly to my mother. It's not that you're unpleasant to her, but sometimes you ignore her and she feels she's in our way."

As usual, Dad didn't confront Mom on her request. Instead, he unloaded his frustration with Grandma K's repeated intrusion into their home life to his diary: "Too bad Grandma didn't feel that way ten years ago, when we could have enjoyed some privacy. Once [I'm] a little friendly, she starts taking over, considering we are living with her instead of her with us. . . . I didn't promise one way or the other."

Having her own bedroom turned Grandma K into a recluse. With the door closed and the shade drawn, she sat alone in her room for hours, never enjoying the view she had insisted upon. For eight months, she refused to wash her hair. She shuffled about in an old gray dress and a torn robe, a raggedy cloth diaper draped over her head, rejecting Mom's pleas to bathe or to wear the new robe Mom had bought for her. Her condition became ever more alarming.

Certain that Mom and Dad stole from her, Grandma locked her bedroom door, even when going to the bathroom or to eat. During disagreements, she flung at my mother

her favorite epithets, "whore" and "streetwalker." If Mom defended herself, Grandma slapped her face as if Mom were a child.

In July of 1956, Mom wrote a long letter to a psychiatrist, summarizing Grandma K's previous fourteen years. After five pages describing Grandma K's insane behavior, my mother wrote, "I hope and pray that she can be helped back to a normal existence." I was dismayed to discover that Mom made no mention of a "normal existence" for her husband and children.

About a month after Mom wrote the letter to the psychiatrist, we were about to leave for our annual camping trip to Devil's Lake State Park in Wisconsin. Dad had spent days preparing, jamming a rented trailer with tents, tarpaulins, fishing gear, Coleman lanterns, a portable stove—everything to make our vacation as comfortable as possible. The night before we were to leave, Mom reassured Grandma, preparing her for our departure with gentle words "so she wouldn't go berserk," Dad wrote in his diary. He continued with what unfolded.

The next morning, Dad was in the alley hitching the trailer to the car, when he heard "an awful commotion and screaming in the kitchen." He ran toward the house. Paul, Billy, and I were shouting at Grandma, "Stop it! Stop hurting Mommy!"

Grandma had Mom by the throat and was pushing her backward onto the porch, screeching, "Whore! Thief! Crook!"—the usual. I can still see Mom, clad only in pants and her bra, her lips pressed together in desperation, slapping at Grandma K, trying to free herself from her mother's powerful, crazed hold. I was frozen, but the paradoxical thought that consumed my wheeling brain was, *You're not supposed to hit your mother.*

At that moment, I saw Dad leaping two steps at a time onto the porch just before Grandma shoved Mom backward down the stairs. Wedging between the two women, prying

Grandma's grip off Mom, Dad yelled, "Hey! Hey! Get your hands off Lil! Stop it! *Stop it!*"

He pushed flailing Grandma back into the kitchen. She grabbed a glass off the table, swinging it in a wide arc toward Dad's head. He ducked. The glass crashed to the floor. Grandma grasped Dad's right thumb and wrenched it sideways, taking Dad to his knees in agony. I was paralyzed. Grandma K stood panting over Dad, glaring at him with hate-filled eyes. Mom was crying. My mind was a spinning whirlwind, my only hope with Dad, who was on the floor.

He found his footing, rose, locked Grandma in a tight embrace, and dragged her flailing body to the dining-room couch, where he forced her to sit. He held her arms pinned against her sides until the fury subsided. I stared mute with fear and confusion. Mom called the psychiatrist, who asked to speak to Grandma. She yelled into the phone, "They're thieves! They're trying to kill me with rat poison!"

Mom spoke one more time to the doctor, then hung up. My mind whirred, but because Dad and Mom stayed calm, I felt grounded. We all gathered at the kitchen table, eating breakfast in silence while Grandma K continued a nonstop tirade until ten o'clock. Then Dad, Paul, Billy, and I waited in the car, while Mom said some final goodbyes to her mother. When she finally climbed into the passenger seat of the car, Mom's face was streaked with tears, her mouth grim. She said nothing.

Dad immediately diverted our minds with car games. "Let's see how many out-of-state license plates we can spot before we get there," he challenged us. En route we sang familiar songs and talked of hiking five-hundred-foot bluffs and what fun we'd have swimming in the always-warm waters of Devil's Lake.

In the pleasures of the week ahead, I didn't dwell on Grandma's physical attacks on both Mom and Dad. Looking back, I would think this would have roused my mother to action, to find a mental institution for her dangerous mother. Nothing changed.

CHAPTER 21: Travels with Dad

Dad teaches Linda to swim in Enid, Oklahoma, July 1958.

1958

Vacations were about the only time during the year when Dad could really connect with his children. Mourning this lack of one-on-one time, he came up with a solution. During our summer breaks, Dad started taking Paul or me with him on National Board business trips. In July of 1958, I traveled with Dad to Enid, Oklahoma. That time with him still unspools like a movie in my memory.

On the highway south from Chicago, we drove straight through Missouri, night drawing down around us. By the time we looked for a motel, every neon sign blinked "No Vacancy." Dad pulled onto the highway shoulder, and we snuggled together in the back seat to sleep. In the morning, Dad apologized for the cramped conditions, but I hadn't noticed.

After arriving in Enid, we checked into the Trail Motel. Dad and I walked to the pool outside. "Honey, I'm going to teach you to swim while we're here," he told me. I peered into that vast expanse of blue, reading "Nine Feet" on the deep end. A knot of fear tightened in my chest.

We arose every day by seven, trekking for miles in the southern heat on inspections. "She's my shadow," Dad wrote to Mom. "No demands. No complaints." Of course not—I had Dad to myself. Every evening, we returned to our motel for swimming lessons. Dad started me out in the shallow end, where I hung onto the edge, kicking my feet and turning my head to his instructions: *Head out, breathe in; head in, breathe out.*

When I developed a modicum of coordination, Dad had me swim the width of the pool. "Daddy, I'm afraid I'll sink!"

"I'll be beside you all the way."

So I pushed away, flailing my arms and legs, gasping, sputtering. Dad urged me forward, not holding me, until the opposite wall was within reach. We both smiled. "Now back," he said. With each width, my breath found its rhythm, my legs obeyed, my arms stretched long.

It was time for the deep end. We swam together across the rosy, twilit surface, the bottom falling away from a touchable three feet to a chasm of nine. Back and forth I went, until I could do length after length. In my dreams, I swam in such smooth, rhythmic strokes, I was faster than Paul.

"Are you ready to swim underwater?" he asked one evening. He held my hand on the first plunge beneath the surface, as I kicked fiercely until my lungs cried "uncle," then tried again. Dad swam under the water with me, back and forth. Then he sent me off alone. Each time I swam farther, enveloped in silence, until I could stay under for an entire length.

At the deep end, Dad tossed in a quarter, challenging me to retrieve it. "What if I have to breathe and I'm at the bottom?" My heart shuddered at the thought.

"Just go a little deeper each time. I'll be watching."

On my first attempt, I barely got halfway, resurfacing like a bobber, sputtering, eyes wide, blinking out the stinging chlorinated water. I pushed deeper with each dive, until I pinched the coin off the pebbly floor, flipped upright, and scissor-kicked hard, breaking through the surface to see Dad's beaming smile.

Dad wrote Mom, "She's a trooper. Tramping with me all day, then working hard on her swimming at night."

I helped Dad with his job by making a fire-limits map based on official records. It was like book coloring. "Good job!" Dad said when I had finished. "You saved me about four hours of work!" I glowed.

One day, we walked three miles to downtown Enid and spent eight hours trudging around on inspections under a broiling sun. On our way back to the motel, we picked up groceries for a "picnic" supper in our room, which seemed like an adventure to me. En route back, I took Dad's hand, kissed it, and said, "I love you, Daddy. I'm glad I've got you for *my* daddy."

I'm not sure how I pulled up these words, which I seldom heard in our family. They must have just emerged on their own from my joy in Dad's company. And I hadn't even recalled this sweet scene or many of these details—until I read Dad's July 12 letter to Mom, in which he also wrote:

> *I am very happy that we have a little girl, especially one like Linda. Little trips like these give me an opportunity to __know__ the children, their moods and thoughts. At home, they are just one of the family and can get very little personal attention.*

I didn't feel ignored at home, but Dad was right about the "personal attention." We kids simply didn't expect it, seeing how hard our parents worked. That's why this trip was so special for both of us, and why Dad continued including Paul or me on summer travels for years to come.

Dad didn't write what he'd said in response to my spontaneous, "I love you, Daddy." He didn't need to.

Dad and Linda at pool, Enid, Oklahoma, July 1958.

CHAPTER 22: The Asylum

Mom and Grandma K, Manteno,
Illinois, 1960.

About a month after Dad and I returned from Enid, Oklahoma, our family made the annual pilgrimage to Devil's
Lake, two years after Grandma K had tried to push Mom
down the back steps. When we got home from Devil's Lake,
we found a soot-laden oven with a charred chicken inside,
the odor of smoke still permeating the kitchen. For days,
Mom and Dad spoke to each other in quiet undertones. I
overheard snippets: "burn the house down," "danger to children," "lock herself in," "take off the door," "straitjacket." I
sensed what was coming.

Mom drove Grandma to the psychiatric ward of Cook County Hospital for evaluation on August 12, and a week later received another court order, like the one from nine years earlier, declaring Louise Koroschetz to be incompetent and authorizing my mother to commit her to an institution. Mom explored several Illinois mental hospitals and chose one located in Manteno, Illinois, a minimum ninety-minute drive from our home. Enamored with Manteno's lovely grounds, Mom rejected closer choices.

The sun shone from a brilliant blue sky on August 20, 1958. Grandma locked her room, as usual, before shuffling to the washroom. Dad worked fast. Using a skeleton key, he unlocked her door, then drove the hinges up and out with a hammer and a screwdriver. He lifted off the door and hid it against a sidewall in the living room.

When Grandma K exited the bathroom, Mom gingerly took her arm. "Mama, we have to talk to you." Grandma looked from Dad to Mom in an oddly calm state, allowing them to lead her to the dining-room couch, where she sat between them. They spoke to her softly—their heads bent, both looking intently into her blank face. I heard words like, "a safe place for you," "a place to get better," "come home for visits."

Grandma said nothing. She seemed not to be listening, just staring from one to the other, then down at the floor, her present calm as inexplicable as her past explosions. The doorbell rang. Dad walked to the front, leaving Mom talking to Grandma K.

As a child, I couldn't have understood the despair Mom must have felt in her unrelenting, and ultimately futile, attempts to cure her mother. I saw Mom from across the room, her face close to Grandma's, their hands intertwined. Mom's voice had a pleading tone, like I might have used if

I didn't want to be blamed for something. I sensed Mom's sorrow, but I had no idea what to do about it. I had learned through my parents' reticence over the years to keep silent.

Two men in white coats wheeled a gurney down the long hallway into our dining room. Mom and Dad stood, one on each side of Grandma K. They each gently grasped Grandma by an elbow, helping her to her feet. "The doctors have come to make you feel better, Mama," said Mom, her eyes glistening.

The men led Grandma to the side of the lowered gurney. "Here, we'll give you a hand getting on the bed," one said, as he helped her sit, lifting one leg, then the other. She lay back, and they covered her with a light sheet. Grandma's blue eyes traced the faces peering down at her. I don't remember if I kissed her.

She said nothing that I recall. I wasn't sad that she was leaving, but I knew this moment was a turning point in our family. She had lived with us for my entire life, wandering at times through the house like a wraith, until she exploded, screeching like a banshee, that banshee now being exorcised. With each progressive step of the process, I felt tension, even fear, lifting from the air. What if Grandma had refused to leave, or had erupted into full paranoid mode? Relief flooded the room, but my mother's sorrow flowed with it.

Mom's eyes brimmed when she stroked her mother's silvery hair and kissed her forehead, saying, "I'll see you soon, Mama." The men wheeled Grandma K down the hall and out the front door into bright, cloudless sunshine, lifted the gurney into the back of an ambulance, and slammed the rear doors in two detonations.

I wish I had known to take Mom's hand and squeeze it.

We all stood silently on the sidewalk, watching the ambulance drive away until it was swallowed in the distance.

At the age of nine, I only knew that Grandma was "not right in the head," that her name-calling outbursts had made Mom cry, that she had physically attacked both my parents, and that Dad had brought her under control, as he himself stayed calm.

Until I read Mom's detailed records and Dad's personal diary entries of Grandma K's bizarre behavior, I couldn't have known the rift Grandma K had torn through my parents' marriage. I hadn't realized the quiet, restrained resentment Dad had felt for Grandma's presence in our lives—or how she had singled him out for her explosive ire. I hadn't understood that, despite Dad's tolerance and control of his mother-in-law's outbursts and physical attacks, despite the gifts and greeting cards he had bought for "Mama" at Mom's request, my mother had wanted more from him. Being "nice" to her mother wasn't enough. She wanted Dad to be "openly friendly" to Grandma K.

My brothers and I were left out of any discussions about Grandma K's mental illness. I don't recall either Mom or Dad explaining to us kids why Grandma heard voices, screamed vicious names, or tried to hurt them both. Maybe they didn't have the words to tell us, didn't understand themselves, or thought these outbursts would be forgotten by a child's mind. But the tension, the anxiety, and the fear that Grandma might hurt them had settled inside me like a chronic illness I could neither cure nor control, but had to bear. How I wish I could go back and demand they tell me, "What's wrong with Grandma?" I realize now how much better off we all would have been.

The three hours of driving required to get to and from Manteno State Hospital to see Grandma, plus time for the visit itself, now created a new source of strife between my parents. In the first two months after Grandma K was committed, the whole family went along on several trips to the institution, but with his brutal travel schedule, Dad increasingly objected to giving up one of his few at-home Sundays.

When we all visited Grandma together, Dad dropped us off at her residential building while he parked. Sometimes female patients came to the window and lifted their gowns, exposing themselves to goggle-eyed Billy, who was only five.

The moment we entered the wide, open waiting area, our noses crinkled, slammed by the odor of stale urine, diminished but not banished by Lysol. I breathed through my mouth. Peppering the air were whines, moans, and repetitive shouts from the patients: "Get away from me!" or, "Let me go!"

A woman dressed in a white uniform greeted us. Mom said, "We're here to see Louise Koroschetz." The white-clad lady turned to a long, narrow file box and picked out a card.

"One moment," the lady said. "I'll bring her." She walked quickly away, her soft tread squeaking in the vast hall.

As we waited for Grandma, I tried not to stare at the patients, listing permanently over wheelchair arms or swaying in the hallways, flimsy raiment sliding off their shoulders. Some women closed in on me to stare or babble about imaginary people. I used all my willpower not to shrink back, possibly embarrassing them, until a nurse led them away.

I wasn't frightened. I'd become accustomed to the odd assortment of types who had come and gone in our rooming house, some living right down the hall and using our communal bathroom. But I knew these women were beyond strange. Grandma had been loudly and aggressively off-kilter, but she was a conscious, if splenetic, even violent, presence. These patients appeared to be in a kind of anesthetized reality, beyond my ken, but expanding my comprehension of where a human mind can go. Seeing these people, lost to the world, I can understand how Mom might have indulged in denial, believing her mother didn't belong in such a place;

how she could have misplaced her loyalty, her fear and devotion to her mother overwhelming the sanctity of our home as a safe place.

━━━━━

When hospital workers finally arrived in the front hall with Grandma, who always wore a loose, flowered housedress, Mom kissed her cheek. "Hello, Mama," she said, entwining their arms. Grandma smiled at my brothers and me. I think I kissed her cheek, but the memory is dim. I knew we were there only for Mom.

In pleasant weather, Mom walked arm-in-arm with her mother, quietly talking while we kids ran around on the wide lawns. Dad infused some fun into the long day by letting Paul and me (twelve and nine respectively) each take turns at the wheel, teaching us to drive on mostly empty roads within the grounds.

After about an hour, we all met Mom to say goodbye to Grandma. She gave us flat-lipped kisses, a wan smile, and waved limply as she was led back by an aide down a long hallway. She seemed content.

On the way home, we usually stopped for dinner at a roadside diner, its neon sign blinking, "EAT." And we did! We seldom ate at restaurants and relished the kind of food Mom rarely cooked. Paul ordered an open-faced roast-beef sandwich with gravy on white bread. Billy and I ordered burgers with everything, a side of fries, and milkshakes. We enjoyed the family time and conversation, but afterward, torpid from the meal, we still had at least an hour more to drive home, always in the dark, from fall to spring.

In her zeal to do the very best for her mother, Mom had chosen an institution so far distant that visiting Grandma was a burden on everyone. We kids had homework and school activities; Dad had little time at home. That November, Mom drove to and from Manteno alone—three hours to brood and curry resentment, which she dumped into a letter to Dad that very evening.

> *November 23, 1958*
> *Dear Fred,*
> *After we were on our feet again financially and*
> *we didn't need that room on the first floor for the*
> *income, if you had been the first to say, "Let's give*
> *that room to Mama now—she's helped us a lot,"*
> *I would have loved you more.*
>
> *Anytime we wanted to go out, we could go,*
> *and Mama would watch the children. We didn't say,*
> *"Would you please watch the children," we just went.*
> *I said, "Thank you, Mama," but if you had ever said,*
> *"It's swell of Mama to take care of the kids"—I would*
> *have loved you more.*
>
> *Now that Mama is in the hospital, if you*
> *were to say, "Mama would probably enjoy seeing*
> *us—suppose I drive you and the kids out there this*
> *Sunday, and maybe we could bring her something.*
> *She's probably lonesome and has no one but us"—*
> *If you had said that, my dear, instead of regretting*
> *the "wasted" day, I would have loved you more.*
>
> *Somehow, someday, if Linda is married and her*
> *husband is "nice" to me as you were always "nice"*
> *to Mama, perhaps I'll die of a broken heart.*
> *Love and tears,*
> *Lillian*

When I read the carbon copy of this letter, saved by Mom, I nearly wept at her blind injustice. I can only imagine what prompted her to write such unfair accusations. Perhaps Mom couldn't bear alone the guilt she must have felt for not being able to cure her mother, and, to ease her own suffering, passed the blame onto Dad. He surely felt the sting of Mom's cruel condemnation.

He could have written a similarly toned letter, wishing for perhaps a smidgen of appreciation from Mom for fifteen years of tolerating Grandma K's psychotic outbursts, her vitriolic, irascible, and dangerous behavior. But of course, Dad would have said nothing. Nurturing his own resentment, he would have withdrawn further from his wife, just as he had from his mother's incessant condemnation. More bricks were added to a wall of bitterness, pushing them apart.

CHAPTER 23: Black and White

Dunk Tank, Riverview Amusement Park, Chicago, Illinois,
http://livinghistoryofillinois.com.

Despite the constant stress created by Grandma K's mental illness, Dad's travel, and the nonstop work on the rooming house, my parents somehow found time for family fun. Both when Grandma lived with us and after she was in Manteno State Hospital, Dad, Mom, and we kids often piled into our maroon Chevy and drove a few miles to Riverview, billed as the "World's Largest Amusement Park." Riverview had dozens of rides, including steep, screeching roller coasters, one so wild that the park displayed a whole trunk of clip-on earrings that tore off women's ears when the "Bobs" careened around curves. A set of parachutes slowly hoisted riders, who peered down at the people below shrinking to bug size. Gut-churning fear built as the chutes rose . . . and rose . . . and rose—until they released with a sudden, violent jolt, dropping screaming passengers to earth, their stomachs left somewhere above.

Scores of barkers called out to visitors walking along the midway, "Try your luck! Just hit the bottle in three tries! Hey, young man, don't you want to win this big teddy bear for your girlfriend?" One of the games encouraged contestants to throw balls at a target, which, when hit, dumped a black man into a tank of water. Over the years, it had been called variously, the "Nigger Dip," the "Dark Town Tangos," the "Chocolate Drops," the "African Dip," and finally, the "Dip."[36] African American men were hired to taunt passing white men, getting many so riled up with insults that the visitors bought ticket after ticket. "Hey, little man," jeered the large black man behind the high wire surrounding his drop seat, to a short guy. "I bet you can't hit the side of a barn!" He attacked the man's diminutive size, pea brain— you name it.

Shouting racist epithets, the white man pulled back his arm and threw the ball with such fury, the target vibrated for seconds after the hit. It was obvious to me that the dunk-tank guy kept insults flying to make sure ticket sales were brisk. Dad made a few throws at the target but then walked away. He understood the psychology and wasn't going to waste his money.

My stomach went queasy watching the white men throw with such anger—red-faced, veins popping, enraged at being insulted by a black man. Surely, I felt, the black men's pride was wounded by the nasty comments and by repeated dunkings, even though they gamely leaped back onto their seat, dripping wet, and started right in on the next dupe.

The game was a perfect metaphor for prevalent racist

attitudes seldom questioned by whites at the time. Blacks and whites were thoroughly segregated: by neighborhood, by opportunity, by the media, and even at our biggest amusement park. At the dunk tank, only blacks were dunked, and I saw only whites do the dunking.

Dunk Tank, Riverview Amusement Park, Chicago, circa 1921, with permission of Derek Gee and Ralph Lopez, authors of *Laugh Your Troubles Away: The Complete History of Riverview Park.*

Chicago's prevailing racist attitudes were at work in our family as well. Whenever a tenant moved out, Mom used a two-pronged approach to find a new tenant. She advertised in the *Chicago Tribune* classified section and also hung a "For Rent" sign on the front door. At home, I was playing with my dolls on the colorful hooked rug Dad had completed during one of his travels, when the bell rang. Walking briskly past me, Mom disappeared around the corner into our short front hallway. I heard the twist of the knob, the creak of the front door opening. "Hello, ma'am. We're interested in the apartment you have for rent," a woman's voice drawled.

"Oh, I'm sorry," Mom responded in a polite tone, "but we don't rent to colored. Sorry."

There was a mumbled response. Mom said, "Goodbye," and the door shut.

Heart pounding, my face went hot. My mother's words, I felt, heaped pain and insult on the woman at the door. When Mom reentered the living room, I looked up from brushing my doll's golden hair and asked, "Mommy, why did you say that—that you don't rent to colored? Didn't that hurt that lady's feelings?"

Very matter-of-factly, Mom gazed down at me and explained, "Linda, we can't rent to colored. If we did, then the whole neighborhood would go colored, and we would lose our house. This is how we make a living."

It was the same reasoning Mom gave a few years later, when she was planning a birthday party for me. I wanted to invite Stephanie, an African American friend I often played with at recess in my first-grade class. Stephanie was smart and fun, but still, I knew to ask if I could invite her, instead of just giving Mom her name with those of the other girls. Mom said no. "If people see a colored girl coming into our house, they might think she lives here, and then there could be trouble."

When I passed out the invitations in the classroom, I could hardly look at Stephanie, I felt so downright mean. She held my eyes with clear and bitter understanding as I passed her desk. She said, "You only invite those little curly-haired girls, don't you?" I wasn't sure why she used those words, but I knew she meant "white." I mumbled something of an excuse, my stomach twisting, wishing I could sink into the floor. Nothing I said could undo the insult.

I couldn't make the connection between my six-year-old friend coming to our house and the idea of trouble. I was as yet unschooled in how deeply whites felt the threat that blacks posed to their communities—that an African American moving nearby jeopardized everything for which the whites had worked and sacrificed.

Mom may have heard of the violent mob action that accompanied blacks entering white neighborhoods in the previous few years, the kinds of attacks that could very well target our home. In 1949, the year we moved into our two-flat, it took only a rumor of African Americans entering a neighborhood to spawn a white riot. In Englewood, on Chicago's South Side, a local labor organizer invited a few black people to the house for a meeting. A neighbor, seeing African Americans entering the home, assumed it was being "sold to niggers." Up to ten thousand whites rioted for four days, pelting the property with stones and beating bystanders. That violence exploded over mere speculation. An NAACP memo documented, between 1949 and 1951, three bombings, ten actual—and eleven attempted—incidents of arson, and "at least eighty-one other incidents of terrorism or intimidation" against blacks.[37]

The federal government had created redlining, which caused the value of whites' homes to fall; fear of losing equity in their homes exacerbated whites' racism and maintained segregation of the races, creating a vicious cycle of stereotyping. Chicago whites had few ways to get to know African Americans as individuals, and prejudice ruled. Whites presumed that blacks would let their property deteriorate, that they would bring dilapidation to their community, no matter what their class, veteran status, or education. That, in turn, ensured that blacks were terrorized out of white neighborhoods, continuing the separation of the races.

In Mom's letter to Dad in 1953, in which she had related the dire warnings from her departing tenant, Birchler, about how North Lawndale had become "mostly colored," she also related her concern about another group:

*You know that rooming house the Birchlers are living
in? It really tears down our neighborhood because
they take all trashy people in, and of course, you
know how the front windows look—trashy. Birchler
told me the building is just about infested with
hillbillies and a lot of the roomers are drunks, let the
bathtub overflow, etc.*

My mother recognized as early as 1953 that all was
not well with the neighborhood, but my parents' hectic lives
precluded action. By the latter 1950s, the large apartment
building at the end of our block was becoming increasingly
populated by "hillbillies," a word my parents only used for
those southern migrants with a slovenly lifestyle.

Many of the children's faces and clothes were a dusty gray,
their ears, neck creases, and fingernails black with grime. Billy,
open and friendly, invited one such boy to play, maybe having
met him in the alley. The kid thanked my brother by stealing his
piggy bank. Mom somehow got the family phone number and
called the boy's mother, politely explained what had happened,
and requested that the bank be returned. "I ain't responsible for
my kid's debt!" was the defiant rejoinder, delivered in a virtually
unintelligible southern twang, followed by a curt hang-up.

In sixth grade, a six-foot-two boy with a strong southern
accent, who was clearly older than the other classmates, said
to my school friend Stephanie, "Shut up, you nigger," when
she objected to him butting in line ahead of her. My heart
thumping with indignation, I cringed and turned to Stephanie, whose mouth twisted with contained anger. She drew
herself up and said, "Only low-class people use that word."
He sniggered and mumbled something incomprehensible.

I put my hand on her shoulder and said, "That boy's a
stupid jerk. He's so dumb, he's flunked a bunch of times. Pay
no attention to him." But of course my words couldn't take
away the pain. Smart and pretty, Stephanie undoubtedly had
been forced to hear these kinds of insults more than I could

have known, from people far less accomplished and classy than she was.

In my seventh-grade class, a girl from Tennessee disrespected our teacher, who sent her to the principal's office with a stern rebuke and a call to her mother. Instead of chastising her daughter, the mom charged into our classroom near the end of school the next day, heaped more insults onto the teacher, and stormed out with the girl in tow. We all just sat, mute and stunned.

Some of our middle-class neighbors caused us trauma as well. When we played catch, badminton, or Ping-Pong, an errant ball or birdie might fly into our neighbor's yard to the west. The owner, Mrs. Beedle, marched scowling out her back door and snatched up the offending missile. With chin-jutting, silent defiance, she stomped back into her house.

Bumping into Mrs. Beedle on the street one day, the usual rush of traffic roaring by, Mom greeted her with a friendly "Hello," then spoke of the toys occasionally landing in the Beedles' yard. "Mrs. Beedle, why don't you tell me if something is wrong, so we can work it out?"

"I have no intention of doing so," said Mrs. Beedle, glaring at Mom. "You're the mother. It's *your* responsibility to make sure your children do no wrong. And if this doesn't stop, there's going to be trouble, and I won't be the one to have it!" She turned on her heels and walked on, leaving my mother fuming.

I only learned about Mrs. Beedle's belligerent confrontation with my mother when I found her letter to Dad, in which she recounted her fury at this obnoxious woman. I was struck by how few of our neighbors were in any way neighborly. I recalled the Stones, the couple who had destroyed my parents' just-furnished basement apartment with cigarette burns on the couch and their filthy lifestyle, and the alcoholic Mr. Ramis, who had bled all over the sheets. Most of the tenants were decent people, but I realized that white people, no matter how slovenly, nasty, or careless, had no problem finding housing in our community.

CHAPTER 24: Brothers and Sisters

Billy with classmates at his Lutheran school, 1963-1964.

1963

As our block was integrating in West Garfield Park, a quarter of a million people gathered in the nation's capital for the August 28 March on Washington, where Martin Luther King gave his iconic "I Have a Dream" speech. In the distance, towering amidst the throngs demanding equality for African Americans, the Washington Monument rose like a giant exclamation point. Our family watched the news that night but heard only a part of King's speech. "Look at that crowd!" Mom said, staring at the TV.

"I've never seen so many people in one spot," I said, awe-struck by the sea of bodies pressed shoulder to shoulder, filling every inch of space, starting at King's podium and stretching far into the distance, past the Washington, DC, mall.

"The man sure can express himself," Dad said grudgingly. With his love of words and poetic mind, Dad recognized brilliant writing when he heard it, but he found it hard to reconcile his prejudices with King's cogent appeals to justice. "He's a good speaker," Dad went on, "but that doesn't mean the time is right."

"This is no time to engage in the luxury of cooling off or to take the tranquilizing drug of gradualism," King intoned in his speech, rejoining head-on the common attitude Dad had expressed.

We gathered in the dining room, which served as our family room, where the broad television, a ubiquitous piece of furniture in middle-class 1960s homes, sat squat at the east side. At fourteen, I absorbed the mesmerizing rhythm of King's language and his repeated calls for justice, but I was too young to discern their real power—in the cadence of his delivery, his southern preacher's gift to raise the stakes for the millions of blacks who heard in his inspiring words a call to action; in his repeated references to the Constitution's promise of freedom and his expanded metaphor of that promise as a "bad check" to the "Negro people," a check the crowd that day had come to cash.

Just about every sentence in King's speech is quotable, but one dream, which he had specifically envisioned for Alabama, had some promise of possibility on our block: "I have a dream that one day . . . little black boys and black girls will be able to join hands with little white boys and white girls as sisters and brothers."[38]

Within days of moving in, the son of our first African American neighbors and my little brother shouted greetings to one another across the yard between them. "Hey!" yelled Billy, hands cupped around his mouth. "What's your name?"

"Junior," came the shout back. "What's yours?'

"Billy. Can you come over to play?" Soon, Billy and Junior, both age nine, were hanging out in our yard or playing basketball in the alley. Junior suggested a game he called "Cops and Niggers," a variation on Cops and Robbers. Both boys, unconcerned about their racial status vis-à-vis one another, took turns at each role. "Now you be the nigger, and I'll be the cop," said Junior, and they happily exchanged parts, running and hiding, shooting back and forth, the black character arrested or escaped. The two races of children weren't the "sisters and brothers" King had envisioned, but for the first time in our lives, whites and blacks, kids and adults, came to know—and like—one another.

But integration wasn't all Kumbaya. Just a week before King's speech, Billy and the boy living in the second-floor apartment rode their bicycles to Madison Street late one afternoon. Earlier in the summer, our garage had been broken into and Billy's bicycle stolen. The thieves left behind a rusty, falling-apart bike. With Dad's help, Billy dismantled the bike—pedals, bearings, wheels, chains, etc.—sanded, primed, and spray-painted it black, then reassembled it. It shone like new, and Billy was rightly proud of his summer project.

After arriving on Madison Street, Billy and Frankie locked their bikes to a couple of signposts and walked into Kresge's five-and-dime to buy the pièce de résistance for Billy's like-new bicycle: handlebar streamers. They left the store around four thirty, and Billy pushed the streamers into the handlebar holes. Now it looked *really* cool.

Billy crouched to unlock the chain he'd threaded through the wheels and around a light pole. He was twirling through the numbers of his combination lock, when a nearby black teen started chatting with him. The instant Billy pulled apart the lock, the older boy punched him in the face, leaped on the bike, and took off. Shocked more than injured, Billy picked himself up, hand to his sore jaw, and watched in dismay as the pride of his summer disappeared into the Madison Street crowds.

Sobbing when he got home, Billy told Mom what had happened. She called the police, who said they'd send over an officer to take a report. We all tried to comfort Billy for his loss, assuring him it wasn't his fault, that the police would catch the thief.

Detectives came to our house that evening. Dressed in rumpled trousers and open jackets over shirts, ties loosened at the neck, they showed their badges at the door and introduced themselves. Mom and Dad led them into the living room, where they questioned Billy and jotted down the details of the crime. Flipping his notebook closed, one said, "Even if we caught the culprit, they'd let him go. The house of corrections is too crowded as it is." They bade us goodbye.

"Well, that certainly was eye-opening," Mom said, after closing the door behind them. "I guess we're on our own."

As far as I knew, we'd always been on our own. More relevant to our situation at the time than the cop's cynical analysis of crime and punishment was what I discovered decades later in Mom's diary.

Mom recorded the basic facts of the battery and bike-theft incident, but made no comment about it. Instead, she wrote this: "Boy, did I have the ironing tonight! Ironed into the wee hours." She continued with a long list of completed chores. Instead of reflecting on her son's safety—whether an assault and robbery in broad daylight might be a signal to move—she focused on her own accomplishments. My father also knew about the attack, but I don't recall either of my parents talking about relocating. But they had decided, even before the assault, to take Billy out of dicey Marconi School and enroll him in a Lutheran grade school a few miles north.

The mugging didn't change Billy's friendship with Junior. He, more than Paul or I, was growing up with black kids; he wasn't ruled by the negative stereotypes that whites had created for blacks. He saw the good and the bad—from personal experience.

But stories like Billy's, an overriding fear of what would happen next, and the continuing decline of their property values prompted other white families to desert the community as if outrunning a wildfire. All of my neighborhood friends either had already moved or were planning to move. Unlike Dad's generation, when West Side neighbors and Bethel Church members maintained close ties with each other's families for decades, the winds of racial change now blew us permanently apart.

CHAPTER 25: Not Unhappy

Bethel Church Sunday School Christmas Pageant: Linda, right; Billy, back row, 2nd from left, 1965.

1964

In February of 1964, just before I turned fifteen, and eight months after the first black family had moved onto our street, our neighbor to the east, Mrs. Day, sold her house for $16,000. She had bought it for $20,000. Mom and I went outside to introduce ourselves to the new owners, an African American family. They were hauling their belongings into the turreted, grand greystone, the most beautiful house on the block. It didn't occur to me to reflect on the irony that the people we wanted to keep out of the neighborhood owned this magnificent home. Mom strode up and extended her hand to the husband and wife. "Hello, my name is Mrs. Gartz. I'm your neighbor." She gestured with her head toward our house and then toward me. "This is my daughter, Linda."

"Hello. Nice to meet you," I said.

"Mr. Lewis," said the tall, thin man in a gentle voice, just a whisper of a smile across his face, "and my wife, Mrs. Lewis. Pleased to meet you, ma'am," he said, nodding to Mom.

"A pleasure to meet you both," said Mrs. Lewis.

"And you, miss," he said, turning to me. This here's my son, Vance," he said, reaching his arm out toward his boy, who was carrying a packed box toward the house. Vance looked a bit older than Billy, tall and lean like his father, with short-cropped hair and milk-chocolate eyes. He put the box on the sidewalk, brushed his hands on his pants, and extended one to mom.

"Hello, ma'am," Vance said to my mother.

"Hi, Vance," I said, with a quick touch and wave off my forehead. "I'm Linda."

"Hi," said Vance, glancing down, then up with a shy smile.

"We're sure glad to be in this nice house. Looks like you take real good care of your property, ma'am," said Mr. Lewis.

"Oh, yes," said Mom. "A house is so much work. Well, better be going inside and let you get on with your moving. Just wanted to say hello—and welcome. See you later."

We said goodbyes all around. We didn't stop to stare at the possessions being unloaded on the sidewalk, but what I did see looked like the same kind of basic furniture we had. Their couch was covered in clear plastic, just like Grandma Gartz's.

"Isn't that Mr. Lewis nice?" Mom said to me, after we were back in the kitchen. "All these colored men are so polite. They always say 'ma'am' to me. Even Vance called me ma'am. I've never had a white boy address me like that."

"I'll bet Billy and Vance will be friends."

"You know, I'm not the least bit unhappy in this changing neighborhood," Mom said, as she emptied coffee grounds into the trash and rinsed out the coffeemaker. She turned to look at me, placing the pot upside down into the dish drainer. "I like Junior and his sisters," she said, gesturing with her left hand to the house that the first black family had bought. "Guess what those girls did the other day? I was loaded down with groceries, walking back from the A&P. They saw me coming down the block and ran up to me and asked if they could help carry something. Then they each took a bag. Wasn't that kind of them?"

"That's *really* nice!" I couldn't think of any one of our previous white neighbors, except Barbara, making such an offer. I liked Junior's sisters, too. They laughed a lot and always smiled when we saw each other, but I didn't get to know them. My life was seven miles north; my school, friends, and activities far away.

Focused on homework, school and friendship, I wasn't paying much attention to the steady attrition of neighborhood icons disappearing right along with our white neighbors. Our favorite local movie theater, the Marbro, where Dad had watched films since the 1930s, closed permanently on October 17, 1963.

Whites were quickly becoming the minority in West Garfield Park, but by this time, my parents seemed unfazed by the reversal. They got along better with the new black residents than they had with our previous crabby white neighbors. The "squeamish" feelings Mom had expressed in her diary when Junior's family had moved in were long forgotten.

Despite good relations with our African American neighbors, West Garfield Park had become decidedly less safe. Blacks *and* whites were less likely to venture out after dark, and local stores responded. Kresge's five-and-dime and the pharmacist both now shuttered their doors earlier than in the past. No wonder neighbors were surprised to find that

Mom ventured out well past the time stores had closed. In her diary, she wrote:

> March 29, 1964
> Lately the streets around here are as deserted as in a western movie before a gun battle. I am not afraid, but I'm cautious. I always look behind me and carry a little can of tear gas in my pocket with my finger on the trigger.

Looking back and reading her words, I'm now aware that the new community, the new people, even the dangerous night—excited her.

CHAPTER 26: Saturday Night Burger

Linda and Bill, early date, summer 1965.

1965

In March of 1965, we attended the farewell dinner for Bethel Church's pastor, Oscar Kaitschuk. Bethel had been an integral part of Dad's fifty years in West Garfield Park. At his last service, Pastor Kaitschuk, in his usual white vestment with a colorful stole hanging around his neck and draping down both sides in front, stood facing a smattering of congregants. Palms facing forward, he started to give his last benediction. "May the Lord bless you and . . . " Tears streaming down his face, he choked, bowed his head, and sobbed. When Dad was a boy, Pastor Kaitschuk's father had been Bethel's minister, presiding over up to four Sunday services accompanied by five robust choirs. Now I sang with a senior choir of three to five other diehards, lifting our puny voices in the cavernous church to no more than twenty or thirty parishioners remaining in the pews, most from my grandparents' generation.

Taking a cue from my parents, I wasn't concerned any longer about the racial change in our community. I was absorbed with typical teen anxieties. At sixteen, I was still clueless about how to attract the attention of boys I liked, marveling at the girls who bubbled in effortless banter and laughter with boys in LHN's hallways before school or during lunch.

Peggy and I were still inseparable friends, growing in our understanding of the high-school social scene, but Peggy was still in the lead. In late May of our junior year, she called me. "Hey, Gartz. John Stock's parents are out of town. He's having an open party next Sunday—on Memorial Day. We *have* to go!" An open party meant anyone could come.

"Oh, man! I really don't want to bump into Bob. I mean, I'm glad to have a date for the prom, but that's all it is—a prom date."

"Come *on*, Gartz! It'll be a blast! He might not even show up, and who knows who else will be there. You'll miss all the fun."

I sighed deeply. "You're right. I should go." Peggy always knew the place to be and tugged me into the social scene.

On Sunday evening, May 30, Dad drove me to pick up Peggy, then on to the party in Park Ridge, a well-heeled northwest suburb. It would be too late to get back to the West Side afterward, so an overnight was planned at Peggy's. She and I both had wriggled into tight white Levi's and slipped into soft moccasins, cutting-edge cool in 1965. Peggy topped her outfit with a faded-blue madras short-sleeved shirt. I wore a sleeveless yellow shell. Dad drove us. "Thanks, Daddy," I said, kissing him on the cheek, before bouncing out of the car.

"Have fun," he called after me, and I turned to see that bittersweet smile of a father watching his little girl grow up.

We followed the rockin' beat of the Kingsmen's "Louie Louie," the titillating lyrics we thought we heard in the slurred words drawing us into a subversive mood. Peg led the way down dark basement stairs into a room heated by a writhing crowd of teens. Some of LHN's coolest kids were doing the "Jerk," convulsing their torsos, hands overhead, looking down, then to the side, then at their partner. It was the latest dance, but I had no idea how to get my body to mimic the motions. I was totally out of it. *No one's going to ask me to dance,* I thought.

A keg of beer was probably somewhere, but it didn't occur to me to look for it. Within seconds, some guy I'd never seen before asked Peggy to dance. She threw a happy smile at me over her shoulder. I was left alone, standing against the wall. *Watching as usual.*

The next dance, that same guy headed my way. Tall, lean, and smiling with a confident stride, he had light-brown hair cut Beatles' length, and he dressed (you guessed it) in white Levi's and a madras shirt. His mouth was at my ear, shouting, "Wanna dance?" *What a relief!*

"Sure." I caught his gentle hazel eyes and smiled broadly. "My name's Linda!" I yelled through cupped palms.

"Bill."

We danced to the driving beat of the Rolling Stones' new hit, "(I Can't Get No) Satisfaction." I tried doing the Jerk, but I felt more spasmodic than cool. Then Johnny Mathis's tender lyrics flowed from the speakers. Romantic, evoking love's uncertainty, "Chances Are" slowed down the pulsing night. Bill drew me toward him. I raised my arms around his neck, and we smiled at each other before he tucked his head onto my shoulder, and we swayed in mellow harmony. I liked the way he cupped the small of my back with his hands, the way we fit each other's bodies together. *I think I'll stick with this guy through the night,* kept running through my mind.

In between songs, we chatted. A friend of his, a senior at Luther North, had brought him to the party. I told him about my family and my fun-loving father. He said that he'd been working since thirteen at a real-estate office and saved his money to pay for flying lessons and scuba equipment. He'd earned his pilot's license and dove in local quarries.

Bill was finishing his sophomore year at Northwestern University, but it didn't occur to me to be impressed that a college guy was spending the whole evening with me. I could tell he liked me—just as I liked him. I didn't have to try to figure out, like I did around other boys, *What's the magic to fit in?* We talked easily, naturally, then danced, then talked more. He never left my side. About eleven thirty, Bill drove Peggy and me back to her house. Before we exited, he asked, "Can I have your number?"

I pulled a scrap of paper from my purse and jotted down my home phone. "Here you go," I said, smiling as I handed it to him. "And thanks for the ride home." I had never given an unknown boy my number before. I felt I had passed an important threshold.

As soon as we left the car, Peggy pumped me for details. "Gartz! A college guy? That is so *cool!* What's he like?"

"Well, he's really funny, and . . . just nice. He goes to Northwestern, but he lives with his parents. He was really easy to talk to. And get this: he has a pilot's license and scuba dives."

"Wow! That's crazy. So do you think he'll call you?"

I thought a moment. "I think so."

The next day was Memorial Day. I had to study for finals, but I couldn't concentrate on German verb conjugations or master the eye-numbing periodic table of elements. Instead, every few minutes or so, I'd stare at the pink Princess phone, sitting silent on the glass-doored cabinet of knickknacks I had painted pink with green trim to match my wallpaper.

Tuesday night, two days after I met Bill, the phone rang at 7:10 p.m. I leaped up from my desk, not shrewd enough to let it ring so as not to seem eager.

"Hi, Linda. It's Bill."

"Hi, Bill. Fun party, wasn't it?"

"The best."

We talked for about half an hour before he said, "I'd like to take you downtown this Saturday to see *My Fair Lady*. I hope you're free." Starring Audrey Hepburn, the musical was one of the most popular of the year. I'd seen it just a few weeks prior with my parents, but I didn't know how to tell Bill that without sounding picky, so I figured I'd just see it again.

"Sure. That sounds great."

"I'll pick you up at seven," he said.

Going downtown was a big deal, so I dressed for the warm June night in a pale sea-green sleeveless chiffon shift and tan-shaded nylon stockings, cinched into place at midthigh with garter clips hanging from a girdle. Always a skinny kid, I sure didn't need a girdle, but I'd never heard of a garter belt. White two-inch heels completed the ensemble. I tossed lipstick, blush, a comb, and some cash into my white purse, then checked myself out in the mirror. I wasn't nervous because we'd clicked so well at the party.

When Bill arrived, my parents joined me to greet him at the door. There was no way I was going anywhere without initial parental scrutiny, so Bill sat down for a conversation with Mom, Dad, and me in our living room, where my parents had set four chairs in a semicircle.

Bill looked more like seventeen than the nearly twenty-year-old he was, so it didn't register with my parents that I was going out with a guy almost four years my senior. He wore a suit jacket and narrow tie, "downtown Chicago" attire in 1965. He looked awfully cute, with his longish hair and lean body. I recalled our easy banter at the party and knew there'd be no problem.

My parents asked him the usual questions: where he lived, what he studied (chemistry), about his family. Leaning forward casually in his chair, his hair just brushing the top of his eyebrows, he spoke with comfortable confidence. His dad was a lawyer, his mom a housewife. Bill lived with them and his two brothers on Chicago's northwest side in a building his dad had constructed to house the family's living space on the second floor and his law practice on the first. They were landlords, too, but rented office space, not rooms.

My parents nodded and smiled throughout the conversation, Mom making punctuating responses of approval ("Oh! That's nice!"). Dad listened intently, as he always did to others, tilted his head or raised his eyebrows in concurrence, and said just the right thing to keep the conversation casual. It was obvious they liked what they saw and heard: down-to-earth and smart, Bill came from an educated, middle-class family, with good values of hard work and ambition.

When we were ready to leave, Mom insisted I take a sweater and gave me extra cash—"mad money," she called it—so I could take a cab home or make a phone call if things didn't go well. As we exited, Mom just had to humiliate me. "Don't forget," she said to Bill, "Cinderella turns into a pumpkin at midnight."

"Of course," said Bill, smiling.

"Okay, Mom, we've got it." I rolled my eyes. We were home by midnight.

On our next date, Bill picked me up in his turquoise Pontiac. I slid over to sit close to him on the bench seat. The car was powerful, with massive fins poking out the back, and Bill drove it fast—showing off as he sped within inches of parked cars. In the back seat were his good buddy, Dennis, and a pretty girl, Susan, whom Dennis was taking out for the first time.

After dinner and a movie in downtown Chicago, we headed home around eleven o'clock in the summer heat and dark. With the windows open, as we listened to Dick Biondi's raspy DJ voice introducing British Invasion hits on the radio, Dennis called out, "Hey, I'm hungry. How about getting something to eat?"

"Sounds good," said Bill. "Are you hungry?" he asked me.

Dennis was cuddling Susan, giving her long kisses in the back seat.

"I'm fine either way," I said.

It was already late, and I didn't dare get home after midnight, so we were on the lookout for the first fast food we could find. In teen oblivion, I wasn't thinking about where we were. Between our West Garfield Park neighborhood and downtown lay East Garfield Park, which was even more crime-ridden than it had been when my parents were scared to send me to Marshall High School. Driving east on Madison, we saw a neon sign blinking "Hamburgers–Hot Dogs" just a block south on Western. It would be fast, and we were a mere two miles from my house as we pulled into the parking lot at 11:20. That gave us plenty of time to down a burger and 7-Up, and still be home on time.

As Bill and Dennis strode into the burger joint to order, I twisted around, facing the rear window, so I could talk to Susan. I wasn't alarmed by the all-black clientele—it looked just like my block. But I thought it was odd the way Bill and Dennis were walking back to the car, their heads down, not talking, taking long, purposeful strides, their hands holding trays of food. I was midsentence, when a hulk of a black man—at least six foot four—emerged out of the darkness. He stepped in front of Bill and Dennis, towering over them and blocking their path. Within seconds, he swung back his huge arm and punched Dennis square in the face. Dennis crumpled to the ground.

"Oh my God!" I shouted. "He hit Dennis!"

Susan whipped around. "My poor baby," was all she could muster, kneeling on the seat and peering out the rear window.

Later Bill told me it had all happened so fast, he hadn't even seen the punch coming and wondered why some guy on the ground, with a twisted nose and gushing blood, wore the same shirt as Dennis. He knew soon enough.

Now the man was going after Bill. Still grasping the tray full of burgers and drinks, Bill backed away, brows knitted, talking to the guy, keeping eye contact. Heart hammering, I felt as if I'd suddenly been thrust into a movie, imagining the next scene—Bill beaten to the ground. The commotion had drawn a crowd, but no one intervened until the African American manager came running outside, his ketchup- and mustard-splattered white apron hanging low over his shirt. At only about five foot eight, he ran right up to the aggressor, gesturing and talking agitatedly. The big man lifted his fist again, moving toward Bill. The manager stepped between them, raising both palms up high against the man's chest, holding him back. Unsteady on his feet, the assailant weaved away and disappeared into the darkness.

Bill dashed to the car, signaled for me to roll down the window, and shoved in the food. "Stay in the car," he barked. "Lock the doors."

"What are you going to do?" I yelled, but he was running back to Dennis before I finished my sentence.

Susan and I locked our doors. I rolled down the window partway to hear. The manager had helped Dennis to his feet, placing wads of paper napkins over his bleeding nose. Bill said something to the two of them, then strode to the pay phone in the parking lot. He dialed "O" for operator. "I need police at Western and Monroe. Hamburger place on the corner. We have an assault."

Susan's bouffant hair had lost none of its lift, but her skin had gone from blush pink to gray. Her eyes, round with terror, darted around the scene while she chewed on her fingernails. My eyes stayed glued on Bill at the pay phone. He was talking into the mouthpiece, when I saw the attacker return and stumble toward Bill. "Bill! Look out!" I screamed.

Bill turned just as the man grabbed the phone from his hand and smashed it onto the cradle. His face contorted with anger, Bill shouted, "Get the hell out of here! I'm calling the police." He picked up the phone again.

"No, you ain't." The guy grabbed the receiver from Bill and banged it, missing the cradle multiple times, until it finally stayed put.

I shouted through the cracked-open window, "Stop talking, Bill! Please! Just get in the car."

Bill was six feet but no more than 150 pounds. The assailant was hefty and muscular. I was sure he'd smash Bill's face—or worse. Then what would I do? Would I get out of the car? Call the police myself? I didn't know. I'd never been in a violent encounter, but Bill's aggressive stance, a revelation to me about his character, reassured me. At least *he* had not lost control.

Bill picked up the receiver. The black man hung it up again. Bill kept shouting, dodging nimbly out of the guy's woozy reach as they each repeated the gestures, like some bizarre vaudeville routine. Out came the manager again, trying to persuade the man to leave. The big guy lumbered off, as if he had time on his side.

Susan's eyes brimmed with tears. She lived in a safe, upper-middle-class suburb and hadn't bargained for a Saturday night date that would end with her boyfriend's nose broken. We heard a siren's wail, like a nearing train whistle. *Please let that be for us!* Mars lights spinning, a cop car pulled into the parking lot and two policemen stepped out, pulling on their hats. They took statements from Bill, Dennis, and the manager. The attacker was long gone.

After Bill and Dennis got back into the car, the cop leaned into the driver's window. "What the hell are you kids doing in this neighborhood?" he asked.

"My girlfriend lives over near Pulaski and Washington," Bill said, gesturing at me.

The officer stared at oh-so-innocent-looking me, and shook his head. "Roll up the windows and keep those doors locked," he said, "and drive right home. Don't stop for anything." He slapped his palm against the side of Bill's car. "Nice ride."

Bill drove fast. We were at my house in less than fifteen minutes, but it was already past one in the morning. He and I got out and hurried up the front steps of my house. Before I could get my key in the lock, Mom opened the door, her face a black scowl. "You're an hour late!" she shouted. "Your curfew is midnight!"

"Mom, listen to what happened."

"I don't care about excuses," she yelled.

"Mom, we were attacked!"

She turned on Bill, her voice rising in fury. "How old are you?" she asked, but interrupted him before he could answer. "Listen," she growled, "she's sixteen and has to be home by midnight. Period!"

"I appreciate your position, Mrs. Gartz," said Bill, "but—"

"Mom," I tried to interject, my voice raised, "Dennis's nose is broken. Don't you understand? We were attacked!"

"If she wants to go out, she'd better be back when I say." She was spitting out the words, bits of saliva spewing into the air between us, her voice cracking with anger.

Mom's tirade and our futile attempts to explain went on for ten minutes, until she finally calmed down enough to let reality sink in. She told Bill she was sorry. She glanced out the front window. "I hope Dennis will be okay," she said sheepishly.

"I have to get him to the hospital," he said. "Goodnight. I'm sorry we were late, but it couldn't be helped." He looked at me. "I'll call you." He shut the door behind him.

"Thanks a lot!" I yelled at my mother. "You don't even care that Dennis's nose was broken!"

"I thought you were purposely staying out late," Mom said, her voice softened now, chagrin creeping into her tone, "just to prove you could do what you wanted—and that made me mad. I'm sorry. I'm glad you're all okay."

"Forget it! I can't even talk to you!" I turned away from her, marched into my bedroom, and slammed the door behind me. *What a jerk!* I thought as I unclipped my stockings and rolled them off. *Her RULES! RULES! She can't even shut up for a few seconds to listen.* Pulling my dress over my head, my mind leaped back to the huge man in front of Dennis, his arm pulled back; Dennis on the ground; the guy going after Bill; my sense of helplessness—not knowing what to do. Guilt began to seep into my gut. *I should have known better than to stop there.*

I opened a dresser drawer and grabbed a nightgown. I had argued the previous week with Mom for a later curfew. She wouldn't budge. I was exasperated with her, but I wasn't a defiant teen; I never gave my parents any trouble. *Why wasn't that obvious to her?*

And both my parents must have known that West Garfield Park was becoming more dicey—and the surrounding communities already had crime and gangs. *Why wasn't she worried, instead of angry?*

As I lay in bed, my thoughts looped mostly around my "unfair mother," but into the loop, images of the attack crept in, evidence that the neighborhood safety we once took for granted was slipping away.

The next day, she and Dad asked me for details. "That's a bad area," Dad said. "Don't ever go that way again."

"Kids can't even stop for a hamburger after a date anymore," Mom said, shaking her head. But neither of them said, "It's time to leave." The following week, they learned of a departure that would tether them more firmly than ever to West Garfield Park.

CHAPTER 27: The Tether and the Dream

Our new home at 4323 N. Keeler Avenue.

1965

The doorbell rang on Wednesday evening, June 16, 1965. Mom strode with her usual quick pace to answer it. From my bedroom, I heard my grandparents and Uncle Will. *How strange.* They virtually never visited during the week. I walked into the living room and heard Mom's tentative greeting, "Hello . . . Come in. Is anything wrong?"

"No, no. We just have something to tell you," said Grandma, moving quickly past Mom with her side-to-side gait. Dad walked down the hallway from the kitchen into the living room. Mom looked to Dad, who shrugged his shoulders and raised his eyebrows in an "I don't know" expression.

Gesturing to our green couch, Mom said, "Won't you sit down?" Mom took a seat next to them. Dad sat on the ottoman, leaning forward with his forearms on his thighs; his fingers spread wide, the tips pressed together; his face all expectancy. I lowered myself onto the rug into a cross-legged position.

"We've bought a house in Villa Park," blurted out Uncle Will. "We'll be moving before July. We just wanted you to know." I'd never heard of this town.

"Villa Park!" Dad said. "That's far. When did you decide to do this?" I saw the concern in Dad's face. I knew Dad viewed West Garfield Park as his family community—where Dad had spent his entire life, working with his parents, through Depression hardships and Ebner's heart-numbing death. Even when his parents had offered so little support to us during Dad's travels, he had stayed loyal to the neighborhood—partly because his parents were still here. Now they were deserting us without a word beforehand, even though whether—or when—to leave the neighborhood was on everyone's mind.

"Well, we wanted to surprise you. We're giving you our six-flat," said Grandma.

"What?" Mom practically shouted, her hands flying to her face. "What do you mean?"

Grandpa leaned forward, grimaced, and flicked his hand to the side. "It means we're giving you our building—a gift."

I pulled back from his annoyed gesture and looked at my silent parents, at their stunned, dumbfounded expressions. I was perplexed, too. Grandma and Grandpa were not known for their generosity. Shifting on the couch, Mom found her voice. "This is . . . so . . . unexpected. I mean, I'm not sure how to thank you, but . . . well, thank you!"

"Yes . . . thank you," said Dad, his fingertips tapping lightly together.

Grandma waved away their gratitude with hardly a smile. "You'll see what it's like." My grandparents talked a little more about their new home. Villa Park lay sixteen miles and about forty minutes west of our house.

Uncle Will drew an envelope of photos from his pocket. "It's a ranch. It'll be easier for Mom and Pop to get around," he said.

"The neighborhood is so *quiet*," Grandpa gestured, sweeping his palms forward, tracing the air in a half arc, as if it were the community itself. He scrunched up his still-alert blue eyes in his usual way to emphasize a point. "No more tenants, and an arbor to grow roses." No matter how many hours Grandma and Grandpa labored, they always had planted a beautiful garden.

Will passed around snapshots of a nondescript yellow-brick house, a tiny patch of grass bordering the front. Inside were two small bedrooms; a compact, eat-in kitchen; a living room with a large picture window looking out on the front; and a basement for storage. "It looks nice," said Dad, but his tone said it all—he was hurt by this bombshell, marginalizing him again.

After a little more talk about their moving date and the logistics of transferring the six-flat deed to us, my grandparents and uncle stood. "Well, we have to get going. A lot of packing to do," said Uncle Bill.

After living in West Garfield Park for half a century, Grandma and Grandpa had been befuddled by the changing neighborhood. Suffering from high blood pressure and tachycardia (a racing heartbeat), Grandma had already had more than one heart attack during the previous two decades. She and Grandpa were both in their late seventies, and they couldn't take the stress of the doorbell ringing with would-be African American renters and harassing calls from realtors.

It wasn't until decades later, after everyone was dead, that I discovered Grandma's scribbles, on random sheets of paper, about the six-flat gift. I learned that the appraised value of the six-flat in June of 1965 was $40,000. She noted that their tax lawyer had advised her and Grandpa to gift some of their savings, "or you'll give it to the government," as he put it. Grandma's notes show that she and Grandpa thought the building would help pay for her grandchildren's college educations, but based on conversations over the years, I know they never told that to my parents.

I recall my mom and dad briefly discussing whether or not to sell the six-flat, but they repeatedly came to the same conclusion: it would be a slap in the face to my grandparents' generosity. I believe now that Dad may have unconsciously feared his mother's acrimony if they sold. *So this is what you do with a gift of a building? You should take care of it as we did!* Grandma's condemning wave of the hand, her sour face and head-shaking disappointment—Dad had seen it all, over and over, since early childhood.

I learned more from my grandmother's notes—facts that I had never known about the six-flat gift. Since my grandparents had given Dad a $40,000 building, my grandparents felt it was only fair that they give Will $40,000, too—in stocks and cash, part of which Will used to buy the house in Villa Park. His gift was a home in a safe neighborhood and thousands in growth investments. Dad's gift was a tether to a community on the skids, with the implication that my parents shouldn't sell it.

By early July, my grandparents and Will had moved, so Dad and Mom tackled the six-flat in earnest. "After all the bragging Grandma did about her great housekeeping, they sure left that place a mess!" Mom told me once she and Dad returned home after spending the day determining what work my grandparents' former apartment required before it could be rented.

Sweating through the July heat, Mom and Dad steamed and scraped off the old, dirty wallpaper only to discover the walls beneath were riddled with cracks. They hired Italian plasterers and, at a cost of several thousand dollars, replaced the failing furnace. Mom scrubbed the floors with trisodium phosphate, then sanded and varnished them. But Dad forgot to lay a drop cloth before prepping the walls for paint, and the newly varnished floor was spotted with primer. Mom wanted to cry.

"You ruined the varnish!" she yelled at Dad. He spent several hours with a turpentine-soaked rag and scraper, removing the errant spots. In most Chicago apartments, especially in African American communities, if landlords even bothered to paint, they certainly wasted neither time nor money cleaning up splatters or smudges. Windows often stayed broken for months or were permanently painted shut. Heat might be unpredictable or inadequate. But my parents' old-world values required that their work was perfect.

Just as they were investing more effort and funds into the West Side, fate stepped in, giving them a clear vision of how to fulfill a dream they didn't even know they had.

It was another building.

About a month after my parents took possession of the six-flat, Peggy and I were walking to her apartment after school. A "For Sale by Owner" sign hung in front of the house one door north of her building. Whenever I visited Peggy, I had walked past and admired this gracious, white clapboard Victorian with its wide front porch, brilliant stained-glass windows, and wraparound second-floor balcony. Even my parents had remarked on its beauty whenever they picked me up after an overnight. "Look at that gorgeous house!" one or the other would say, as if it were far out of reach.

When I got home, I said to my parents, "Guess what? You know that really pretty house next door to Peggy? It's for sale!" I was grinning, talking fast. "Here—I took down the phone number from the sign." As far as I knew, they weren't actively looking to move, although it had come up in desultory conversations—with no real plan attached. With my grand-parents' departure, and the extra dangers we had recently encountered in and near West Garfield Park, I figured they were open to finding a safer place to live.

I handed Mom the slip of paper as she sat making notes at the handsome oak Victorian desk she had refinished.

"Hmmm. I've always loved that house," she said, staring at the number. She got up and handed the information to Dad, who extended his arm backward from the couch, pausing from the *CBS Evening News* with Walter Cronkite. "What do you think, Fred? We should at least take look."

Dad sat up, turning his back to the TV. "That *is* a beautiful home," he agreed. "Sure, let's go. Can't hurt to look." Mom made the appointment, and early the next evening, our whole family piled into our Ford station wagon and drove from Washington Boulevard, five miles straight north up Pulaski, then two blocks west at Montrose to Keeler, for a visit.

The owners were an elderly woman, Mrs. Trandell, and her son. Stooped with age, Mrs. Trandell greeted us at the front door, her white hair wisping about her heavily lined face, her tentative smile appraising us as a mother might evaluate potential adoptive parents for her baby. She ushered our family through the crescent-shaped entryway, bordered on two sides with leaded-glass windows, then through another oak door, opening to an expansive entry, in front of a wide, light-oak staircase winding out of sight to the second floor.

Mrs. Trandell began her tour of the first floor: parlor to the left; sitting room to the right, leading into a dining room, which opened to the kitchen; then the mudroom with a back stairway leading to the second floor. Off the mudroom was a real luxury: indoor access to an enormous basement. Mrs. Trandell spoke in reverential tones tinged with nostalgic longing: "I've been so happy here," she said, her eyes misting over. "I would never leave, but my son says it's just too much for me to handle."

We climbed the front winding staircase, which ended in a small sitting area, bathed in a golden glow by the western sun. Light poured into all four second-floor bedrooms, each with at least two windows and a view. The master bedroom was huge, with a walk-in cedar closet—definitely for Mom and Dad. Across the sitting area was a bedroom that seemed ideal for Paul—plenty of room for a big desk, where he could spread out his books to study. Everyone agreed the bedroom directly across from Peggy's room next door had to be mine. "You and Peggy could just lean on your windowsills and gab with each other!" Mom said.

At the back was a smaller bedroom, with built-in cedar drawers under the raised bed. Billy, age twelve, looked to Mom with a wide grin and spoke quickly, the words pouring out. "This looks just like where the captain of a ship would sleep! And I can look out the window to the backyard—as if it's the sea!"

"It would look so nice with nautical wallpaper," Mom chimed in. We were talking as if we already owned the place.

Across from the home's only bathroom and right next to "Billy's room," we opened the door leading to the attic. At the top of the bare wooden stairs, we reached an expansive space, the center soaring up fifteen feet. We tilted back our heads, our eyes sweeping around the hugeness of it all. Even up here, sunlight played its magic, the rays illuminating dust motes that floated and bounced about like fairy dust.

"We could have parties and balls up here," Dad said in a whisper, his creative mind always turning things over in the most unlikely way. We looked at one another and smiled. Our hearts were already aching.

My parents had just spent the previous month upgrading the six-flat, but the effort that this nine-room home (plus a barn, a basement, and a yard at least six times as large as the one on Washington) required didn't deter them. Besides, it was understood that all three of us kids would roll up our sleeves to help refurbish this faded beauty—if we bought it. After our tour, we asked Mrs. Trandell the price. It was non-negotiable at $24,600. Why? "Well," she said, "the digits of the price and the digits of the house address (4323 North Keeler Avenue) have to add up to the number twelve."

"I see," said Mom, but she and Dad shot each other a glance that showed they didn't see. Neither did I, but I knew that was irrelevant. Despite Mrs. Trandell's bizarre reasoning, the price was affordable, especially now that we had the six-flat as additional equity. Not one of us held a poker face. "We just love this house," Mom effused. "We'll get back to you as soon as we check on the loan." Our family had stumbled onto a new life that we hadn't even been looking for.

But Mrs. Trandell's odd price requirement wasn't the only weird thing about the purchase. We were in for an emotional roller-coaster ride. Mom called Mrs. Trandell the next day. "Hello, Mrs. Trandell, this is Lillian Gartz calling about the house. We're ready to offer you your asking price. When can we work out the details?"

"Well, I don't know," said Mrs. Trandell, wavering. "You see, another nice family wants this house, too. I think we have to sell it to them."

Mom's face twisted as if she had been kicked in the stomach. "Oh, no, Mrs. Trandell, I don't think you want to do that," Mom said. "We're the absolute perfect family for that house." Mrs. Trandell listened to Mom's arguments and agreed to sell to us.

Later that afternoon, Mrs. Trandell's son called. "No," he said, "we really have to sell it to the other family. They looked at the house first."

Mom was pacing around the dining room when Dad called from a pay phone, en route to Fireman's Fund inspections. "Hi, Lil. I just happen to be in the Trandell's neighborhood. Should I drop by to talk to Mrs. Trandell?" He was unaware of Mom's most recent conversation.

"Oh, please, do whatever you can! Trandell's son just called to say they're selling to that other family. I think I'll *die* if I don't get that house."

Dad parked in front of 4323 North Keeler Avenue and rang the bell. I can picture the scene. Both Mrs. Trandell and her son were home and welcomed him in. Dad always leaned

forward slightly when he engaged with a recent acquain-
tance—not quite a bow, but humble, friendly, he smiled with
his eyes—sincere and warm. "May I come in? Just to chat
with you both for a few minutes?"

"Of course. Come in. Come in." The Trandells led him
into the parlor, where he sat, elbows again resting on his
knees in his casual way, his hands poised between his thighs
or gesturing in rhythm with his conversation. His gentle,
easygoing manner put people at ease. He told them about his
family and his own childhood. "We're devoted to taking care
of property. Even our kids work with us, and they're eager to
keep this home as beautiful as you've always loved it."

He shared a few of the stories and jokes he knew would
put his audience at ease. Somehow, by the time Dad left, the
Trandells had agreed to sell the house to the Gartz family
after all. It was July 27.

Dad went back to the pay phone. "We've got it!"

"Really? Oh, really? Oh, that's the *best* news! Fred,
thank you. Thank you! I'll call the bank." Mom let out a
whoop and later wrote in her diary, "This is one of the most
momentous days in our lives!"

In the lawyer's office on the day of the closing, Mom's
tongue stuck to the roof of her mouth. Both my parents and the
Trandells had arrived early, but the lawyer was late. Fearing the
old woman might change her mind about selling, Mom chat-
tered at her nonstop, her saliva going down in hard nuggets.

The lawyer finally showed up, discussed a few details,
and handed a pen to Mrs. Trandell, saying, "Okay. It looks
like we're ready to complete this sale." Mrs. Trandell looked
at her son, her eyes moist, the pen poised over the contract.

Mom tried to keep the desperation out of her voice.
"Could we just sign now, please?"

Everyone signed. Mom and Dad were all smiles, floating
on the lightness of relief. The closing marked the high point of
their summer. Less than two weeks later, we found ourselves
in the midst of a maelstrom.

CHAPTER 28: Up in Flames

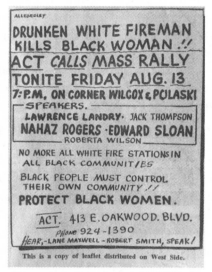

Chicago Daily News, August 14, 1965 p4.

On Wednesday night, August 11, 1965, police in the Watts area of Los Angeles stopped a young black man, Marquette Frye, on suspicion of driving under the influence. Just as in Chicago, blacks had poured into Los Angeles from the South during the years of the Second Great Migration.[39] And as in West Garfield Park, and dozens of other large cities, blacks were segregated. Government redlining policy meant mortgages became unavailable when blacks moved into an area, so whites had deserted Watts in a mass exodus once African Americans moved into their neighborhood.

Often harassed and intimidated by the virtually all-white Los Angeles police force, excluded from jobs, housing, and politics, blacks in Watts were a community powder keg, ready to explode. Frye's arrest lit the spark. After Frye's mother and brother got into a physical confrontation with the officers, the local crowd of onlookers burgeoned into a mob, hurling rocks and chunks of concrete at the police. Violence escalated as up to thirty-five thousand rioters looted, set fires, and attacked police and white motorists. By Friday, August 13, rioting was so intense that as many as thirteen thousand national guardsmen were called in to maintain order.

The evening after Watts convulsed in riots, on August 12, a fire truck pulled out of its station at Wilcox and Pulaski, just south and east of our buildings and near the neighborhood's main business district. That simple routine turned into tragedy.

Neighborhood blacks perceived the Wilcox all-white fire department as racist. One African American woman who went to Providence St. Mel School, just south of Garfield Park, recalled why: "City services were such that you didn't want to call the police or fire department; they would treat you with disrespect."[40]

Despite numerous petitions by West Garfield Park African Americans to the city to hire more blacks to serve in the Wilcox firehouse, the requests were ignored. Just like Watts, WGP was a tinderbox of resentment. A fire alarm that Thursday night of August 12 struck the match.

A hook-and-ladder truck was dispatched to respond to the alarm, but the tillerman, whose job it was to control the ladder, never took his place at the back. He was supposed to press an "all-clear buzzer," telling the driver that he was in position and that it was safe to pull out of the fire station. The driver mistook another sound for the buzzer and raced out of the firehouse without the tillerman in place. On a sharp turn, the uncontrolled ladder swung free, ramming a stop sign, which struck and killed twenty-three-year-old Dessie Mae Williams, a young African American woman.

The day of the fire-truck incident, I was spending a couple nights with a friend in a northwest suburb, focused only on teenaged fun. The next morning, unaware of Williams's death, Mom and Dad decided to take a needed break from their non-stop work on the six-flat and the tense negotiations to buy the house on North Keeler. They, along with Billy, took one day off to relax at Lake Geneva, Wisconsin, an hour and a half north.

The glow of owning their first single-family home was still fresh in their minds. In between brief swims, they discussed plans for remodeling, indulging in their dreams on that bright Friday afternoon of August 13. Swimming in Lake Geneva's cool, calm waters under a cloud-puffed August sky, Mom and Dad had no idea of the fury fomenting after Williams's death, just blocks from their apartment buildings.

Rumors had flashed through the neighborhood that the fireman whose ladder had hit and killed the young mother on Thursday night had been drunk. On Friday, angry leaflets circulated, fueling the rage. One screamed for attention in huge, bold type:

DRUNKEN WHITE FIREMAN KILLS BLACK WOMAN.
ACT CALLS MASS RALLY TONITE
FRIDAY, AUG. 13, 7 PM, ON CORNER [OF]
WILCOX & PULASKI

(In tiny print in the upper-left corner is the word "alleged-ley." [*sic*])[41]

The *Chicago Daily News* reported that Lawrence Landry, chairman of an activist civil-rights group, ACT, addressed a large group of African Americans in front of the Wilcox firehouse. Landry exhorted his listeners to take action against the injustices blacks had suffered, saying, "Black people must control their own destiny," and, "You're being misused because you're in a white-controlled society." The crowd swelled. Clusters of angry youths took to the streets.[42]

My parents and Billy left Lake Geneva as the western sky blushed mauve and purple. Seldom having time to simply talk to one another, they didn't bother to turn on the radio. And they had so much to discuss: the new house, the six-flat repairs, and catching up on Billy's life and interests.

As the conversation shifted, the ongoing riots in Watts came up. Mom later told me they had wondered aloud whether such violence could happen in our neighborhood. Just the previous year, Harlem and Rochester, New York and Philadelphia had erupted in devastating race riots. Why not Chicago, too? An hour later, they were traveling south on Pulaski in the summer dark, clueless about the anti-white rage that was already boiling over just blocks from our home.

As the crowds swelled, the police cordoned off Pulaski Road at Washington Boulevard, our street. After twenty-four hours of furor and decades of frustration, black West Siders vented their outrage in volleys of missiles. From housetops, curbs, and doorways, in all sections of the community, youths pelted police with bricks, stones, and bottles. The crowds surged into the business district, just a few blocks away.

Two *Chicago Daily News* reporters, one black, one white, entered the fray. The black reporter, Burleigh Hines, donned old clothes and mixed with Chicago's West Side rioters. He wrote about what he saw as my parents and Billy, oblivious to the melee, made their way toward home:

> *Young punks swarmed in the area, yelling and cursing. Some of them seemed almost hysterical with hatred. The hatred was directed at white men—all white men. . . . "KILL THE white _____" the punks screamed whenever a white person made the mistake of showing his face in the area.*[43]

(Whatever epithet the reporter left blank in his story, it apparently was too raunchy even to allude to in a family newspaper in 1965.)

The paper's white reporter wrote, "I'll have to rate it as the most dangerous newspaper experience in fifteen years of covering stories in this, my hometown. . . . A young Negro boy stuck his head in the window of my parked car at Wilcox and Pulaski and shouted, "You get out of here, white man, and don't come back . . . don't ever come back."[44]

Scores of drivers and passengers were struck by bricks that crashed through the windows of their moving cars. In one of these cars rode the Reverend David Nelson and his sister, Mary Nelson, both white, who were just arriving on the West Side. The children of a Lutheran pastor, both were devoted to helping the downtrodden. David was coming to West Garfield Park to be the new minister of our virtually empty Bethel Church. Mary came along to help him settle in and work on community development. Their welcome to the community they had come to serve was a brick through the window of their Volkswagen Beetle.

It was after nine thirty when Mom, Dad, and Billy approached the intersection of West End, a block north of Washington, where police cars blocked Pulaski. An officer directed Dad to turn west. Turning slowly, Dad peered south. Dozens of flashing blue lights scattered the darkness. In the distance rose tongues of flame and billows of smoke.

He drove down our alley, backed the station wagon into the garage, then started east on foot, calling over his shoulder, "I'm going to find out what's happening."

"Fred, please. Don't go. This is not your business. With all those cop cars, it must be dangerous," Mom pleaded.

"I'm going!" he shouted, and walked toward the whirling lights.

When Paul heard the back door open, he dashed from his bedroom into the kitchen. He looked to Mom and Billy. "Where's Dad?" he demanded.

"A slew of police cars were blocking Pulaski," Mom said, gesturing east. "I begged him not to go, but, as usual, he wouldn't listen!"

"What? The radio said there's a race riot going on. I've got to find him before he gets killed!"

Mom grasped Paul's arm. Her voice cracked. "Paul, don't go. Please. He'll come back. If you go, then you'll both be out there. I don't want to lose my husband and my son!"

Paul pulled free of her grip and ran to the front. The door slammed. He leaped down the steps and strode east, half running, half walking. He knew Dad would have gone straight to the action. Dad's years in the business of fire protection and underwriting had made him a junkie for conflagrations and firefighting tactics. Paul ran south to Madison Street, then turned toward Pulaski on deserted sidewalks. The eastern sky glowed a lurid, smoky red. Slowing his pace as he approached Pulaski, he couldn't absorb what was happening on the streets where he had grown up, shopped, and played with friends. *All hell is breaking loose*, he thought. Fear clutched his throat tighter with each crash and whoosh in the distance. As he approached Madison and Pulaski, a scrum of young black men rounded the corner ahead and blocked his path.

"Hey, white boy?" one guy said to him. "You don't wanna go down there." He gestured at the red sky. "Don't you know they killin' your kind?" In moments, Paul was surrounded by at least seven black men, with many more behind them.

"I'm looking for my father," Paul said, keeping his eyes on the guy who had spoken to him. The young man had bright eyes. *Smart guy*, Paul thought as he appraised his situation, even as he felt the sweat gathering under his arm-pits, his heart moving to his throat. The man confronting him stood about five foot nine, had a moderate build, and appeared to speak for the group. Next to him stood a guy, drunk or high on drugs, wide and muscular. He locked his bleary, empty eyes on my brother and didn't move or say a word. Paul thought, *This guy could kill me in a second—like squashing a fly. I can't let them think I'm afraid.*

The leader did all the talking, expounding of the injustices the black man had suffered at the hands of white people. He told Paul that blacks were better than whites. "You can only make white babies. We can make any color we want."

Paul listened and nodded, saying little except an occasional, "You have a point."

After about fifteen minutes, Paul said, "Well, I understand your position, but now I really need to go." He backed away. The men behind him parted to let him through. He walked back west, toward our home, dazed and not certain what had just happened or if he might still be in danger. Not daring to look back, he hunched his shoulders and kept a purposeful pace. He was followed only by the crackle of flames and the roar of water gushing from fire hoses, until the din faded to a dull muffle.

By the time he arrived at our flat, Dad was back, too.

"Dad!" exclaimed Paul. "What happened?"

"The cops wouldn't let me go any farther after I got to Washington and Pulaski, but it sure looks like a riot," he said.

"Paul! Thank God you're back safe," Mom cried, throwing her palm to her forehead, her dramatic gesture when relieved. She paced the room. "Just don't anyone go out again!" she commanded.

Only I wasn't home. She picked up the phone. "I've got to call Linda and tell her what's happening, tell her to call us before she comes back home tomorrow."

Race riots were the focus of the entire front page of Saturday's *Chicago Daily News*. The upper three-fourths was devoted to Watts, introduced by this enormous headline:

TERROR IN L.A.
16 Dead; 2,000 Troops Fail to Stop the Rioting Mob

The article at the bottom, "In Chicago, Scores Hurt in Riot," reported that seventy-nine people had been injured during the Chicago riot, including eighteen police officers. The headlines conveyed the shock of both black and white reporters who had been on the Chicago scene: "Hysterical Hate on the West Side" and "A Night of Shame on Pulaski Road." The *Chicago Defender*, Chicago's venerable newspaper for African American readers, headlined less volatile sentiments in its August 14 issue, "Civic Leaders Condemn Violence."

It seemed as if the entire country were disintegrating into racial hatred and violence, while we lived side by side and got along fine with our African American neighbors. The day after the riots, Mr. Lewis, whom Mom had always referred to as "the nicest man," was helping Paul work on our car. This is what Mom recorded:

Police from all over the city were stationed on every corner of our neighborhood, ready for trouble. The strangest thing of all was that, on this day of racial tension, Paul and Mr. Lewis next door were working on [our] station wagon, doing a new valve job. So here they were, both black and white, working together, sweating together, while this racial situation was just waiting to explode. Later in the day, I brought up the subject, just casually, and [Mr. Lewis] said, "I just hate this worse than anybody."

A new era had begun in our neighborhood—and our lives.

CHAPTER 29: An Island in a Sea of Destruction

The riots erupted just a couple of weeks after Mom and Dad had toiled through the July heat to bring my grandparents' former six-flat apartment into pristine condition for rental. In June, the building had been appraised at $40,000, but what would it be worth after the angry destruction wreaked on our community's once-bustling commercial district?

Searing images of the deadly and devastating Watts riots in California melded with the fires, looting, and virulent anti-white hatred on Chicago's West Side into one amorphous threat. Gripped by visceral fear, remaining whites and middle-class blacks fled, creating a vacuum that sucked in an ever-poorer population. Amid rising crime, a glut of homes for sale, and continued blockbusting, property values plummeted. My parents soldiered on, but not without consequences.

Over the next several years, the demands of overseeing four houses (our home on North Keeler, the six-flat, our former home, and a second two-flat they had bought in 1958 on Washington Boulevard) multiplied their workload. Grandma and Grandpa Gartz had routinely worked sixteen-hour days, so the extra labor my parents took on seemed normal to Dad.

But he had scant experience managing all the moving parts, which Mom did. The increasingly complicated paperwork and income-tax preparation, the coordination of repairmen and the management of tenants, as well as her own household and children, boosted her stress—and her ire against Dad, whom she blamed for her predicament. In the early days of his travel, Dad had repeatedly tried to mollify Mom with compliments and appreciation, but by the time he had secured a non-traveling job with Fireman's Fund in 1962, the pattern of their relationship had reset into one comprising Mom's complaints and Dad's increasingly cavalier attitude, figuring he couldn't do anything to please her, so he might as well please himself.

My parents had arrived at a crossroads, both personal and historical. The riots were not isolated neighborhood tremors that would subside, but rather part of a societal earthquake, cracking open and challenging long-held beliefs on a national scale. We teetered on a fault line of radical change, and America rocked from one upheaval after another—every value and institution under scrutiny and dissent. As a young teen, raised by a traditional family and attending a conservative Lutheran school, both of which reinforced values of good behavior and obedience to authority, I couldn't understand the turmoil, the decades of simmering black grievances that boiled over into riots, the slow-burning fury that exploded and embroiled cities across the nation. As I came of age, I felt like I was gasping for understanding, as if gasping for air, in the flood of change overwhelming us.

Returning to the West Side the day after the riots, I exited the bus at Pulaski and Madison, where Dad was waiting for me. Smelling the lingering odor of stale smoke in the air, I scanned still-smoldering buildings, broken windows, and glass-strewn streets. "Wow, Dad!" I said, gaping at the destruction. "What *happened* here?"

"People run amok. Just run amok. Hating white people, throwing Molotov cocktails, burning down buildings." He swept his arm in a wide arc. "We used to chase butterflies through open prairies in this community when I was a boy. Everyone wanted to build the place up, not tear it down."

"But why? Was it like Watts?"

"Not that bad. Today's paper has an overview. Something about a fire truck hitting a colored woman. I'll show you when we get home." We walked west to a chorus of hammers clanging on nails and grunting men lifting plywood boards to cover smashed windows. Broken bottles, some with charred rags hanging out the necks, littered the street. The world was coming undone just as I was getting old enough to enter it.

"I just don't get it, Dad."

Putting his arm around my shoulder, he said, "Let's talk about something more pleasant. What were you up to last night? Mom tried to call you, but no one answered."

I told Dad how my friends and I had skulked around a cemetery, dressed from head to toe in black to emulate the characters in the TV show *The Man from U.N.C.L.E.*

"That seems so stupid now. You guys really could have been hurt—and I was acting like a little kid!"

"It's never stupid to enjoy yourself at sixteen," he said. When we reached home, he kissed my cheek before pushing his key into the lock.

We walked through the house and into the kitchen, where Mom was making lunch. "Well, it's my long-lost daughter," she said, smiling ruefully and looking over her shoulder from the stove.

Dad showed me the *Chicago Daily News,* its front page plastered with photos of riots and mayhem in Watts and Chicago. A shadow of dismay crossed his face. "What were they thinking?" he said, looking up from the paper, gazing at nothing. "They've burned down their own neighborhood."

Mom sliced celery, adding it to the bowl of tuna salad. "If

they owned property, they'd understand the effort required to care for buildings—they wouldn't be so quick to just destroy everything!" she said as she smeared the salad onto pieces of bread, added cheese, placed them side by side on a cookie sheet, and slid them under the broiler.

After lunch, I walked to my summer job at Baer Brothers & Prodie, a fine-clothing store on Madison Street. Just a block from the worst rioting, its display windows were boarded up.

I rode the elevator to the women's department and started my day as usual, moving the overdue layaways from the stockroom to the sales floor. I hated returning those clothes to the rack, wondering what happened to the women who had dreamed of owning a pretty dress or skirt, put money down, but never finished paying. Now their money *and* the clothes were gone.

Just in case of further trouble, Mom and Dad picked me up from work. Taking a cue from my parents, I wasn't fearful, but I was flabbergasted at the wanton destruction of property. We certainly didn't see ourselves as capitalists who exploited poor people. But that was how the ACT activists had portrayed landlords on the night of the riots. Their pronouncement that owning and caring for buildings had something to do with subjugating others was incomprehensible to us.

In my naïveté, I was clueless about the centuries of intimidation and humiliation blacks had endured at the hands of whites. Years later, sociologists and historians concluded that decades of thwarted dreams had exploded into violence in cities across the country. It wasn't until I gained some distance from then-unfathomable events and better understood the racist housing policies and the bigotry African Americans had endured from a white-controlled society, in which my family had been complicit, that I could gain perspective and put the riots into context.

Whites continued to abandon West Garfield Park by the thousands. We stayed, and my parents came to know our new neighbors and their histories. The insights were often heartbreaking, especially since many had every reason to be consumed by fury, yet hadn't rioted.

Eddie Bass was one of these. He labored seven days a week at the local butcher shop. Eddie was a squat African American with close-cropped hair and an anguished look, as if sadness from somewhere deep inside seeped out to his face. He spoke kindly to all his customers. Mom admired his direct, honest manner and liked to chat with him when the butcher shop wasn't busy.

One day, she asked Eddie what he thought about the civil rights movement. Folding the white butcher paper over her ground beef, he shook his head and said, "I just wants folks to call me 'Eddie' or 'Bass' and shake my hand, but not call me nigger." He handed her the package and wiped his brow. "When I was growin' up in Mississippi, I did all sorts of low work for the boss man." He sighed. "That weren't the worst of it. Every Saturday night, that man was *drunk*. He made me run around in the dark so he could do some target practice—on *me*, shootin' at me with his pistol."

Mom's eyes welled up. Little had been written in mainstream newspapers about the oppression of blacks in the Jim Crow South—until the civil rights movement placed the injustices squarely on the front pages and led the evening news. When she came home, she told us Eddie's story.

"Man's inhumanity to man," said Dad.

"He made me want to cry," said Mom, her voice choking in the retelling.

Mom showed an apartment to Mr. and Mrs. Darden, a mid-
dle-aged black couple. Mrs. Darden carried herself with an
air of dignity and privilege. As she and her husband walked
from room to room, she just nodded and said, "Mmm-hmm."
Mom was crestfallen at Mrs. Darden's lack of enthusiasm for
the beautiful apartment.

That evening, the smell of pork chop suey filled our
kitchen. As we each passed our bowls to Mom from seats
tucked around the table, she talked about her day. "That
Mrs. Darden I showed the apartment to today?" She scooped
rice into each bowl, then ladled her steaming chop suey on
top. "She kept asking about the heat." Mom finally pulled
out her own chair, squeezed against the stove, to sit down.

"The heat?" asked Dad, after blowing on a hot spoon-
ful. "What did she want to know?"

"Well, get this. It turned out her last apartment was so
cold, she had to put on a coat every morning when she got up
and even when she came home from church!"

Dad, his parents, and his brothers had awakened in
the middle of the night to keep their coal-burning furnaces
functioning perfectly. He stared at Mom, his spoon poised
above his plate, his eyes wide with surprise. Looking down
in disgust, he said, "I guess that's how these other landlords
make a killing—just don't heat the place!" Mom assured the
Dardens that the heat worked fine, and they signed a lease as
of October 1.

Mom rented another six-flat apartment to Samuel and
Dorothy Headd, an African American pair in their thir-
ties. "They're such a darling couple," she said. "They didn't
ask, but I repainted the kitchen and dining room for them.
A lovely pale pink. She kept thanking me for the beautiful
apartment." It was the first time Mom was renting to African
Americans. She felt on shaky ground and wanted to be sure
everything went smoothly with no ruffled feelings.

That fall, Mom advertised, fielded phone calls, showed
apartments at the six-flat, typed up leases, and worked late

into the night to keep up with increasingly complicated book-keeping. Dad drove around the city during the day, making inspections as a loss-control engineer for his job at Fireman's Fund. Nights and weekends, Dad went to the West Side, comfortable with the kind of work integral to his family pride. He dusted hallway banisters, mopped tiled vestibules, glazed new glass panes into rock-smashed windows, and cleared the sidewalk of broken beer or whiskey bottles—and then, something new—used needles.

Acquaintances and friends assured him and Mom, "The colored will wreck those apartments," but my parents ignored them. "We're going to take care of those buildings like we always have, and I believe we'll get tenants who do the right thing, too," Mom said. After the hectic summer of beautifying the six-flat and interviewing potential tenants in autumn, my parents hadn't had a spare moment to think about the shabby condition of our newly purchased North Side home and all the work *it* needed.

CHAPTER 30: Be Still, I Am Thy God

Every room in our new home needed fresh paint or wallpaper. Even without the West Side properties, it could have overwhelmed the time and energy of most fifty-something couples. But Mom and Dad had nurtured more than buildings over the years. They had taught my brothers and me the skills of home maintenance, the value and satisfaction of a job well done, the patience to stick with long-term projects from start to finish, the optimism and confidence to keep our eyes on the prize. Paul, Billy, and I were so thrilled to have a home of our own, we willingly dove into whatever effort was needed to uncover the hidden beauty in our Cinderella house.

In our family's version of "quality time," we teamed up to refurbish the house during the December 1965 holiday break. Paul volunteered to paint every surface of the enormous sixteen-hundred-square-foot unfinished basement, beams and all. The week before Christmas, he rented a paint sprayer and worked around the clock for two full days, stopping only to eat the sandwiches Mom brought him when he refused to come home until he was finished.

When Paul finally walked into the back door on the West Side, he was like the mimes who stand motionless in European city squares, stiff and white as a statue. His lashes, heavy with paint, blinked oh-so-slowly. Every hair on his

181

body was a bristly, sticky white: head, arms, hands—even up his nose. Only his eyeballs weren't white. They were red, bloodshot from the insult of spray paint.

My bedroom was next. Wrestling rented wallpaper steamers, we pressed the awkward, heavy rectangles of metal against the walls for thirty seconds at a time. Vapor hissed out, clouding my room with the cloying smell of melting wallpaper paste. Despite frigid outside temperatures, we threw open the windows, releasing intense steam and heat.

Pressing rigid putty blades against softened old paper, we scraped off layer after layer. Press. Hold. Scrape. Repeat—until we were down to the bare wall, each of us shouting a loud "Hooray!" upon reaching the base level. Sometimes the massive steamer plate fell against an arm, causing a blistering second-degree burn. An expletive, a quick trip to the bathroom for Mercurochrome and a Band-Aid—then back to steaming, a vision of the end product firmly in mind.

Mom found beautiful wallpaper, a closeout at a dollar per roll—enough for the parlor, entry, and hallway up to the second floor. One of her tenants recommended a contractor, Mr. Henderson Ford, a large, heavyset African American man, who dropped by to give an estimate. Ford arrived in a paint-spattered coat, which, when unbuttoned, exposed overalls stretched by his rotund belly. Garrulous, funny, and with years of experience, he explained to Mom how he'd approach the work. She liked his forthright style, his attentive ear, and his good suggestions. They hit it off instantly, and she hired him on the spot to paper the first floor and all the bedrooms.

Amidst all these complicated projects, Mom still had to figure out what to do with our present two-flat on Washington Boulevard. We had to pack up sixteen years of family living and the accumulations remaining from Dad's Depression-era

mentality. "Never throw out anything you might need someday," was his parents' mantra and a guiding principle still
embedded in Dad's psyche. It was how his family had survived, then thrived, during lean times. He saved everything—
scraps of wood (for repairs), old buckets (still serviceable), a
two-foot stack of 78 records ("These will be priceless someday"), multiple sets of dishes and cheap Revere pots and pans
he collected at Salvation Army stores ("The kids will need
cookware when they move"), and hundreds of other items,
from rolls of plastic to bottles of nails and screws, each type
labeled and sorted into its own baby-food jar, and multiples
of every tool imaginable: ten varieties of saws, fifteen screw-
drivers, wrenches of all sizes and uses.

How were they going to get everything packed and then
manage their rooming house, with a total of twelve individual tenants, from five miles away? That winter of 1965, Mom
panicked at her predicament. Heart racing, mind ajumble,
she saw lying on the dining-room table a small pamphlet by
Norman Vincent Peale, the author of *The Power of Positive
Thinking,* probably ordered from a magazine ad. Inside was
a Bible passage, Psalm 46:10, offered as a solace in times of
crisis: "Be still, and know that I am God." Mom remembered
it as: "Be still. I am thy God." She lay down on the dining-room couch, repeating this passage over and over until
her thoughts and pounding heart calmed. "That's when I
began to *think*," she later told me, "and figure out priorities.
Before that, it was always work, work, work."

"We can't possibly run a rooming house from five miles
away," she told Dad.

"Well, we'll see," he said, unwilling to make a decision.

Mom wasn't religious and seldom went to church, but
the Peale epiphany would inspire her invocations of the
Almighty in the years ahead.

The following March, Mom was moving boxes to our
new home, when she found a contractor's soggy brochure
on the front porch. "Divine intervention," she declared, and

called the man and hired him to remodel our rooming house. Within ten days, his crew tore down the sleeping-room walls and restored the second floor to a single-family, eight-room flat with two bathrooms. They turned the three basement studios into one multiroom flat, all completed as our family packed its possessions. Now she would have to cope with only three tenants in our two-flat, instead of twelve.

A month later, the moving van pulled up in front of the only home I'd ever known, loaded up our furnishings, and headed out of West Garfield Park, where Dad had lived his entire life—more than half a century. But Dad wasn't *really* letting go of his old neighborhood. He remained tethered to the past by three buildings.

CHAPTER 31: A New Life

Dietmar, Peggy, Bill, and Linda: dressed for
Luther North Homecoming Dance, 1966.

I was fine leaving the West Side. All my grade-school pals were long gone, and my high-school friends lived on the North Side. I loved our new single-family house and was proud that I had found and helped to beautify it. On moving day, we trailed the huge truck carrying all our furniture until we arrived at our North Keeler house in Chicago's Old Irving Park neighborhood. The community comprised apartment buildings, modest bungalows, and grand fin de siècle Victorian homes, fronting streets shaded by old-growth trees.

Peggy, now my new neighbor, dashed out of her doorway when we pulled up. I jumped out of the car, and we grasped hands, leaping up and down in teenage glee.

"Can you believe it?" I said.

"This is so cool!" grinned Peggy. "Let's talk to each other through our windows."

I raced around the movers scrunched over my parents' oak dresser, dashed upstairs to my bedroom, now wallpapered in glowing yellow-and-orange daisies, and threw open the window facing Peggy's. Across the divide, Peggy lifted her sash, and we both stuck out our heads, waving to each other in mock greeting.

"Hi, Peggy!"

"Hi, Gartz!" We laughed at the unlikelihood of our proximity. After almost four years as best friends, with five miles dividing us, we now lived next door to each other! We could ride the bus together to Luther North in fifteen minutes—but not for long. Graduation was a few weeks away.

I'd been dating Bill for almost a year by this time. He'd asked me out for every Saturday night since we'd met at the Memorial Day party in 1965. Before meeting Bill, I'd gone out with only a couple of boys, but they didn't interest me. With Bill, every weekend was a blast; we never ran out of things to talk or laugh about. His self-deprecating humor and witty retorts were funny not only to me, but also to my parents, who found Bill engaging and down-to-earth. Except for the fiasco at the hamburger joint, I always arrived home happy, most dates ending with a few kisses on the front porch.

I just liked being with him, and it didn't matter what we did. On our second date, we went to Kiddieland, a small-scale amusement park, where (he later told me) the roller coasters gave him an excuse to hug me tight. But he could also afford to take me on all sorts of cool dates because he had worked since the age of thirteen at a local real-estate office. By the time I met him, he was the owner's man Friday. Bill did bookkeeping (he was a whiz at math), addressed hundreds of postcards for direct marketing campaigns, washed the office windows, made repairs—whatever the boss needed, Bill did. With his earnings, he took me to the movies, local teen dance clubs, and out for a nice dinner or a simple pizza.

But I was really thrilled when he scored tickets for a Beatles concert that summer of 1965 at Comiskey Park, which was home to the Chicago White Sox. Like most teens at the time, I was enamored with these long-haired, "wild-looking" guys with their new musical sound and memorable lyrics— truly "the soundtrack of our lives."

Once the concert started, no one could hear the music or the Beatles' voices. Thousands of young girls screeched, screamed, and pulled their hair as if possessed; they jumped in place like frenetic windup toys or bent over in paroxysms of sobs, tears streaming, hugging each other in the prepubescent sexual thrall of their idols. I gazed around in astonishment, mesmerized as much by the performance of the crazed girls as of the Beatles. I had just turned sixteen a few months earlier, but I couldn't imagine putting on such a display. Bill and I nudged each other, discreetly gesturing to one wacky teen after another.

Another time, he rented a Cessna 150 and we flew over all of Chicagoland, giving me my first aerial view of our sprawling city and its glittering lakefront. A private pilot since he was sixteen (he'd paid for lessons with his own money), Bill dove the Cessna into spiraling, downward turns so he could practice pulling out of a spin, and pointed the plane's nose straight up into the air until it stalled, motionless for a few seconds until we plunged toward earth, regained lift, and straightened out. Both maneuvers are critical pilot skills, but they made me so dizzy, I thought I'd vomit. He stopped. But I wasn't worried: I trusted his skill and judgment completely and always felt safe.

Later that summer, and for the next several years, we wrote letters and sent cards to each other, even though we only lived a few miles apart. We've saved them all. Just as my mother's diary introduced me to her young heart as she fell for Dad, Bill's and my letters whisk me back to our youthful love. I wrote how much I missed him, asked him about his studies, made goofy jokes, or griped about the chore of reading *Moby Dick* for Honors English.

I bought a coloring book of French words and phrases, designed for about a six-year-old. Every week, I colored in a picture of a little kid demonstrating a French word, made some silly comment on it relating to Bill and me, and mailed it to him. (It was obviously a procrastination tool as well.) He kept them all. They remind me of how truly naive and childlike I was at sixteen. We had an innocent romance in those early months. We made out, but we mostly just kissed; it was a long time before any petting started. I would have been shocked—and reluctant—had he expected sex.

In the fall of 1965, his junior year at Northwestern, Bill was working with early computers (huge monstrosities that took up entire rooms). He often mailed me IBM punch cards, each printed with a short love note that he'd programmed. I tore open each envelope, warmed by his sweet and clever greetings.

We were necking on my parents' living-room couch on November 11, 1965, when Bill pressed his cheek against mine and whispered, "I love you." A short pang of fear stabbed my chest. My family seldom used those three little words, and I didn't know what to say. I hugged him tightly and continued kissing him, my emotional reserve holding me back. About a month later, I confessed that I loved him, too.

By the fall of 1965, Peggy had captured the heart of a former Luther North basketball star with the German name Dietmar Faust. Graduating a year before Peggy and me, Diet (DETE) was finishing his freshman year at DePaul University, where he played forward under fabled basketball coach Ray Meyer. Bill and Diet had met the previous fall as both waited to pick up their respective best girls when Luther North let out. Pretty soon, we were double-dating every weekend.

For the first time as teens, it was easy, not scary, for our friends to visit us. Both Dietmar and Bill lived just a couple of miles away, and Paul still lived at home, commuting to the Illinois Institute of Technology (IIT), on Chicago's South Side. Our Keeler house became *the* place to hang out. Diet introduced to us his family tradition of card-playing. All the young people, including twelve-year-old Billy, now played rounds of pinochle on weekends. Even Mom or Dad would take a break on a Saturday night and join in. Diet usually brought over a couple of six-packs, sharing a beer with Mom or Dad. Enjoying the youthful camaraderie, neither of my parents gave a thought to his underage status.

In between the good times, I was engaged in the serious business of applying to colleges. To keep costs down, I never even considered a school outside of Illinois. The University of Illinois was the most logical choice, with Northern Illinois at De Kalb as a backup, but one school kept popping up in my imagination. Northwestern University first blipped onto my radar screen in fall of my junior year, when our majorette troupe performed there on High School Band Day.

A school bus drove us north along Sheridan Road under an arch of golden elms, shimmering in the low autumn sun. Spangles of light danced off Lake Michigan's blue waters. Books cradled in their arms, girls in pleated wool skirts and angora sweaters sashayed in groups of three and four along the tree-studded campus. Northwestern's whole atmosphere seemed to me an idyllic representation of what I pictured college should be. I imagined myself carrying those books, learning from those erudite professors—opening up a whole world of ideas. I was smitten, not by just the beautiful campus and the shiny-haired coeds, who seemed, at first glance, no different to me from Luther North girls, but by the complete package of the university. I didn't worry about fitting in. I just went with my gut and persuaded my parents to visit.

A campus guide led us along meandering paths snugged by foliage. Bells pealed from University Hall, a Gothic limestone edifice. A bit farther north, we entered Deering Library, another Gothic structure, where our footsteps echoed on the stone floor. I wasn't hearing much of what our guide said. I was absorbing an emotion, a longing to be part of this beautiful university, to sit among the tight knots of students, discussing history or art or some great book.

But would I be accepted? I was a good student, but not the very top of my class. Financially, it was a huge stretch, but more affordable if I didn't live on campus. Bill commuted from home. Maybe I could, too. I applied.

The following April, I came home from school to find Mom and Dad putting dishes into kitchen cabinets. Mom pointed to an unopened envelope—from Northwestern. I stared at it for a long time, preparing myself for disappointment. "Well?" asked Dad, smiling as he handed me a pair of scissors.

I slit the envelope, pulled out the letter, scanned it, and looked up at them, grinning like a maniac. "I'm in! I can't believe it!"

Mom, then Dad, hugged me. "Oh, congratulations! That's wonderful!" Mom effused. "My little girl!"

"Good for you," said Dad, embracing me. But beyond that, they didn't make a fuss. Now they had to figure out how to pay for it. Tuition alone was a whopping $600 per quarter, $1,800 a year. We agreed I'd live at home.

Most of my friends were going away to college, but Paul and I still lived at home, available and willing, along with Billy, to help ease my parents' enormous workload. Over the years, we kids had also evolved into a buffer between them, softening the blows their marriage had endured from Dad's absence, Grandma K's insanity, and their time-sucking devotion to building maintenance. The newly gifted six-flat from my grandparents, an increasingly dangerous West Side, the Keeler home, and, ironically, Dad's Chicago-based job, further battered their marriage.

CHAPTER 32: Unraveling

A new kind of estrangement between Dad and Mom arose out of Dad's job at Fireman's Fund, where he'd worked since the fall of 1962. During his years at the National Board of Fire Underwriters, he'd seldom enjoyed peace or appreciation. Mom told him he wasn't part of the family; Grandma K erupted in paranoid accusations when he came home; Dad's boss and supervisor at the NBFU had harangued Dad and caviled over petty grievances. At Fireman's Fund, Dad was surrounded by people who adored and admired him.

When he started at FF, he was already forty-eight years old, with neither the temperament nor the desire to climb the corporate ladder. He worked with a pool of guys who were years his junior, many fresh out of college. The younger men were captivated by Dad's out-of-the-box thinking, his ready jokes and cache of off-color limericks, his raconteur nature, and his crazy menagerie of pets. They called him "the Eccentric," a moniker he accepted with prideful pleasure.

The atmosphere and culture of Fireman's Fund Loss Control Department was a perfect fit for Dad. FF gave him a company car and a list of businesses to visit during the week to be certain each had adequate fire and theft prevention to minimize or eliminate losses. He was the department's expert on fire prevention, the nuances of which he'd mastered at the National Board.

No one tracked his comings and goings. As long as Dad finished the assigned inspections each week and wrote up the reports, he was golden. For a guy like Dad, who loved kibitzing with people, it was heaven. Perhaps he chose to spend three hours at a fishing store while the owner regaled him with arcane details about scores of flies. Maybe he'd compare his knowledge of bullet caliber with the proprietor of a gun shop. He could be lost for hours in a used bookstore, poring over volumes of poetry or European history. He made about the same money as at the NBFU, for about a third of the time.

The young men he worked with included him in their after-work barhopping. "He wasn't a father figure," one of the guys told me years later. "He was just one of the boys." For Dad, the camaraderie was heady. Sometimes he'd call Mom to say he wouldn't be home for supper, which she had already made. Angry and hurt, she ate alone. It evolved into a pattern: Mom excoriating Dad for his callous behavior, her anger driving him to stay with "the boys." The barbs of resentment, sharpened by this vicious cycle of accusations, ripped further at the fabric of their marriage.

Dad invited the impressionable young men from his office, many from small towns, on a tour of the West Side. As they drove from downtown Chicago past block after block of abandoned, burned-out buildings, the guys locked the car doors, staring wide-eyed out the windows. In the six-flat basement, Dad showed off his host of ancient collectibles: an old Victrola record player, his collection of vintage stained- and leaded-glass windows, a crossbow he had refurbished, scores of twin photos positioned side by side to create a 3-D image on an early twentieth-century stereoscope. The younger men were enthralled by Dad's stories, but mostly they were astonished that he owned three buildings in this desperate and dangerous community. "No big deal," he always said, shrugging. Deep down, he still believed it was *his* neighborhood.

Mom had a different motivation for her continued work on the West Side. Never a volunteer or missionary type, Mom was driven by a sense of duty and accomplishment. She wanted to prove to herself, and to naysayers, that by providing well-cared-for apartments, their African American tenants wouldn't "destroy everything," as was the prevailing belief among most whites. Mom had faith that both the property and her hard work would be respected and appreciated by the tenants. She was big on gratitude, which she felt was lately in short supply from Dad. During his first years of travel, he had written her heartfelt poems to show his devotion. His early letters, and even his personal diary, had been filled with loving sentiments and admiration for her ability to hold down the home front during his long absences. But by now Dad's expressions of tenderness and praise had been supplanted by avoidance and withdrawal.

During the next several years, they could barely keep up with the criminal assaults on their West Side properties and renters. In February of 1968, Dad repaired and rehung a tenant's door that had been smashed in a burglary attempt. Another tenant was robbed at gunpoint. Thieves regularly yanked the mailboxes out of the wall in the front vestibule to see what was worth stealing, or used the vestibule to shoot up smack, leaving used needles strewn about the tiled floor. Dad replaced the mailboxes nine times before he found the solution. He exchanged the glass door with a sturdy, solid one. At his tenants' requests, he added bars to all first-floor windows. The six-flat was taking on the appearance of a fortress.

The same month the bars went in, Mom hired a plumber to fix a leak and water damage in the bathroom of Lonnie and Annette Branch, who rented one of the six-flat apartments. Mom stayed for several hours to supervise the repair, returning the following week to be sure the pipe was no longer leaking. It was.

"Why isn't this fixed yet? It's been two weeks. I wish the plaster had hit me on the head so I could sue you!" Lonnie shouted, patting his inch-high, neatly trimmed hair for emphasis. "I'm going to call the Board of Health and report you!"

"Be my guest!" Mom retorted, getting hot, glowering at her tenants. "Listen! This isn't an instant job. It took me four days to find a plumber who would even set foot in this neighborhood! Each step takes time." When angry, Mom's mouth turned down and her eyes narrowed, her whole face contorting in fury and hurt.

"You two have stabbed me in the back. We try to provide a good building for our tenants, but no matter what we do, it doesn't work. You've both completely disillusioned me." Her eyes filled with tears.

In turmoil all week over the confrontation, Mom called Mr. Ford, the African American painter who had become her friend, and shared with him her anguish. "Who would have thought Lonnie and Annette would turn on me like this!" she said.

The following week, Mr. Ford arrived at the Branches' apartment to finish up the decorating. "I almost didn't let you in because it took you so long to get here!" Lonnie railed.

"Listen," said Mr. Ford. (I can see him straightening his wide, bulky frame and looking down into Lonnie's eyes.) "I'm only here as a favor to Mrs. Gartz. If it was up to me, I'd just let you sit and look at that hole in your bathroom ceiling. I'm not doin' this for *you*. I'm doin' it for *Mrs. Gartz*. If you don't like it here, you should just move on. This apartment can be rented fifty times over. You won't find another landlady like Mrs. Gartz in the whole city of Chicago."

When Ford later related this conversation to Mom, he added, "You're just too good to those tenants, Mrs. Gartz— offerin' to scrape off all the paint and start over. I don't want to say you're crazy, but you are."

"I just don't like to be aggravated," Mom said. "Besides, I have a strong sense of responsibility."

We had all witnessed Mom's loyal nature over the years, to both family and tenants. When Dad was on the road, she wrote him letters, no matter how tired or overworked she was. When our basement flooded the kitchenettes one summer, she and Dad invited the tenants to sleep in our flat for days until my parents could clean up the water. When an elderly roomer who had no family died, Mom arranged for him to have a "very creditable funeral," as she described it. She had invited her uncle John to live with us when he was too frail to care for himself. And, of course, she had demonstrated unending loyalty toward her mentally ill mother. That last duty had come to an end.

CHAPTER 33: Riots Redux

Aftermath of April 1968 riots on Chicago's West Side.
Photo © Jo Freeman

In September of 1967, a few months before Mom's confrontation with Lonnie and Annette Branch, Grandma Koroschetz died at the age of eighty-one. Mom had made the three-hour round-trip drive to visit her mother at Manteno State Hospital about once a month. Dad and we kids joined her off and on, even when Grandma K no longer recognized any of us. In the last few years of her life, she had developed full-fledged dementia, staring at us with blank, shimmering eyes and speaking only her native Austrian dialect. At the news of Grandma K's death, Mom didn't cry. "I've shed oceans of tears over my mother. I have none left." She said this with a bitterness that kept me at a distance.

I felt little loss at Grandma K's death. She had lived in our home as a troublesome, sometimes violent, enigma for the first nine years of my life and then, for another nine years, was at Manteno, where I saw her only occasionally, as a duty to appease my mother. I was relieved that the battles over visiting Grandma K would now be behind us, but I was sorry for Mom. I had seen how hard she tried to be the good daughter, but in her loyalty to her mother, she'd thrown a net of guilt over the rest of the family for not possessing the same devotion to Grandma K as she did.

We had a wake and a funeral, but Mom never buried her resentment against Dad for failing to join her on every Manteno visit.

Grandma's death occurred just as I was starting my sophomore year at Northwestern, where virtually every girl lived on campus. Living at home, I had made almost no friends, a foreign experience for me. I decided my only option for connecting with other coeds was to join a sorority, so I subjected myself to the painful ritual of Greek rush.

Rushees walked from one sorority house to the next, where beaming members greeted the visiting group of would-be pledges with wide smiles and rehearsed songs. Once inside, we had fifteen minutes to "get to know" the women. Some of my conversations were so superficial and strained, my stomach flipped in an agony of stalled chitchat and painful seconds-long silences. At other houses, the girls and I warmed to one another. That's what happened at Delta Delta Delta, where I was offered a bid to join. But with limited space, new pledges weren't allowed to live in the sorority house, and I still longed to feel as if I were truly a part of Northwestern.

Walking out of my French lit class late in the fall quarter, I chatted with Marge, a girl who knew I wanted to live on campus. When one of her four roommates transferred out of NU, Marge arranged for me to meet the remaining two on a gray November day. Seated in an oak high-backed booth in the gloom of the university's antiquated cafeteria, we exchanged backstories and fell into comfortable conversation. Rikki, Joannie, and Marge invited me to be their fourth roommate.

"Mom! Dad! Guess what?" I shouted, dashing through the house and dropping my books on the kitchen table. Mom was ripping apart iceberg lettuce and dropping it into a bowl. She looked up. "You certainly seem excited. What is it?"

"That girl I told you about—Marge? Well, I met her other roommates today, and they want me to be the fourth girl in their dorm! Oh, I really want to do this. Can we swing it?" I'd spoken with Mom before about the isolation I felt living off campus.

Mom picked up a tomato and sliced it into wedges. "Well, that's great news," she said, and cut up two more chunks before catching my eye. "But we'd have to figure out how to pay for it."

I was prepared. "I stopped by NU's finance office. I can take out some low-cost student loans, as long as you cosign them."

"Hmmm . . . it'll be a stretch. Let's talk it over with Dad." She handed me a couple of carrots and the vegetable peeler. "In the meantime, would you please peel and chop these carrots for the salad?"

After dinner, Mom, Dad, and I reviewed the price of room and board for two-thirds of the school year. They agreed that with loans, they could handle the extra cost for the winter and spring quarters. Mom, as the family CFO, would fill out the prodigious loan paperwork.

In January of 1968, I moved into the Northwestern Apartments, where Marge and I shared one of two bedrooms; Joanie and Rikki the other. We all used the common bathroom. I kept quiet when I learned the generous allowances each had. They often skipped breakfast or chose to order pizza for dinner instead of eating the dorm food. With my meals already paid for, I never missed a single one.

Marge—zaftig, smooth-skinned, smart, and focused— had beautiful clothes, lovely lingerie, and an open smile. She had brought her record player, which she invited me to use anytime, the first gesture of many that made me feel welcome in the group. And what wonderful albums she had! Joni Mitchell, Judy Collins, Bob Dylan, the Beatles—all the sixties greats, none of which I owned. I played them all, over and over.

Rikki, a high achiever, had been president of her high school's senior class and had scored the prestigious role as director of NU's Freshman Carnival. A drama major, she won leading roles in university productions, where her powerful intensity spread goose bumps across my skin. Her thick, black hair fell to her waist, swaying with the vigor of her brisk, purposeful walk, on to the next endeavor.

Our fourth roommate, Joanie, was often away for a long weekend with her boyfriend. I heard her sobs from down the hallway when she returned on Sunday nights, and ran out to greet her. Tears streamed in black rivulets from her mascara-drenched lashes surrounding large blue eyes, the heavy suitcase she carried listing her to one side. I gave her a long hug, took her suitcase, and, with an arm around her shoulder, listened to her heartsick laments.

Girls from other rooms came to ours to chat, gossip, and share their traumas. One hated the food (I thought it was fine); another despised Northwestern and planned to quit. Thrilled to be able to attend NU, I was perplexed by her petty grievances. Some girls were just psychological messes, anxious and sobbing over a project due the next day, about other girls stealing their boyfriends, about fights over money with their "horrible" parents. Some talked openly about their sexual escapades with this guy or that, sometimes boys in the same fraternity house. With my anti-premarital-sex upbringing, I was flummoxed. They all seemed like perfectly nice girls, not "whores," as my mother referred to women who slept around.

As January came to a close, I was getting comfortable with dorm life and the widely disparate characters I'd met. I had no way of imagining the upheavals that lay ahead.

Nightly news programs beamed the Vietnam War right into America's homes and college dorms across the nation. War was a vague concept I had studied in history class. I knew Ebner's death after World War II had permanently scarred Dad and my grandparents, but I had experienced none of it. Now TV gave all Americans an eyewitness view. I saw scared, mud-splattered boys about my own age hunkered down in swamps. Many of these soldiers confessed to interviewers they didn't know why they were in Southeast Asia.

I watched CBS news reporter Morley Safer broadcasting from a small Vietnamese hamlet that had been burned to the ground by American troops. Children and elderly women, stunned and blank-eyed, wandered like ghosts among the charred ruins. I felt sick at the images—at the thought of my brothers, friends, or Bill moldering in those swamps; killed, blown apart, or tortured in a POW camp.

Day after day, television showed us body bags being unloaded at airports; I tried to comprehend the young men dead and rotting in gray zippered plastic. We saw footage of helicopters—the "whop-whop-whop," a soundtrack to countless scenes—spraying Agent Orange, defoliating thousands of acres of farmland. We learned only later it had poisoned our own troops.

Meanwhile, our nation's generals and President Johnson assured us that all was well—we had the enemy on the run and were winning this war. But after the Tet Offensive, well-coordinated North Vietnamese attacks against more than a hundred towns and cities in January of 1968, Americans realized the Communist Viet Cong were far from defeated. We'd been lied to, and a longer war was inevitable.

The specter of being drafted and sent to Vietnam hung heavy over every young man, including Paul, Bill, and Dietmar. As college students, they all had deferments—for the time being.

I watched tens of thousands of young Americans march and demonstrate in antiwar protests across the nation, denouncing the war as immoral. I was not politically astute, and read the conflicting opinions of the "Hawks" and the "Doves," unsure of what to believe. But the lies and dissembling, the scenes of innocent children and farmers killed, their livelihoods destroyed, drove me into the antiwar camp.

The mood of NU's campus had flipped since I'd enrolled. When I was a freshman, in the fall of 1966, Greek life was all-powerful. The mostly wealthy population of coeds had dressed for class in expensive skirts and sweaters, even tying color-coordinated bows into their hair. By 1968, dressing up was becoming passé, replaced by a uniform of jeans and T-shirts, better suited to the spreading mood of defiance. Students focused on the war and the civil rights movement instead of sororities and fraternities, a transition still in flux when I pledged.

We questioned everything. In the spring of 1968, women protested the paternalistic curfews governing female students. Northwestern men could come and go from student housing as they pleased, but women had to be in their rooms by eleven o'clock on weekdays and midnight on weekends. Just a couple months after I moved onto campus, NU introduced more gender-equal hours, but only with parental approval for the females. Mom felt the more lenient dorm rules were an "invitation to temptation."

Since my childhood, Mom had lectured me against premarital sex, adding admonitions like, "Why buy the cow when the milk is free?" I know her intention was good—to protect me from an unwanted pregnancy. Abortion was illegal, and use of birth-control pills (FDA-approved in 1961) was severely restricted. As recently as 1972, when the U.S. Supreme Court declared the state's "Crimes against chastity" law unconstitutional, it had been a felony in Massachusetts to provide birth control to unmarried people.

Dad believed in as much freedom as possible for his kids,

so I had to persuade only my mother to sign off on the unrestricted hours, which she finally did. But dorm rules turned out to be the least of my parents' problems that spring.

On April 4, an assassin gunned down Dr. Martin Luther King as he stood on the balcony of his hotel room in Memphis, Tennessee. Riots exploded in cities across the country. West Garfield Park again went up in flames, but with far more destruction than in the 1965 riot. Looting and arson engulfed the community where I had walked and played. One of the six-flat tenants called my mother as the mayhem unfolded that first night. She told Mom she had just returned from taking her husband to Garfield Park Hospital. On his way home from work, he had been ensnared in the rioting and shot in both hands.

"Don't come down here to collect the rent," she told Mom, her voice rushed and staccato. "They're turnin' over white people's cars, throwin' rocks at any cars. Mobs of folks are just lootin' the stores on Madison. They're comin' out with armloads of clothes, TVs, dressers, furniture. The police are just ignorin' them. It's like they're directing looter traffic!"

On TV, I saw rioters smashing windows and smiling looters hugging TV sets with both arms. Some pushed shopping carts loaded with goods down the sidewalks, fire and smoke rising behind them.

Years later, I talked to Barbara Lilly, an African American woman and member of my former church, Bethel. She had moved into West Garfield Park about the same time we'd moved north. After more than forty years, the 1968 riots were still seared in her memory. Here's what she recalled:

People were burning up houses. They were just rollin' clothes out of Robert Hall [a Madison Street clothing store]. . . . The National Guard was right there. . . . They had tanks in front of my house and down the

*streets on West End. I had to get my kids out of
school. My kids saw all those tanks going down West
End and said, "Look, Mommy! Look! What's that?"
Then at night, when we looked out the window, you
would have thought it was Vietnam!*

Neighbors climbed up to their rooftops for a better view
of the eastern sky, where flames stabbed through swells of
rolling black smoke. Barbara Lilly also recalled that mayor
Richard J. Daley commanded his police, "Shoot to maim
looters and shoot to kill any arsonists." The order outraged
many in Chicago, but it especially incensed African Americans like Lilly.[45]

"It was terrible," said Barbara Lilly, as she recalled the
riots. "We were already devastated by the whole thing. He'd
a never given that order if they'd been white."[46]

While the riots and flames engulfed the West Side,
Mom and Dad drove to the six-flat to fix a furnace problem.
Annette Branch greeted my parents with more bad news, her
voice frayed with fear. "Someone got shot just north of the
six-flat—right here on Keeler Avenue," she said.

Dad patted the gun in his waistband. "We're being extra
cautious," he assured her.

The King riots had reduced our once-vibrant commercial district to ashes. After more than forty-eight hours of looting,
arson, and attacks on firemen and police, eleven Chicago citizens were dead, forty-eight people had been wounded by
police gunfire, ninety police officers were injured, and 2,150
people had been arrested. Thousands were left homeless,
and a two-mile stretch on West Madison Street was reduced
to rubble.[47] Two weeks later, my parents' last white tenant,
elderly Mrs. Dilzer, moved out.

CHAPTER 34: Convulsions

Bursar's office takeover by NU black
students, May 3, 1968; white sympathizers
outside. Photo © James Sweet

Racial tensions had been simmering at Northwestern University for several years by the time King's murder heated them to the boiling point. NU had admitted only five blacks to its 1965 freshman class. When I started at NU a year later, fifty-four African Americans entered. At the time of King's murder, Northwestern's total student population comprised approximately 8,000 students; about 160 were black—now restive and angry. They felt isolated, that prejudice permeated NU's education and representation on campus. King's assassination galvanized them. On May 3, about 100 to 120 of

Northwestern's black students took over the bursar's office, refusing to leave until a list of demands was met.[48]

At the time, I didn't know what the demands were, but rumors claimed that serving soul food in the cafeterias was at the top of the list. Raised to respect property, I was furious at the audacity of *any* group occupying a private building, and viewed the takeover as blatantly illegal.

Adding to my consternation, my studious, far-from-radical roommates joined scores of other white students to sit outside the occupied building in solidarity with the black kids inside. At the end of the day, back at the NU apartments, my roommates, their friends, and I stood or lounged on the beds in my dorm room and debated for hours. For the first time, I heard a point of view different from the conservative philosophy espoused by my parents. Many of the girls articulated persuasive arguments about the rationale behind the takeover. One, a chain-smoking, fur coat–wearing, seldom-smiling, cynical girl from New York, spoke most forcefully. "Those same people who claim 'soul food' is the main issue completely miss the point. If they were to sum up Christ's message, they'd boil it down to 'Eat fish and bread.'"

I learned later what some of the actual demands were: set up a home base for black students to congregate and pursue their own social, cultural, and political agendas; increase the number of blacks accepted into the university to be more in line with the percentage of African Americans in the country's population; offer courses in black history; increase financial aid; create dedicated student housing for black students; and desegregate NU's real-estate holdings in Evanston—among other demands.[49]

After the passionate debates in my dorm room, I saw beyond what at first struck me as criminal behavior. I came to view the occupation as a "civil disobedience" model of dissent, like Rosa Parks breaking the Jim Crow law requiring blacks to sit at the back of the bus.

The next day, I brought snacks to my roommates as

they sat outside the continuing occupation. They greeted me with smiling enthusiasm, thinking I would be joining them, but I said, "I disagree with this takeover, but I admire your conviction." Thirty-eight hours after the standoff began, the black students left the building. The university had agreed to virtually all of their demands. Some alumni were furious, but I learned later that the administration felt the demands made sense and were easy to accommodate. NU's president had seen the outcome of confrontations on other campuses—it had gone badly for all.[50]

King's murder won changes for black students at NU and raised my and many other white students' consciousness, but his assassination had also rung the death knell for changing neighborhoods in large urban centers across the country.

Barbara Lilly, the woman who lived in West Garfield Park at the time, said of the rioters after King's death, "They were just destroying their own. I guess they felt they didn't have anything else when Martin Luther King was murdered—like he was their savior. . . . [After the riots], A&P and Madigan's . . . a Jewel . . . all prominent stores—Robert Hall, Fish Furniture—all those stores left. We had to go out of our community to shop."[51]

Seeing the images of Madison Street and the stores I knew so well, most now lying in smoldering ash, desiccated my heart. I had warm memories of those places, walking or riding my bike with Barbara, buying my first bra at Madigan's Department Store, hauling a wagonload of groceries every Saturday from the A&P, shopping for school clothes with Barbara and her mom at Robert Hall. My former neighborhood was now a wasteland, a place where I could never again see the touchstones of my childhood.

The entire nation was still reeling from the riots and horrors in the aftermath of King's death, when another assassination rocked the country—and my world. Just after midnight on June 5, Bobby Kennedy was shot three times at close range, just after finishing a presidential campaign speech at the Ambassador Hotel in Los Angeles. I stared at the newspaper photo of Bobby, taken right after the shooting. He lay on the floor, a bright light casting harsh shadows over his face, his arms outspread, as if he were surrendering, his eyes open. A young man cradled Bobby's head. My gut twisted. He died twenty-six hours later.

Alone in my dorm, in between final exams, I slid down the wall of my room onto the floor, pressed my head against my scrunched-up knees, and sobbed for a fraying, incomprehensible world of brutality and murder. King's death, riots, takeovers, protests, bombings, war, and now this. Life was the opposite of all my brothers and I had been taught to believe: that we—and all people—were in charge of our lives, our fate. That outlook now seemed like a fantasy.

More violence was just two months away. The 1968 Democratic National Convention was scheduled to be held in downtown Chicago. Hippies, Yippies, and protestors were planning huge antiwar demonstrations to disrupt the convention and take advantage of the media spotlight. I was back at home for summer break, working downtown at First Federal Savings & Loan. When the news hit that Yippie leader Abbie Hoffman threatened to spike Chicago's water supply with LSD, panic flamed through the city. It sounded wacky to me, but nothing seemed too far-fetched that year. Why would anyone consider poisoning an entire city? Dad said, "They're anarchists. They want to destroy everything. They're just sick people and should be put away." I had to agree.

Mayor Daley was leaving nothing to chance. I later learned that he had dispatched nearly 12,000 police officers on twelve-hour shifts, ordered 5,649 Illinois National Guardsmen with 5,000 more on alert, and up to 1,000 FBI and military intelligence officers at the ready. The 101st Airborne Division and 6,000 army troops, equipped with bazookas and flamethrowers, were waiting as backup in the suburbs.[52]

By August 23, thousands of young people settled into Lincoln Park, a few miles north of the convention site on Michigan Avenue. I had zero interest in taking part. The nightly news turned into a kind of bizarre theatre. Mayor Daley was determined to clear out all protestors by eleven o'clock, the park's official closing time. Ordered to disperse, the crowd defied baton-wielding police officers, who shot tear gas into the throngs. The protestors took to the streets, chanting anti-war slogans and marching south toward the convention center.

With this backdrop, Grandma Gartz called Mom to chide her and Dad for not keeping the fence at the six-flat properly painted. Grandpa had driven by his former building and said if we didn't paint it, he'd go there himself to do it.

In her lifelong attempt to mollify her impossible mother-in-law, Mom said to Dad and Billy, "Well, if it will make her happy, why don't we go and paint the fence?" Dad refused, but Mom found a willing accomplice in Billy. They spent three days painting that fence while mayhem unfolded five miles to the east.

Between August 23 and 28, confrontations escalated between twenty thousand Chicago police officers and as many as ten thousand protestors—and television again brought it all home. Police roughed up reporters, innocent bicyclists, residents in their doorways, and a young man who stripped a flag from its pole. Demonstrators responded by throwing food, rocks, and concrete at the officers, as crowds of young people shouted to the cameras: "The whole world is watching! The whole world is watching!"

In the fall of 1968, there were no open slots in campus housing, so I was living at home again. But I did have the sorority. I met Katy from North Carolina during fall rush. At her first visit to our Tri Delta open house, Katy's huge blue eyes fixed on mine, her lilting North Carolinian accent sweetly unique among the throngs of girls coming through. We hit it off immediately, discovering we were both German majors. She was voted in and became my pledge daughter. With her advanced-placement credits and an extra load of courses, Katy's plan was to achieve junior status in one year—and join the Junior Year in Munich program. My commuter status had again left me uninformed. I had never heard of *any* year abroad program. After making some inquiries, I discovered that I could still participate in the program the following school year as a senior.

To live in Europe someday had been only an inchoate dream, one I couldn't name or grasp. Perhaps it was the pride with which Dad always spoke of his German heritage, which had influenced me in choosing my major. Now the dream turned real, from a misty thought to a tangible brochure and application—a goal I could actually pursue.

Persuading my parents was the next step. The sponsoring university, Michigan's Wayne State, had cheaper tuition than Northwestern, and the German government subsidized University of Munich dorm rooms, which cost students only twenty dollars a month. All my credits would transfer to NU, but because the Munich semester ended in July, after NU's graduation ceremonies, my diploma would be mailed to me. A year studying in Europe or dressing up in a cap and gown? No contest. My mother's biggest concern was that her daughter would live away from home without a chaperone. Dad, of course, was all for it.

I had lived amicably with my roommates in the Northwestern Apartments, but we hadn't become close friends. We parted ways after the quarter ended. In Katy, I had a real pal on campus. We hung out in her freshman dorm, drinking

Constant Comment tea and smoking Marlboro Lights. Bill often rode up to Evanston on his newly purchased cherry-apple-red-and-white Honda 350, which Katy thought was the ultimate in cool. She'd hop on the back for a fast ride up Sheridan Road and back to the NU campus, her red hair flying behind her. Sometimes I'd ride back home with him from Katy's dorm, roaring up to my parents' house.

Even Dad showed his displeasure. "It doesn't look right for a young lady to be on the back of a motorcycle," he said.

Mom was more direct. "You're embarrassing us! You look like hoodlums on that motorcycle."

As finals week approached at the end of the fall quarter, my despair over the traumatic events of the previous year was fading, but an ongoing war was still being waged on the West Side. Victims were residents like my parents' tenants. When burned-out businesses left, the West Side's economic base was destroyed. Anyone who could afford it moved to safer areas; they were replaced by an increasingly impoverished population, followed by escalating crime. Mom and Dad were on the front lines of coping with the results. In Mom's diaries, I discovered details neither Mom nor Dad had shared with me. Reading those entries decades later induces admiration for their fearless devotion, but raises questions about their choices.

In early December, a crook jimmied open the six-flat outer-door lock. He unscrewed the light bulb in the vestibule—and waited. When a tenant, Mr. Murry, entered the darkened foyer, the assailant beat him to the ground and stole his wallet. In the one day it took for my parents to get the lock repaired, a thief walked into the building, broke into the Murrys' apartment, and stole their television.

Mom recorded that event and more in her diary:

*Our tenants all have the jitters with these robberies
and purse snatchings going on. Headd has had the
tires stolen off his car, which was in a garage down
the alley before he moved into ours. Then his car was
stolen out of a repair shop recently. Darden had been
robbed in the alley right by his garage about a year
ago, and he just begged Fred to install a lock on the
front outer door because he said teenage gangs are
roving the streets and stealing light bulbs out of front
halls and then later breaking in.*

*I find that the situation has become much,
much worse since the April riots after Martin Luther
King's assassination. Mrs. McKinney said she's so
tired of hearing women scream when their purses are
stolen. Darden said "I'd rather die than be fenced
in," meaning fear is forcing everyone to stay in the
house. The neighborhood is starting to go.*

I'll say we're awfully patient.

Starting to go? Mom had been noting problems in the
neighborhood that could affect their property values since
1953, when she had written about the "trashy" appearance
of a nearby building and the racial change in a border community, North Lawndale. Now after two riots, its infrastructure destroyed, and the middle class in frenzied flight,
West Garfield Park's slide had accelerated into a plunge. The
nation as a whole had been traumatized by assassinations
and riots throughout the year. We all said a grateful farewell
to 1968 and hoped for a better 1969.

But for the tenants in West Garfield Park, 1969 held the
same horrors as the previous year. In May, thieves broke into
Lonnie and Annette Branch's apartment at the six-flat. "Annette's
a nervous wreck," Lonnie told my mother. "She's worried those
crooks will come back here, and she's too scared to even take the
bus from work anymore. I have to pick her up at her job."

1969 was a turning point for Mom. Incessant West Side

lawlessness and the added work of maintaining our North Keeler home accelerated her stress. Dad seemed to take the crime and craziness in stride, even though he labored for hours after work and weekends to repair the damages. Dad's work was tangible. He did extensive on-site physical work, but Mom bore the brunt of coordinating repairs and tenant communication.

And another major change in her life was imminent. The gaggle of young people who'd filled the North Keeler house and pitched in with major projects during the past three years would soon be moving on. The previous year, Paul had earned a full scholarship from Bell Laboratories to pursue a master's degree at Stanford University in electrical engineering. The research and development subsidiary of AT&T at the time, Bell Labs was considered the most innovative scientific organization in the world. After his first year at Stanford, Paul headed east to New Jersey for his summer job at Bell Labs before returning to the university in the fall.

His work on military contracts shielded him from induction, but the Vietnam War still hung like the sword of Damocles over Bill's head, more menacing than ever. In 1968, at least sixteen thousand American troops had been killed in action—more than in any previous year of the war. All young men, and the people who loved them, were scared.

In the summer of 1969, Bill had two years of law school behind him, but pursuing a degree no longer guaranteed a deferment. Talk of a lottery to choose draftees was gaining traction, and no draft-age men would be exempt—unless they were in another branch of the armed forces.

Bill applied to the Army Reserves. His application included his recently earned commercial pilot's license (the lessons were a college-graduation gift), which impressed the Reserves' aviation unit. He was invited to join. At the end of July, he boarded a plane bound for Fort Benning, Georgia, to complete basic training for the next five months. A month later, I would leave to study in Munich for a year.

Mom threw a farewell party for me, replete with a bon voyage cake, decorated with a confectionary ship. But Grandma Gartz didn't come. "She hasn't earned the right to go to Europe!" she told Mom and Dad. "She should stay home and help her mother!"

Linda with Bon Voyage cake at farewell party, August 1969.

Shortly after my farewell party, Peggy and I flew to visit New York for a week before my ship departed. We stayed with Paul in Newark, New Jersey, near his Bell Labs' offices. Seven days later, Katy and I boarded the ocean liner SS *Rotterdam* for the nine-day overseas voyage to the ship's eponymous city.

I was the last to leave of the older kids who had brought so much verve and fun into my parents' home, and to Mom's life in particular. Only Billy, sixteen, remained behind. For Mom, the trauma of being overworked was soon augmented by the desolate emotions of a woman whose home, once vibrant with youth and laughter, had become quiet and nearly empty.

CHAPTER 35: **News from the Front**

Katy and Linda prepare to cross the Atlantic, August 1969.

While I was in New York, I was unaware that flames had ravaged an apartment in the six-flat. A swift fire-department response contained the blaze to the one unit, but for my parents, the night dragged on. After rushing to the scene, comforting their tenants, filing police reports, and calling a board-up service, it was after three in the morning when they wearily tramped up the steps to their North Side home.

Instead of reaching a peaceful haven, they were greeted by angry phone calls from neighbors. Our dog, Buttons, had run away again and was shrieking at the back door. The confluence of aggravations triggered Mom's fury toward Dad and our hapless pet. "If you can't contain that dog, then put him to sleep!" Buttons had been the family's faithful companion for thirteen years, but now Dad was acquiring animals at an astounding rate.

Dad had always brought a steady stream of animals into our lives, from orphaned ducklings and baby hawks to a raccoon he'd rescued from an illegal steel-jaw trap. Now he had Hermann, the flying squirrel; two ferrets; three adult rabbits; five baby rabbits; an orange cat, Marmalade; and the four kittens she had birthed in the summer of 1969. Dad considered neutering animals to be "cruel."

In one of his "I'm just looking" forays into a pet store, my father bought a baby boa constrictor, the size of a common garter snake, but it would eventually grow to more than six feet in length and eleven inches in circumference. To provide a steady food supply for the snake, which he named Lucifer, Dad began raising rats in the basement. "The snake has to eat," he insisted when Mom complained.

The animals were amusing for us kids and Dad's friends ("That Fred! What an eccentric!"), but they wore on Mom, especially after huge water beetles joined the pet party in the basement, undoubtedly drawn by the odiferous rat cages. Whenever we flipped on the basement lights, scores of shiny black bugs scurried for corners and crevices, their little legs tap-tap-tapping along the concrete floor. "I've had it with all these animals!" Mom shouted. Dad shrugged his shoulders, and his face lit up with a scampish grin.

Mom's letters to me in Munich were mostly cheerful, newsy pieces about—what else? Work on the West Side. "I have a new title now," she wrote in the fall. "I'm the contractor for the burned-out apartment remodel. I have to say, I'm pretty good at it."

When her October 29 letter arrived, it brought a more somber tone and disturbing news. Mom started with the backstory. Her tenant, Mrs. McKinney, told Mom her phone and electricity had been cut off for lack of payment. Mrs. McKinney had "hit rock bottom" and had to give up the apartment. When she broke down in sobs over her predicament, Mom cried with her.

The following Tuesday morning, Mom drove to the West Side to oversee Mrs. McKinney's move. After parking on Keeler, just north of the six-flat's alley, she walked south toward Washington. She saw two men eyeing her on the west side of Keeler. Her heart jumped when they crossed toward her, but before she could react, one yanked at the strap of her purse. "Help! Help!" she cried out. She struggled to hold on. "Please don't take my purse! Please don't take my purse!" It held the huge sum of fifty dollars in cash (about $325 today), all her credit cards, the new keys to the McKinneys' apartment, as well as keys to another apartment. When one thug drew back his fist to punch her in the face, Mom ducked and let go. The men dashed off down the alley.

Panting in fear and exhaustion, she ran toward Washington Boulevard and hailed a passing cop car. They cruised around for several blocks, looking for the thieves, but had no luck. "My tenants had warned me," she wrote. "Somehow I wasn't prepared for a purse-snatcher at 11:00 a.m., but what do I expect? Special hours?"

Her next letter, dated December 9, had a more frightening story. David Nelson, the pastor of our former church, told Mom and Dad about an attack on his sister, Mary. Pastor Nelson and Mary had been working side by side to bring relief and hope to the increasingly impoverished West Side community ever since their arrival during the August 1965 riots.

Mary was working late in her office at the Christian Action Ministry, CAM, founded after those riots. At ten thirty, she finally left to drive home, but her car wouldn't start. She returned to the office, unaware of the man skulking behind her. She dialed her roommate for a ride, but before she connected, the man leaped from the shadows and brutally assaulted her, kicking her repeatedly in the head and damaging her eye.

Frightened by the abrupt end to the phone call, Mary's roommate drove to the office, burst in, and scared off the attacker. She called for an ambulance and the police. For twenty-four hours, Mary lay unconscious in the hospital, and several more days passed before she recuperated enough to return home. After her recovery, she went right back to work at CAM. "I'd have to live in terror if I didn't get back to my mission," she later told my mother.

The dangers were real, yet Mom's letter contained no sense of fear—just the quip after the purse-snatching anecdote, "What do I expect? Special hours?" My entire life, Mom and Dad's West Side work had always been integrated into our lives, and I accepted it, even after the neighborhood changed. Now I was 4,500 miles away from home, and all communication was via letters, which took five to ten business days to reach their destination. To really discuss anything would require a fifty-dollar phone call for a twenty-minute conversation. I was focused on schoolwork and negotiating a foreign country. Besides, Mom was not about to take advice from me.

Their friends implored them to sell, but Dad wouldn't discuss it. Mom had no real say in the matter, even though she managed the whole enterprise. My grandparents had gifted the six-flat in Dad's name only. Despite this blatant slight, Mom exhorted me, in this most recent letter, not to be "vindictive" toward my grandmother. "Grandma really has almost never offended me," she wrote.

It was as if she were on an emotional mother-in-law pendulum, swinging between hate and praise. "Don't forget," she continued, "she's had a very hard life. Who are we to judge?" Mom ended the letter with a sentence that tipped me off to the underlying motivation behind her inexplicable change of heart: "Always be open to criticism and advice. Someone else always knows something you don't know." I got it. She was hoping to soften me up to accept *her* advice and criticism, especially on the subjects of sex and marriage, points of increasing tension between us in the age of the sexual revolution.

CHAPTER 36: Sexual Politics

Linda and Katy join in sing-fest, Austrian Alps, 1969.

Had I become pregnant, I would have been just as fearful of my mother's wrath as I would of my own ruined future. From early childhood on, Mom taught me to preserve my virginity until marriage. However, Mom was no prude about sex *after* marriage. In one diary, she entered a section on sexual positions (written in shorthand); Billy was conceived in a moment of passion in the bathroom. When I was a toddler in the crib, Mom and Dad entertained me with their "bing bong" game, as they sat half-naked on their bed. In 1940s and '50s photos, I've seen the sexy looks they threw each other; their happy smiles, filled with sexual innuendo.

I have every reason to believe that my parents had a robust sex life.

But I'd also seen how Grandma K had demonized women's sexuality in her angry and psychotic rants. When Mom was a teen, her mother had screamed at her, calling her only daughter a streetwalker or a whore, ludicrous accusations. But these slanders against her character must have penetrated deeply into Mom's psyche, creating a rigid sexual morality, where premarital sex was the domain only of prostitutes. I think I could have been convicted of murder, and she would have been less horrified than had I become pregnant without the sanctity of marriage.

And it wasn't just Mom. In the 1950s and '60s, society heaped opprobrium on unwed pregnant girls, who were whisked out of town "to visit an aunt in Kansas," returning months later. Their babies had been placed for adoption, all records sealed.

In my Lutheran high school, as in most 1960s high schools, sex education didn't exist. We girls were taught about our menstrual cycle and the process of pregnancy as part of physical education (girls moaned in embarrassment at even the mention of the word *menstruate*), but that was it. Any discussion of preventing pregnancy was out of the question. Abstinence was expected.

Except for condoms, which I hadn't even heard of, when Bill and I met in 1965, birth control was still denied to unmarried couples in twenty-six states. That same year, the Supreme Court finally overturned a Connecticut law that had made it a felony for married couples to use birth control. Abortion was illegal, but I didn't even know about such a procedure.

Bill, too, had been raised by a mother worried about premarital sex. She had warned him of girls who "trapped men into marriage" by getting pregnant. He and I weren't sophisticated enough to talk on any level with each other about sexuality. On our first date, Bill kissed me goodnight. His lips were full and soft. But would he think I was loose for kissing him back so early in our relationship?

We went on several dates before our kisses turned passionate, deep, and long. We found privacy at drive-in movies, where we kissed, our tongues tangled and insistent. Bill's hands roamed freely over my body and mine over his; a pulsing heat swarmed from my groin to my chest to my arms—until I was enveloped in desire. "I wish we were older," Bill said one night, as we paused, panting from our heavy necking and petting. We were ready to go further, but the fear of pregnancy held us back. We somehow stopped ourselves before going all the way.

As Bill and I approached our fourth year together, we still hadn't "done it." My college friends were baffled, asking, "What's holding you back?" Many of the young women said that their mothers had never even talked to them about sex, so they just followed their hormonal instincts and did whatever felt good. I was stunned. Didn't their mothers want their daughters to be informed? To protect them? Mom had never portrayed sex to me as "evil" or "bad." Just sex before marriage was immoral—and then there was the possible horror of a young girl becoming an unwed mother.

"You can get birth-control pills at the student health center," Katy assured me when I explained our situation. Birth control was so new, only recently available to unmarried women, I hadn't even considered it, but now a switch flipped. I visited a campus gynecologist, wearing a conservative skirt and button-up blouse, my hair tied in pigtails, all contrived so he wouldn't think I was a trollop. I got my prescription for birth-control pills. I had shed my mother's rigid sexual mores and feared only pregnancy.

On the fourth anniversary of the day we met, Bill and I drank champagne in his bedroom long after his mom had gone to sleep in a faraway part of the house. We kissed and petted and shed our clothes in marijuana-infused mellowness while Bob Dylan's languorous, sexy "Lay, Lady, Lay," played on a cassette tape.

"I didn't know it would be like *this*!" I blurted out, returning his thrusts as we found perfect rhythm. Climaxing, we both cried out—grinning like fools, trying hopelessly between giggles to shush one another so as not to wake his mother. Breathless, we spread kisses over each other—face, neck, chest, breast, belly—laughing, crying, and declaring our love for each other, again and again and again.

Two months later, at the end of July, he would head into basic training, just a month before I would leave for Germany. The synchronicity was fortuitous; both of us would be away from Chicago at the same time. I also thought it would be good for us—for me, especially—to be apart for a while. I had transitioned directly from childhood and adolescence into my relationship with Bill. I loved him, but felt I needed to be independent from both my parents and the steady boyfriend I'd met when I was only sixteen. I wasn't looking for a new romance, but a place where only *I* was responsible for my life and I could embrace adventure. I didn't share these thoughts with Bill. For him, our separation held nothing but dread and loneliness. Four weeks after Bill left for Fort Benning, Georgia, I was on a ship to Europe with Katy.

The evening after arriving in Rotterdam, the entire Junior Year in Munich group boarded a train to Munich, jostling and squeezing ourselves in among the crowds. When we arrived in Munich, Katy and I settled into our respective dorms, but we didn't explore the city. Katy had a much more ambitious plan. Within a couple hours, we had packed our bags, taken a bus to the autobahn, and thrust out our thumbs, taking turns holding up our cardboard sign with *GRAZ, AUSTRIA* emblazoned in huge letters.

Katy's father, Duke University's chemistry chair, had included the family on several yearlong sabbaticals, once to France and most recently to Graz, where Katy had attended her senior year of high school. Visiting her former school buddies was her highest priority, so off we went on day one. It was the first of many such forays. Fearless and experienced, Katy led the way on adventures I never would have considered on my own. Her blazing, long red hair, extending halfway down her back, blew wild in the wind as she leaned casually on one leg, stuck out her right thumb, and coolly dragged on the cigarette in her left hand. In Katy's mind, nothing bad could possibly happen, and her confidence rubbed off on me.

With my book-learned German, I jabbered for hours at truck drivers, businessmen, and workers, amazed and thrilled that they understood me, as if I were breaking a code. At day's end, my face muscles ached, sore from contorting my mouth to form a host of new sounds.

At University of Munich lectures, I learned to take notes in German. On the weekends, we explored the Bavarian countryside, riding buses on excursions to iconic castles like Neuschwanstein (the inspiration for Disney's Fantasyland castle) or to small towns with tongue-twisting names like *Garmisch-partenkirchen.*

One weekend, Katy and I hiked in the Austrian Alps with a couple of Bavarian boys amidst clumps of wildflowers under an azure-blue October sky. We ended up at a farm, where the ruddy-faced farmer's wife served us steaming *leberknödel* soup and hearty stew. After dinner, a toothless, sun-scorched farmer plucked a worn guitar, leading us and other hikers in Austrian folk songs around a rough-hewn wooden table. We downed hefty steins of beer, banging them together with ever-increasing gusto as the night went on.

Our bed was the straw-covered barn loft, where the

heavy scent of animal manure and fodder wafted among the rafters. Clanking cowbells and dawn's early rays, slicing through the planked walls, awakened us. I was having the best time of my life. Bill was having the worst.

His letters arrived several times a week, each one filled with loneliness, longing, and love. He hated the army: belly-crawling for hundreds of yards in the red Georgia dirt, nettled by insects probing his sweat-soaked skin in the stifling heat—sweat so profuse that he could drink two gallons of water each day and seldom urinate. The recruits arose at four to run a mile before breakfast, followed by physical training while being harassed by their drill sergeant, who screamed at them: "Maggots, pussies, and ladies!"

"What's the purpose of a bayonet?" The drill sergeant shouted at the young men. In unison, they chanted back, "To kill! To kill! With cold blue steel."

"This is what they're teaching us," Bill wrote to me. We had to keep reminding ourselves how lucky he was not to be slogging through Vietnamese mosquito-infested swamps, shot to pieces, or captured. But that truth didn't keep his heartache at bay. In one letter, he told me, "I want to eat with you, sleep with you, make love to you, and awaken next to you." I was pricked by guilt—that his life was so miserable, he could think only of me, while I enjoyed my adventures. I wrote him at least weekly. I missed his ready laugh, his sweet kisses, and his warm hands across my skin, but I was giddy with my newfound independence.

Bill arrived in Munich on December 27, 1969. He had completed basic training just two days earlier. Waiting outside the jet bridge, I sat twirling my hair, biting at my cuticles, wondering if we'd still get along after five months apart. When I saw him striding through the airport gate in his familiar dark-brown winter coat, I leaped from my seat, ran up to him, and threw my arms around his back, pressing our chests together. I tilted my face up to his, and we gave each other a long kiss. His army-regulation buzz cut was a stun-

Bill arrives in Munich, December 27, 1969.

ning change from the Beatles' hairstyle he'd sported since I'd met him. "I'm so glad to *see* you!" I said, holding his arms and leaning back to get a good look at him.

"Me, too! I got my hair cut for the occasion." A man with a sense of humor! He'd always made me laugh, unlike the men I'd met in Munich, who were obsessed with leftist politics and the upcoming "revolution."

Bill stayed in my dorm room, its bed about three-quarters of a twin size. Of course, I didn't tell my mother. "Now, don't get carried away without a chaperone there," Mom had written to me in all seriousness.

At the end of January, when Bill had to return to Chicago to finish law school, I went with him to the airport. We kissed and held each other until the flight attendant called for final boarding. I cried and waved to him before he disappeared into the walkway. My flight of freedom had paid off. He was the one.

Back in Chicago, Bill often dropped by my parents' house to say hi, as a way of feeling connected to me. On a visit at the end of April, he unwisely told Mom that Katy and I were planning to get an apartment together when I returned in the fall. Then, in my mother's words, he "expounded on the antiquity of the marriage system."

Mom typed a five-page, single-spaced letter to me in response to Bill's comments. "I am completely shook up about the false thinking of the young," she wrote. "It seems that the one of our children who is falling by the wayside and not adhering to moral standards is the one where Dad has had his way in rearing her."

What? Dad had traveled six months of every year, starting shortly after my birth until I was thirteen. In her letter, Mom dragged up (or made up) events from the past of which I had no recollection, as evidence of my spoiled and "immoral" nature.

Distraught by Bill's ill-advised comments, Mom even quoted her much-despised mother-in-law as a paragon of brilliance. "Grandma told me I shouldn't send you to Europe because you hadn't earned it and should be home helping your mother! I realize she was always right and actually my best friend. I just didn't know it." Mom ended her letter with, "I do hope when you return that you plan on living at home, even though there might be a few restrictions, which, in the end, is better for you."

I wrote back saying that I had been studying for a big test when her letter arrived: "I couldn't concentrate or think straight, I was so upset." To her comment that if Bill didn't want to marry me, I should just tell him to go to hell, I said, "That will never happen." In the end, her letter was certainly persuasive—there was no way I'd be living at home.

When the University of Munich let out in mid-July, Katy, her roommate, and I borrowed a friend's eleven-year-old Volkswagen and took to the road for six weeks of travel. We headed to Berlin for a few days, then Denmark, Sweden, Norway, and back south to Cologne, where we sold the car. After hitchhiking to Belgium's coast, we ferried toward the chalky White Cliffs of Dover, and ended up in London for the last ten days of our trip.

In between attending plays with Katy, I picked up a copy of *Time* magazine. I lay on the narrow bed of our pension, reading the cover story about Kate Millett's new book, *Sexual Politics*. Millett argued the radical notion that different rules and expectations controlled men and women in society; that women had been steered into specific roles and discouraged from seeking any meaningful work outside the home or beyond limited "female" career options.

It suddenly all fell into place. I couldn't believe it hadn't occurred to me before! I thought of Mom urging me to take typing and shorthand so I could make a living and "never be solely dependent on a man." But I knew many girls who were told the only reason to attend college was to find a husband. Mom's advice to be prepared to work was forward-thinking for the time, but what path might I have chosen had all been open to me? Secretary, teacher, or nurse—these were the big three career options for women in the 1950s and '60s—all fine, upstanding professions, but basically considered to be the *only* work of which females were considered capable. A few extraordinary women broke free of these models, but they were the exception, not the rule.

My mother was a classic case of the thwarted career woman. "I've always hated repetitive 'women's work,'" Mom often said. She enjoyed the more interesting activities required to run our small business, so she ended up doing "men's work" in addition to women's.

Before we departed from Europe for America, Katy and I solidified our plan to share an apartment. Mom's advice to learn typing and shorthand was serving me well—but not as she had anticipated. When I needed an immediate job to pay the rent for my apartment with Katy, my German degree was useless. It was the secretarial skills I had honed over years of summer employment that bestowed independence—not from a man, but from my mother.

I landed a job as a secretary to five managers at Arthur Andersen, at that time one the world's top eight accounting firms. Only men were accountants. I tested well in the interview, despite my rusty shorthand and speedy but less-than-perfect typing. Mom, however, could pound out letters, leases, and income-tax forms, with multiple carbon copies, virtually error-free.

I now know what I never even thought to ponder at the age of twenty-one. She would have made a far better secretary than I, for more money, pleasure, and pride than she received for her work on their West Side properties. In 1970, I was making $7,800 a year at AA, more than double what my mother's executive skills, combined with her and Dad's hard labor, netted from the West Side buildings.

In January of 1951, when she had argued vehemently in letters to Dad against his insistence on creating basement apartments, she wrote, "Honey, if I have to work for a living, I think secretarial work is much more enjoyable." Despite her cogent arguments against the basement plan, she had acquiesced to please my unrealistic father.

Now, after almost twenty years of managing their properties, she was trapped by their earlier decisions and couldn't see her way clear to get out from under it all. With the kids mostly grown, she could have nabbed a secretarial job like mine and paid for a building manager, since Dad refused to even discuss selling the buildings. Such thinking never occurred to either of them.

How much happier they could have been had they been able to let go of old habits and recognize the toxic influence both their mothers had on their lives: Grandma K made our home unwelcome for my traveling dad; Grandma Gartz's constant and belittling criticism drove Dad, and later, Mom, to relentlessly try to prove their worth through physical labor.

With today's hindsight and understanding, I would have advised Mom to seek counseling for herself, from both a therapist and a lawyer, the latter to understand her options with the six-flat, so as not to let Dad's choices and hang-ups control her.

CHAPTER 37: Moving On

"Oh, by the way, Mom," I said, holding up her new gold drapes as she inserted pins into the pleats before hanging them, "Katy and I think it would be fun to get an apartment together. She's finishing her last year at Northwestern and needs a roommate so she can afford a decent place."

Pinching out the T-shaped pins from between her lips, Mom stepped down from the ladder and faced me, her face a bitter scowl. "You mean to tell me you're not going to live *here* and pay me rent? Don't you think you owe me that after a whole year living in Europe?"

I knew this was coming and tried to sound casual, matter-of-fact. But her guilt-inducing, accusatory tone churned my gut. I took a deep inner sigh and stood my ground. "Mom, I'm twenty-one years old. I spent all year living independently. Besides, Katy needs a roommate to share rent. I'll still be close to home."

"I can't believe you're doing this to me!" She jabbed at me with her index finger. "After all I had to contend with last year—the fire in the six-flat! Running back and forth to the West Side! When I finished high school, I gave my parents seventy-five percent of my salary when I got *my* first job. Aren't you being just a little selfish here?"

"Mom, that was the Depression! Your parents couldn't find work. Besides, it's time I was on my own."

"We're barely squeaking by with those buildings. There's always extra expenses and one headache after another."

I tried to keep my voice calm and even, but a pleading tone had crept in. "Mom, I've promised Katy. I'll be able to help you when you need it."

I didn't mention that I had no intention of tolerating the curfews Mom would surely impose on me, or her furious harangues if I ever stayed overnight at Bill's new apartment. "You young people are all mixed up," Mom ranted. "It's the Communists—I know it! Undermining America by morally corrupting our youth! Khrushchev said he'd bury us—well, this is how he's doing it!"

<hr />

The heady days of buying our "little mansion" (as Mom proudly called the house on North Keeler); the sense of cama- raderie effervescing from our family's teamwork, which had turned the fixer-upper into a beautiful home; the vitality and energy of riotous youth that had infused the house—that era had passed, and along with it, the extra helping hands had disappeared.

Smitten with his office crowd, Dad wanted an escape from Mom's relentless criticism. Gone were the days when he had written her love poems, told her how much he appreci- ated her holding down the fort, and encouraged her "not to do anything unnecessary." He had withdrawn emotionally and now seemed not to understand (or care about) Mom's roles as homemaker and business manager. "What do you do all day?" he queried resentfully when she wanted to purchase a dish- washer ("a three-hundred-dollar storage cabinet," he groused).

Mom was nursing long-held grudges and new realities. She stewed about Dad's lack of appreciation. "He saddled me with that rooming house when he was gone six months of the year," she sputtered in exasperation. She also claimed he'd never been "openly friendly enough" to Grandma K, choosing to ignore Dad's patient tolerance and management of Grandma's psychotic and threatening outbursts in their home for fifteen years.

Now Paul was gone (and the "ingrate" didn't write or call), and I was moving out. She began demanding recognition. "I'm an executive," she shouted at us, "doing dirty work! No one knows what the housewife does. It's all taken for granted." A housewife, okay, but to call herself an "executive?" We all found this statement ridiculous hyperbole. Yet that's exactly what she was—managing the finances and logistics of the three West Side buildings *and* our twelve-room house with a barn, an attic, and a basement, all of which Dad was filling with his junk at an alarming rate.

It's not surprising to me now that Mom began drinking.

Having a couple highballs at the occasional gathering of her friends and at her monthly club meetings—or waking with a hangover on New Year's Day—had been the worst of her indulgences. When ironing, she sipped from a can of Budweiser set on the end of her ironing board as she watched TV. I never saw her drunk.

Now she was downing mixed drinks or sipping Four Roses whiskey for a couple of hours nightly while she sat at the kitchen table, puffing cigarettes, stewing about the injustices that had been foisted upon her. It was bad enough that she had to put up with her manipulative, judgmental mother-in-law and an insensitive husband, who didn't treat her with "kindness and consideration," but now, her lousy, selfish daughter was moving into her own place instead of paying Mom rent!

While still living with my parents, I came home from my weekly Saturday night date with Bill. Walking from the front door through the darkened foyer, I saw a puddle of light leaking into the dining room from the kitchen. My heart pounded. I dreaded seeing Mom inebriated but went into the kitchen anyway to say hello.

She sat at the Formica kitchen table in her usual late-night mode, chair positioned slightly askew so she could extend and cross her legs at the ankles on another chair. In her left hand, she held a tumbler of amber liquid; a filtered menthol Salem, smoke twisting toward the ceiling, drooped between her right middle and index fingers. Next to the half-empty Four Roses whiskey bottle, a butt-brimming ashtray overflowed onto the table. I entered into a miasma of stale smoke. "Hi, Mom," I said, trying to sound pleasant, but inwardly shrinking—as if I made myself small enough, I could disappear.

"Oh, *hello*," she replied in a bitter tone, her eyes droopy and unfocused. Dragging deeply on the Salem, then blowing the smoke over her shoulder, she set her mouth into a grim, tight-lipped, ironic smile. On the floor lay her girdle, removed so she could drink and brood in comfort. Night after night, her thoughts looped, forever circling to the same playlist: how much she'd suffered; how her despicable mother-in-law had duped her with a purported "gift" of a six-flat in a now-riot-riven ghetto; her horrible children, who'd abandoned her.

"Are you okay?" I asked. She waved the cigarette hand as if dismissing me. I knew a conversation was out of the question. "Well, I think I'm going right to sleep," I said. "I'm exhausted."

I turned to go upstairs.

"That's right. Just go to bed. I know you're far too busy and important to talk to me."

"Mom, that's not fair. I'm just tired."

I headed up the back steps to the second floor, washed my face, fell into bed, and pulled the covers up to my chin. As I nodded into a half sleep, I heard Mom's heavy footfalls on the back stairs, her unsteady tread entering my room, where a desk lamp cast a soft, low light. Opening my eyes in tiny slits, I saw her in the shadowy glow, hovering over my bed, swaying a little; her face sagged, her nose crinkled, and her mouth turned down as if she were looking at an object of disgust.

Ptew. Ptew. She'd spit on me!

I lay silent, stunned—more embarrassed for my mother than furious at her vulgarity. One part of me wanted to leap up, grab the front of her blouse in my two fists, shake her, and scream, "How *dare* you!" But another part cringed at the humiliation she'd feel if I confronted her—if she had to face how low she'd sunk in her desperation to blame someone else for the emotional wasteland of her life.

I pretended to sleep. She spit on me again, muttering, "Whore. After all I've sacrificed for you."

Heart thumping in my throat and chest, eyes still shut, my breath came shallow and fast until she wobbled out of the room. Sleep was elusive; anger, sadness, and helplessness all washed over me. *What was wrong with her?*

Perhaps the years of living with Grandma K's madness, her mental illness encased in a chrysalis of silence, had inured me to not thinking of a solution. Avoidance of the subject had left me bereft of an emotional larder from which I could draw nourishing words and empathy to help my mother. The only way I could respond to Mom's emotions was to steer clear of her.

The next day, Mom said nothing about the incident. Had she been too drunk to remember, or was she too embarrassed to own up to her horrid behavior? Whatever the case, I chose not to bring it up. She was already such a mess, so angry with Dad (for exactly what I didn't understand at the time), and now my drive for independence was sending her into even deeper crisis. She repeatedly circled back to her role in supporting *her* parents. It was the creed and faith of her personal religion: you sacrifice your own happiness, and your family's, to do the very best for your parents. I was an apostate.

I recognize now the damage Mom's single-minded devotion to Grandma K had wreaked on her marriage; that Mom had been flailing her whole life in a river of guilt. She was trying to tug me into the same current that engulfed her. I had to resist the pull, or drown. But there was no point in forcing her head deeper into the torrent, so I just let the spitting incident pass—and planned my escape.

CHAPTER 38: Disgraced

Dad easily accepted my apartment decision. Even Mom calmed down a bit after she got used to the idea of my own apartment, especially when she realized the tangible benefit to her: an opportunity to unload scads of Dad's compulsive saving. He felt vindicated that his prediction had come true: "Someday, we'll need this stuff!"

He and I walked down into the basement, where a dim yellowish glow was cast by fluorescent strips Dad had hung from the ceiling with thick chains. Off a tall shelf, he hoisted plastic blue and red milk crates, packed with an assortment of wooden spoons, pots, pans, bowls, dishes, and other tableware. Holding his treasures, he grinned. "Here's all you'll need for your kitchen." It was.

After poking around to find mops, brooms, dustpans, and an upright vacuum cleaner, he drew out one wooden drawer after another from his self-constructed tool bench and found picture-hanging supplies, flashlights, and baby-food jars of screws and nails.

Mom had her own stash of extras. She gathered towels, pillows, and several sets of weary but perfectly usable bed sheets she'd saved from the rented bedrooms of the former second-floor rooming house. In the basement of the six-flat, Dad and I picked up a couple of bedframes and mattresses,

a medley of lamps, chairs, a Formica table for the kitchen—
even pictures for our walls.

After loading up our station wagon with all my apartment goods that could fit, Dad smiled proudly at his hand-
iwork: the legs of a dresser, a floor lamp, and an oak desk
stuck out the rear of the station wagon, with red cloths, for
safety, flying off the ends of each. He closed the rear-hatch
door as far as possible, then secured it with rope tied to the
bumper. Pillows and bedding scrunched into large garbage
bags blocked the side windows. Later, Dad would bring us a
cast-off couch he'd found who knows where.

Katy and I had settled into our apartment on Paulina
Street in a Chicago neighborhood on the border of Evanston,
affectionately known as "The Jungle." Because Evanston was
dry (home of the Woman's Christian Temperance Union),
Paulina was lined with bars and liquor stores. Within two
blocks were ill-kept multistory apartment buildings, Laun-
dromats, and a popular Mexican restaurant, La Choza, that
served delicious and inexpensive food. The Jungle came by
its name because of alcohol-driven visitors, crime, and pros-
titution, but I knew how to watch my back.

The lower-end neighborhood meant Katy and I each paid
only eighty dollars a month for a two-bedroom, third-floor
flat with a kitchen, a dining room, and a living room. Unlike
my parents, who gave tenants one freshly painted room every
year, Heil and Heil Realty said they'd provide paint, but the
labor was up to us. I painted my room Dresden blue.

I started my secretary job seated right behind the secretari-
al-pool supervisor, Libby, a woman of about sixty, who rolled
her chair up to mine, invading my body space. I drew back a
little, trying not to be obvious. Her upper lip twitched, and
she repeatedly touched her graying curls as she talked, her
eyes squinting behind narrow, out-of-date glasses. "Arrive

well before nine o'clock, when the office opens. Never be late. Your duty is to be fresh and ready for work every day. Address all your managers by 'Mr.' and their last names. Every letter that goes out must be error-free. No erasures. Start over, but of course, you'll make few mistakes." *Uh-oh. Trouble.* I always made some error.

"Do you have any questions?" She raised a penciled-in, narrow eyebrow.

"Um, no. I understand."

"Good. Well, welcome to Arthur Andersen!" Visibly pleased, she gave me a tight-lipped smile, and turned to her desk.

That first afternoon on the job, my shorthand five years rusty, one of the five managers I worked for called me on the phone. "This is Mr. Robinson. Is this the new girl?"

"Hi. Yes, my name is Linda."

"Okay. Take a letter." Robinson rattled off sentence after sentence as I scrambled to keep up, panic freezing my brain and fingers. After his curt introduction, I was afraid to ask him to repeat *anything.* The other four managers were pleasant. They at least said "Good morning" after buzzing me into their offices, usually to take dictation or to bring them coffee. Robinson never even looked up when I brought the morning mail to his desk.

By early spring, I was ready for my next move. I'd always loved little kids, so I applied to Northwestern's Master of Arts in Teaching program and was accepted. In May of 1971, I gave Libby notice. Her rheumy blue eyes bored into mine, her red lips twitching as if writhing insects crawled inside them. "Think of what you're giving up! There's a glut of teachers out there. You won't find a job."

"I'm pretty sure I will." Two weeks later, I bade her goodbye.

With student loans and government programs that supported teacher training, I could pay for the master's program myself. I knew my parents couldn't help out. Despite their nonstop work, and the incessant repairs to keep their West Side buildings in perfect condition, they were barely making ends meet. The previous November, they had spent $4,000 on a new six-flat heating plant and rewiring one of the apartments.

In the spring of 1971, as I was planning my move to NU, their checking account was overdrawn, and Mom had to borrow eighty dollars from our next-door neighbor. In March, she wrote in her diary, "Quite broke this month." It was as if they were *paying* for the privilege of running themselves into the ground in the increasingly dangerous neighborhood.

Accustomed to their kids finding their own way, Dad and Mom seemed only mildly interested that I was pursuing a master's degree. Dad was enjoying his second youth at his Fireman's Fund job. Mom's biggest concern was my marital status. After all, at twenty-two, I was done with college (and Bill, at twenty-six, with law school). We had been dating six years, so, in her mind, marriage was next.

Bill and I had been together for more than five years, yet neither of us was ready for marriage. In the 1960s–'70s zeitgeist, my generation was scrutinizing every institution, including marriage, for meaning. Marriage was "just a piece of paper" and didn't confer love or commitment. In 1970, one-third of all marriages ended in divorce,[53] so what kind of "commitment" was that? And did we want to be tied down so young? According to some feminists, marriage was just another means for men to control women. Instead of making marriage my ultimate goal, I focused on building a career.

I knew Bill was my guy. He had proven his devotion to me over and over. Dad had always encouraged his kids to think independently. So we did.

One day that summer, I was working on lesson plans for my student-teaching job when Mom called me.

"Hello?"

"Hello, Linda. I've called to tell you something that's

been bugging me for a long time now. You and Bill have an immoral relationship. You've disgraced me!"

"I don't know what you're talking about!" My throat contracted, raising the pitch of my voice.

"If you each have your own apartment, something immoral is going on!" she yelled. "Why aren't you getting married?"

"Mom, this is outrageous! What the hell? You're calling me to tell me this nonsense? We're not ready to get married. Someday we probably will, but we're not ready yet."

"And I'll tell you another thing. I'll be damned if I'll spend three thousand dollars on a wedding and then never be invited over afterward!"

"Mom, you need to calm down. I'm just trying to prepare for my classes."

"Well, you've chosen your path. Now we'll see where it leads!"

She slammed down the phone. Mom had *always* liked Bill. She often commented on how polite, witty, or smart he was. They frequently engaged in philosophical arguments— about politics, Communism, religion, and morality. It was the fact that we weren't getting married that set her off on rants like the phone call.

Mom used the same approach to control Dad's behavior. She screamed, "You son of a bitch!" when he brought stuff home. She threw it out the back door, or into his study (Paul's former bedroom), then wrote everything she had said and done in her diary. It became her ersatz psychologist—but with no feedback to encourage reflection, she remained stuck in the same loop of recriminations.

Not privy to their personal world, I often broke down in tears over their rows. "I just want you both to be happy," I sobbed to whichever one I was with. Dad embraced me, saying, "It's okay. It's okay."

Mom insisted, "How can we get along if he won't discuss anything?"

When I asked Dad why he wouldn't talk things over with Mom, he said, "There's no point. If I express an opinion, I'm one hundred percent certain the discussion won't go my way. If I keep quiet, there's a fifty-fifty chance I'll get what I want."

On occasion, Mom acknowledged Dad's relentless toil in a diary entry. After a broken pipe in the backyard required digging up a deep trench, Mom noted: "Fred works hard! He moved all the dirt after the plumbers dug a trench. He has unlimited energy."

But the bulk of her journaling from this era reveals a bitter, unhappy woman. When I first read her entries, three to five decades after she wrote them, I was plunged right back into the heart-thumping whirlwind of her tortured psyche and unfettered fury. Some sentences are followed by multiple bold exclamation points. Her handwriting is dark and agitated, the words embossed onto two or three of the following pages.

Unlike Grandma K, my mom didn't suffer from psychosis, but like her mother, she became a screeching maniac, ranting accusations against Dad, me, and to a lesser extent, my two brothers. As men, the rules of sexuality didn't apply to them. Paul was living with a woman in New Jersey, but Mom said, "That's her mother's problem."

Older now than Mom was when she wrote her angry entries, I'm torn in my reaction to her diary rants. In one moment, I'm in tears over her frustration and plight; in the next, dumbstruck by her repetitive focus on her own certitudes and suffering, her lack of perspective toward young adults: "This is the most selfish generation. I can't believe Linda walked out on me." Reading Mom's diary entry, I instantly thought of that judgmental letter Grandma Gartz had written to Dad's younger brother, Ebner, in 1943, in which she'd declared, "Lil is only for herself."

In the early seventies, I was too young to comprehend the complex torments and quotidian pressures that could gnaw away at a couple's happiness during thirty years of marriage. Add in Ebner's untimely death; thirteen years of Dad's travel while Mom coped with the rooming house alone; fifteen years of dealing with Grandma K's madness; Dad's parents' callous treatment of our family; the riots that undermined my parents' greatest financial investment; and their continued devotion to buildings in a neighborhood tumbling into an abyss of poverty and crime—it's no wonder their happiness unraveled, leaving behind a ragged trail of torn hopes and frayed dreams.

Mom wrote on July 21, 1971: "All the fun is gone because of the abandonment of moral values." She was reading newspaper and magazine articles about the sexual revolution and free love with increasing horror and consternation. When a friend mentioned that her divorced daughter's young son had blurted out, "My mommy is on the pill," Mom was disgusted. "Unbelievable!" she wrote. Ever since she had found the Norman Vincent Peale Bible passage back in 1965, which had helped her cope with the stressful move from the West Side, she had been "hooked on the power of God," as she often said. When Jehovah's Witnesses left copies of their pamphlet, *Awake!* magazine, in her mailbox, she embraced its ultraconservative message about the Bible, God, and especially sex among youth. The latter, above all, reflected her own views. Sometimes she just picked up on a single phrase and sent me the whole article, obviously without reading it all the way through.

In one such article, a daughter asked her mother what made a good marriage. Mom underlined the sentences on the immorality of premarital sex, but obviously had read no further, skipping the section urging women to bend to the will of their husbands. She also overlooked the full page devoted to the evils of drink, her nightly habit.

I returned the article to her with the anti-drinking and "submissive to husband" paragraphs underlined in red. "Thank you for sending me this article," I wrote on an enclosed note. "I've marked some parts you may have missed, so you're sure to get its full message."

Mom never responded, but when I pored through the family archives, I found she had saved my note still attached to the article, on which she had written, "Thank you, Linda!"

Early in 1971, Bill and I dropped by my parents' house midweek to visit. We were watching television with Dad and Billy in the second-floor family room while Mom sat alone in the kitchen downing whiskey, dragging on Salems, and brooding in her bitter loop of suffering. Her often-expressed dismay at the "new morality" and her diary entries, often the exact same words she said aloud, give me a direct link to her thoughts. They go something like this: "These lousy kids today—how dare they! They use all these dirty words; think it's just fine to have free sex. All the parents are working their asses off, and the kids are screwing around."

Her mind twisted, exploding at the gall of today's young people—thumbing their nose at *her* values, her *generation's* values! It was all too much! She marched up the back stairs and entered the sitting area, where Billy, Bill, Dad, and I were watching television. Shoving her index finger into the air to punctuate each sentence, her face contorted with rage, she shouted at us, "Give me an *F!* Give me a *U!* Give me a *C!* Give me a *K!* GO TO HELL, YOU FUCKING BASTARDS!"

She turned, stomped down the stairs and out the front entry, the door slamming behind her. Our mouths dropped. Dad shook his head in disbelief, then shrugged his shoulders and turned back to the TV. The rest of us looked at each other. "What was *that*?"

It was just the beginning.

CHAPTER 39: A New Roommate

Bill and Linda, 1973.

I searched through Mom's diary entries years after her death, trying to understand the source of her misery that was beyond my ken at the age of twenty-two. I learned she did have moments of clarity, which she promptly lost, drowned in a torrent of self-pity. One day, she notes, "Linda is a great disappointment to me." A few days later, she writes, "Now we get along beautifully. She talks real nice to me now." In reality, I was the same. In one entry: "I understand Fred. He's ambitious but can't achieve his goals." In another: "He treats me like a dog." Another: "Fred has a change of attitude. . . .

I'm finally understood after all." Her almost-daily entries were seldom positive.

In June, she and I enjoyed two outings together: a ballet and a wedding shower for the daughter of a family friend, but her emotional psyche was like a sieve—any attention I paid her just drained out. When Bill and I drove up to Wisconsin for a weekend getaway with Peggy and Dietmar, Mom asked me, with hurt eyes and a childish pout, "Why didn't you invite me along?"

"Mom, it was a weekend with friends our age. You wouldn't have enjoyed it."

"Well, after all the times I entertained you young people, I'd think you'd want to include me." Tears welled in her eyes.

"Are you serious, Mom? What twenty-two-year-old invites her parents along on a double date?"

———

In September, my NU master's program assigned me and another MAT student to share teaching duties in a fourth-grade classroom at a North Side Chicago public school. Katy started Northwestern Law School at the downtown campus, so we went our separate ways, vowing to keep in touch. I found a perfect, light-filled, one-bedroom, third-floor apartment in a three-flat just a short bus ride from my school. Before classes started, I went to my parents' house to borrow their station wagon and load it up with school supplies.

Mom met me on the sidewalk outside our Keeler home, a grim expression marring her face, still pretty when it wasn't warped by bitterness. She greeted me with, "I don't even mention your name to my friends because I'm so ashamed of you."

"Ashamed! How can you be ashamed of me?" I cried out, tears spilling, my voice cracking. "I'm getting a master's degree—and paying for it all myself! I graduated from Northwestern with great grades. I'm supporting myself. I just spent a whole day with you and Billy painting screens. I always help when you ask. I can't believe you said that!"

"What am I supposed to tell my friends when you're not getting married and have your own apartment?"

"You don't have to tell them anything!" I tried to explain to her that Bill and I were trying to figure out if marriage even mattered. "We need some time. Besides, I only came to borrow the car. I have so much to do before school starts. Don't you understand? This is my first teaching job! I have to be prepared!"

Mom shook her head. "Well, you're ruining your life." We went inside to get the car keys.

Mom thought about the conversation and later wrote in her diary:

> It's unbelievable! She thinks she's a pioneer of sorts, breaking through with a new concept. I know they're good kids, but they're all mixed up with this new philosophy floating around. To me, it's been promoted by the Communists, trying to corrupt our youth.

Mom didn't have a life outside of her work on the West Side and home. Dad still had two jobs, his day job at Fireman's Fund and his on-call and weekend West Side duties. The West Side brought in some money, but Fireman's Fund gave them a steady income, retirement benefits, and good insurance. It was also a source of daily camaraderie for Dad, but Mom benefitted, too.

She had a couple of friends she phoned now and then, as well as the Tri Psis, a group comprising mothers of my NU sorority, which met for outings about once a month. Other than that, my parents' social life—boat trips, picnics, pig roasts, and weekend gatherings—were either through FF or friendships Dad had nurtured. Despite Mom's constant nagging and screaming, he was making his own happiness, as he had since his youth, skirting her attacks by strategically including friends for all holidays and events.

Mom, unable to recognize how Dad was managing their relationship, took to calling him Alfred E. Neuman, after the iconic character in *Mad* magazine. "What, me worry?" she mocked. "Sure, he's everybody's pal. He doesn't have to solve any problems. It's all dumped in my lap!" In the division of labor, Dad did all the physical work on the West Side, but the problem-solving, finances, and responding to tenants' concerns fell mostly to Mom. When one tenant told her, "Mrs. Gartz, I just want you to know that we do appreciate all you do," it was better than any tonic.

In September of 1971, Bill moved into a large one-bedroom apartment a couple of blocks from Wrigley Field. He had finished law school, passed the bar exam, and was working as a Cook County public defender. After six years together, we still didn't see any need to get married, and it wasn't because we feared falling into my parents' pattern of acrimony. Our temperaments and approach to life were simply different from theirs.

Bill was logical and understood finances in a way my dad didn't. Bill never would have worked so hard at a business that wasn't making money. I had a more even-keeled temperament than Mom; I was neither quick to anger nor as excitable and emotional as she. Dad hated confrontation; Bill would engage with anyone if the situation called for it. Unlike Dad and Mom, Bill and I could talk through disagreements (we had few in the early years), but later, when conflict between couples is inevitable, each of us (usually) listened to one another and (usually) expressed opinions respectfully.

So avoiding marriage had nothing to do with my parents. But I *did* want something to change. I was sick of our dating routine after so many years together. One fall evening, we sat at the Formica kitchen table in my apartment, sipping white wine while '50s and '60s rock and roll played from my turquoise transistor radio.

Bill's hair had grown back steadily since his army-regulation buzz cut, and it hung just below his ears. I looked up past his large-framed glasses into his eyes. My stomach clenched a little. I had a hard time making demands, but it was time. "I think this weekly dating is kinda juvenile after all these years. I'm tired of it."

"What's the problem?" He seemed truly puzzled—which made me talk faster.

"What's the problem! Are we supposed to just 'date' forever? I think we should move in together and see if we can make a go of it."

He raised his eyebrows. "Really? Your mother's already acting nuts. This could put her over the edge." He took a sip of wine, looking down into the glass.

I shrugged. "I just won't tell her. She's already accused me of immorality for having my own apartment—so what's the difference?" After three glasses of wine, self-righteousness had kicked in.

He pulled me toward him and kissed me, a long, open-mouthed kiss, his smell clean and fresh. His hands moved under my shirt; mine under his. "You're such a little trollop," he said with a grin and the teasing tone I loved. We kissed all the way to the bedroom.

I didn't want to rub Mom's nose in what would be devastating news for her, so I continued to pay rent on my apartment, hoping to put off her discovery for as long as possible.

About three months after I'd moved into the Wrigleyville apartment, the phone rang one Saturday. "Hello?"

"Linda?"

I knew what was coming. "Hi, Mom."

"Linda, I've been trying to reach you, but you never answer at your apartment. Are you living with Bill?" She spat out the words.

"Look, Mom, yes, I am. I know this is upsetting to you, and I'm sorry, but it's for the best. We'll get married some-day. Just not yet."

She growled into the phone, "I should have sent you to work when you were seventeen. That was my mistake, letting you go to Northwestern!" She slammed down the phone.

Mom's ideal daughter was herself—the daughter who, at the age of seventeen, had worked to support her unemployed parents during the Depression; who had put her mother's well-being before that of her husband or her children, and never questioned that choice. I was not that daughter. I was putting my relationship with Bill above my mother's values.

I was certain I was taking the right path, but I knew how deeply my cohabitation wounded Mom and violated her rigid morality. She couldn't possibly understand. There was only one response: I folded my arms onto the desk, pressed my head against them, and cried.

CHAPTER 40: No End in Sight

Rats killed by Dad and Billy at the West Side six-flat.

After sending out dozens of résumés to Chicago-area school districts, I was interviewed and hired to start in the fall of 1972, teaching sixth grade in Winnetka, a North Shore suburb renowned for its innovative, child-centered approach to teaching. Even Mom was happy, responding with real joy. She wrote in her diary, "Linda got a wonderful teaching job at the wonderful salary of $9,600 per year."

Winnetka was then, and is now, one of the nation's richest suburbs, with a well-educated populace, lots of trees, large homes, expansive lawns, and safe streets. When I began teaching in 1972, it was virtually all white, including a smattering of Jewish families. The children were scrubbed, casually well-dressed, and privileged (though not necessarily spoiled). Most of my students were kind and motivated. Their parents held them to high standards of both achievement and behavior, but several kids still needed a good deal of guidance and a teacher's loving attention.

It was a solar system away from West Garfield Park, the stark difference manifested in my father's recent close call. The same fall I started teaching in Winnetka, Dad was heading home after checking on his three buildings, all within half a block of one another on Washington Boulevard. Driving a couple minutes east, he saw lights flashing from a scrum of cop cars. The news reported that a twenty-seven-year-old man, his father-in-law, and an employee of a salvage company on Pulaski had been shot to death—just minutes before Dad drove past. The murders occurred shortly after fire had engulfed the nearby historic Guyon Paradise Ballroom, and around the same time the A&P, our family's go-to grocery store on Madison and Keeler, had burned to the ground. Investigators suspected arson in both blazes.

Not long after the shooting, Mom was collecting rent on the West Side, when she learned more frightening news from one of her tenants, Mr. Brooks. "A reliable source" had told him that fifteen women had been raped in just one week within a two-block radius of our six-flat. "A man sees a woman he wants and, as in days of old, just takes her," Mr. Brooks told Mom. He added, "There's a definite deterioration in the kind of people in the area in the past nine months."

"It looks like the West Side is headed for total destruction," Mom wrote, as if this were big news. She told Dad, "We'd better sell that six-flat. We're playing Russian roulette."

Believing that the West Side was still *his* neighborhood, Dad refused. But perhaps he also worried about his mother's disdainful reaction should he sell the six-flat "gift." I think he also relished how his fearless confrontation of daily dangers impressed his coworkers.

Mom, however, was personally invested in doing her part to make the West Side buildings a success—to prove to herself, and naysayers, that their meticulously cared-for property would be respected by their tenants. Responding to every complaint, spending money on repairs and upkeep in no way commensurate with their income from the buildings, she was determined to do the right thing. Her biggest payback was recognition and appreciation, which she felt was in short supply from Dad. I've become convinced that the West Side, with all the fear, crime, and aggravation, somehow fulfilled both my parents' deepest needs left over from childhood.

As an only child, Mom had been showered with personal attention. Despite Grandma K's fierce temper, Mom knew she had always been the focus of her parents' lives. Why wasn't Dad giving her the same kind of attention now for her intense efforts?

I think Dad still felt the lifelong sting of his mother's scorn. She had grabbed precious possessions from his hands and thrown them into the furnace; she had belittled his ideas. I believe that Dad, despite his college chemistry degree, unconsciously tried to garner his mother's approval by maintaining buildings like his janitor parents had. It was a futile endeavor.

In spite of my parents' commitment to their tenants and property, some West Side problems were intractable. One tenant held back on signing her lease because of roaches in her unit, despite repeated visits from an exterminator. The vermin simply invaded again from neighboring apartments that weren't kept clean. "Roaches have nothing to do with the lease," Mom said. "I can't come over there and hit them with my shoe!"

Near their buildings, rats drank openly at a dripping faucet in the middle of the day. The city ignored West Garfield Park, as it had for years, so Dad fell back on his parents' philosophy, *selbstständigkeit:* self-reliance. He had provided lidded and locked rat-proof garbage cans. But at the large apartment building next door to their six-flat, garbage was strewn all about, making easy pickings for rats. Each female procreated at the prolific rate of six to fourteen babies every three weeks.

The rat dens were easy to locate in the yard by simply following the dozen or more paths that crisscrossed the back lawn, the grass worn away by the steady trudge of rats on the move. Dad enlisted Billy to attack the problem head-on.

Dad found the location of a lively rat burrow, including its multiple ingress and egress holes. He plugged up all exits, save two. Into one he inserted a length of garden hose attached to a basement-sink faucet; at the other, he stationed my brother with that useful extermination tool, a two-by-four. Dad turned on the hot water. With a narrow tunnel their only escape route from the raging flood waters, the rats had to scurry one at a time to where Billy stood at the ready, whacking each with the weapon as it charged into the bright sunlight.

Watching the spectacle like an audience at a Colosseum event, neighborhood kids sent up a rousing cheer for every rat killed. It's no wonder: rats had terrorized them and their families. After nineteen direct hits, rodent carnage lay all about. Boys and girls ran into the yard, poking their dead adversaries with sticks, giving them another thwack for good measure. Always one for documenting major events, Dad carefully set out the curled-up corpses into three rows, like a series of apostrophes and quotation marks, for a photo op—a visual aid for another good story percolating in his brain.

Perhaps Dad could have found a more efficient way to deal with the rats, but he seldom focused on efficiency. Besides, rat poison posed risks to other animals and children; it killed the rats over a period of days from inner hemorrhaging—a far crueler way to die. For the time being, he had rid his corner of rats, and he had another story to amaze his friends and coworkers. Providing entertainment for the neighborhood kids was a bonus, just as Dad had done for me and my friends in our childhoods. He always found a way to spark up the tinder of life's tedium with a flicker of humor, a whoosh of drama, a crackle of the bizarre.

But the animal problems were less volatile than the explosive situations that could arise like a thunderclap among residents.

One warm summer day, Dad and Mom were trimming the bushes in the front yard at our former two-flat, when an altercation arose. They both told me what happened, each filling in vivid details. Ruby Montgomery, the twenty-something daughter of the man who rented the first-floor apartment, stood on the front porch chatting with my parents in the yard below, when a woman walked by and started talking trash. "Hey, Ruby. I seen you with that man I was sweet on. What you doin', girl? You the hood ho now?"

"Hey, bitch," retorted Ruby. "Why'd he even look at you—with that shitty wig you always wearin'?" One hand on her hip, the other pointing at the woman, Ruby's head moved in rhythm with her insult.

Her voice rising in fury, the woman grabbed a fistful of her own hair, yanking on it repeatedly as she moved up the walk toward Ruby. "What you call this, bitch?" Riveted to the spot, hedge clippers midair, Mom and Dad hardly had time to register how quickly a few sentences were evolving into a physical confrontation.

Before the woman reached the stairs, Mr. Montgomery stepped out the front door, shotgun in hand. He pushed his daughter to the side, simultaneously raising the weapon, nestling it into position against his shoulder, and taking a bead on the woman. "Move over, Ruby. I got her in my sights."

Dad leaped up the front steps, directly in front of his tenant, and shoved the gun to the side. "Fred! Fred!" Mom screamed. "Don't get shot!"

"Mr. Montgomery!" Dad shouted, his left hand grasping Montgomery's shoulder, shaking him. "*What* are you doing?" Dad pressed down the gun-wielding arm to Mr. Montgomery's side, looking him in the eye. The woman on the street backed away, screaming epithets back at Ruby as she walked east down Washington.

Montgomery sighed deeply. "You're right. You're right." He then turned and walked back into the flat where I used to live, his shoulders hunched, the shotgun dangling at his side, his daughter following behind. "Thank you, Mr. Gartz," she said quietly before closing the door behind her. Mom and Dad finished their work, Mom chastising Dad for his rash behavior. Then they drove home.

Dad's friends and coworkers were once again agape at this latest story. "Freddie, don't you think you ought to get out of that neighborhood?"

"Nothing to worry about," Dad said.

Yet one winter night, while shoveling coal into the furnace, Dad had left the basement door open behind him to release the intense heat, the blaze's flames casting a gleam that rose up into the darkness and shone like a beacon. The basement entranceway, where Dad was working, was down several steps in a dark, cramped space, shielded from view by back stairs that rose overhead—no escape.

A couple of young men moved silently toward the light, catching Dad unawares. "Hey, ol' man." They grinned wide at Dad, who had just laid down his shovel, about to close the furnace door. He turned to see their features flickered by flame; the gun, agleam with reflected firelight, pointed at his chest.

"What do you want?" he asked quietly.

"We want your wallet," said one, extending his palm toward Dad. "Put it right here, and we won't hurt you. Slow now. Just go slow." Dad kept one hand in the air, pulling his wallet out from his back pocket with the other.

"Why don't you two get jobs?" Dad asked, extending the wallet, holding eye contact. "Then you wouldn't have to bother with people like me who are just doing theirs."

"Just stay here, and don't say nothin' till we're gone." They turned and disappeared into the night.

When Dad calmly related this story to me, he said, "I was so mad, my heart was pounding! I was more mad than scared."

"Dad, that *is* scary. If it happened once, it'll happen again."

"I'll be ready next time," he said. "That won't *ever* happen to me again. Punks!" His eyes turned fierce and steely.

Dad later told me of how he planned to thwart future robbers and burglars at the six-flat basement. He would set up a crossbow on a trigger so that anyone who forced open the door (tenants didn't have a key) might be skewered. Bill told him that it was against the law to create a potentially deadly trap, even against someone engaged in a crime.

"A man has a right to defend his property!" Dad retorted.

One day, he arrived at the six-flat to find the trigger tripped, a trail of blood spotting the steps. "I haven't had a break-in since," he said triumphantly months later. "Word travels."

"Dad!" I said, sitting at my parents' kitchen table, looking at my aging father with alarm. "That's dangerous! What if that guy comes back with friends and tries to get you when you're there alone?" He waved away my worries.

Others chided him, too. My father's best buddy since his teen years, now a surgeon, said to Dad, "Sell those damn buildings! You're pouring money down a sewer."

Even the family lawyer said to Mom, "You'd better get rid of that six-flat before you're wiping Fred's brains off the sidewalk."

The dangers were real—rapes, burglaries, muggings, purse snatchings, and Dad's armed robbery. Mom focused on unloading the six-flat, the building with the most tenants and the most trouble. "Fred, we have to talk about selling that six-flat," was her greeting when Dad returned home from work.

His evasive response was maddening. "When do we eat supper?"

Taking up Mom's cause, I said, "Hey, Dad, you really should talk with Mom about selling the six-flat. We're both worried about your safety."

"There's no point in discussing anything with your mother," he said. "She has to get her own way, so there's no point in expressing my opinion."

CHAPTER 41: **Home Alone**

Billy preparing to leave for Seattle, 1974.

That September of 1972, I stared at the blank walls of my corner classroom, light pouring in from a wall of windows, an expanse of trees and trimmed grass across the street. In just two weeks, this room would hold twenty-seven eleven-year-olds, the children of educated, achievement-oriented, and mostly wealthy parents. Winnetka teachers were expected to be creative, to individualize lessons, to *engage* students in their learning. Fear crawled from my chest to my brain. My only experience had been the previous year of teaching fourth grade in a Chicago public school, where I shared one classroom's teaching duties with another MAT student.

That year, we had far exceeded the expectations of the working-class parents. Instead of dividing up the responsibilities, we divided up the class into small groups to maximize each kid's learning. With no school music program, we led the students in weekly songfests, accompanied by my partner's guitar, as well as organized an all-school assembly and, later, a science fair.

I asked Dad to bring his boa constrictor, Lucifer. Engaging his usual flair for showmanship, he pulled the snake's six-foot length out of a burlap bag to a chorus of oohs and aahs and fake shrieks by some of the girls. After holding the snake above his head and wrapping it around his neck, Dad moved slowly down each aisle of desks, allowing the kids to feel the snake's scaly skin and muscular coils, to see up close its reptilian, tawny, vertically slit eyes as he explained its habits and habitat. Feeding the boa was *not* in the lesson plan.

After placing Lucifer back into the sack and knotting the top, Dad again walked among the desks, holding in the palm of his hand five hairless, sightless, day-old baby rats, their tiny pulsing bodies virtually transparent. "Co-ol! Co-ol!" declared one boy, as he rocked back and forth in his chair.

But despite these successes in Chicago, I worried if I could be creative enough for the demanding Winnetka parents. Panic fired up my neurons, and plans began falling into place. First I had to make the room cozy and welcoming. I turned to Dad and his junk. He rented a trailer, loading it with a worn but usable couch, a large carpet remnant, a couple of bookcases, an easel, and two glass tanks—one for fish, the other for reptiles. Out of these cast-offs, a reading corner emerged. I stacked books on the cases' shelves, and prepared folders with questions the kids could answer about each book to get reading credit.

"Don't smile till Christmas," urged one book on maintaining classroom order. I couldn't do that for even the first hour of my first day. As I got comfortable in my role, the whimsy I'd absorbed from Dad popped out. To the kids' delight, I repeatedly sat on the whoopee cushion they placed on my chair, arm-wrestled the boys, and joined all the kids at recess in "maul-ball," a rendition of football. One parent told me at the open house, "When my friends ask what kind of teacher you are, I tell them you're a cross between Mary Poppins and a drill sergeant!"

Just as I started teaching, Bill bought a three-flat with a fire-gutted coach house at the alley. It was located on Chicago's Near North Side, in a transitional neighborhood named DePaul, after the nearby university. An old Italian immigrant owned the corner grocery store, and fireworks shot off well into the night on Puerto Rican Independence Day. The community was a little dicey, with dog poop marring the sidewalks fronting small, weary apartment buildings, but its proximity to downtown Chicago and the university made its future bright.

Following our upbringing, we became landlords. I was in my element—eager to jump in and help with everything from showing apartments to patching drywall. Bill tackled the coach house, devouring how-to books on HVAC and electrical, hiring other tradesmen for the skilled work he couldn't learn quickly. Dashing home from his public defender job, he started in on the construction, working late into the night and devoting every weekend to the renovation. At the end of my teaching day, I came home to a cacophony of banging hammers or the high screech of bending metal— Bill was screwing together and installing metal HVAC ducts or calibrating a special tool to bend electrical pipes into just the right angle to traverse the inner walls.

Once drywall was up, I took over taping and plastering the seams, painting walls, and grouting tile, skills I had learned working with my parents. My efforts gave Mom another tactic for imploring me to get married. "You have no security or guarantee for the work you're doing," she said. "Don't you see, without that 'piece of paper,' as you call it, you have no legal rights—and all your efforts are for nothing!" I understood her point, but I also knew Bill would never leave me.

We moved into the finished coach house in July of 1973.

One of Mom's favorite tenants, Mrs. Barlow, was also moving that summer, from the basement of our former home. Mom was especially pleased that Mrs. Barlow cut and watered the grass—and had even planted a garden—unlike many of the neighbors, whose yards were weedy patches of dirt. "It's an achievement to have everyone's cooperation," Mom later wrote. "Patience and politeness win out in the end."

After admiring the robustly growing collards, mustard greens, and cabbages growing in the backyard, Mom launched into a torrent of complaints. "Today's youth have no morals," she bemoaned. "My older son has moved in with a woman, but that's *her* mother's problem. It's my daughter that bothers me. She's living with a man she's not married to, and won't listen to logic!"

Mrs. Barlow said, "Sense cannot be taught. It has to be bought." She spoke of her own children. "I ain't gonna try to change them so long as they leave me alone. If they wants to listen to my advice, they can, but I ain't forcing them. Like my daddy said, 'If you makes your bed hard, you sleep hard.'"

"I really like my tenants' down-to-earth philosophy," Mom told me more than once. "They have a maxim for everything, and they're so true!" Mom probably had nodded in agreement at Mrs. Barlow's comments, and then, just as quickly, had forgotten them. The opinions of others blew away like chaff in the wind, leaving only the original kernels of Mom's own ideas settled in the basket of her mind.

When Mrs. Barlow moved, her apartment had been left in "immaculate condition," Mom wrote. "Our tenants surely take excellent care of everything. My faith has been restored." Nothing could have bolstered Mom's pride more.

Her and Dad's nurturing attention had borne fruit. "My success on the West Side is the greatest achievement of my life!" she wrote in her diary.

Mom found the admiration and approval she so craved only in the suffering, beaten-down West Side. One tenant told her, "I envy you, Mrs. Gartz. You know how to do everything."

When Mom explained in great detail how leases worked to Lonnie Branch, he said, "You're a good salesman, Mrs. Gartz." (Apparently, he was as well. A few years after he moved from my parents' building, Branch was arrested as one of the city's biggest heroin dealers.)[54]

Another tenant called my mother "glamour girl." Mom loved her tenants, despite the risky neighborhood. "I never feel as alive as I do on the West Side," she said. "And the tenants are all so nice to me." One had given her a gift of flower vases. "I get respect from my tenants, not from your father." She ignored or overlooked the fifteen years he had respected psychotic Grandma K's presence in our home—and the multiple times he had intervened, saving Mom from her mother's physical, sometimes life-threatening, attacks.

After Bill and I had settled into the now-finished coach house, we invited Mom and Dad to see its transformation from a burned-out shell to a bright, two-floor, two-bathroom living space. We gave them a tour, made a gourmet dinner, and then took them to the movies. In a brief moment of clarity, Mom wrote after the evening, "I accept their relationship because he is good to her, and they are happy. I'm happy to have them in Chicago, with Paul in New Jersey, and Billy going away."

The previous four years, Billy had been the only kid still living in my parents' house, during which he had spent two years as a student at the University of Illinois at Chicago campus. He had developed coping skills to survive in a household that seemed like a set for the play *Who's Afraid of Virginia Woolf?* Mom screamed. Dad responded by tossing out subtle zingers, escalating her fury. When Mom went on a rampage, Billy sat down at the piano, drowning out the cacophony of anger and bitterness by banging out the theme from the movie *Exodus*—appropriate since he had been planning his own escape. He and Paul had taken a cross-country trip together in 1970, including a stop in Seattle, where Billy fell in love with the city. He decided to move there for his junior year and complete his degree at the University of Washington.

After saving money from part-time jobs, he bought a 1967 Buick LeSabre for $750. He'd drive to Seattle, move onto campus, and start a new life in the Pacific Northwest, close to the great outdoors and far from Chicago. Neither of my parents questioned whether their nineteen-year-old son could safely drive a used car solo the two thousand miles from Chicago to Seattle. They took their children's self-sufficiency for granted. We, too, were *selbstständig*.

On Monday, September 10, 1973, the Buick was packed. Crying, Billy hugged Mom. "Goodbye, my little Billy," she told him.

"Don't leave me alone with her," Dad whispered when Billy embraced him.

"It's time for me to go, Dad," he said, pulling away from the hug, but keeping his hands on Dad's shoulders. "You two will be all right. Just be nice to each other." He gave Dad a final slap on the arm, walked down the front steps, climbed into his car—with every available space packed to the brim—and headed west.

Contemplating her youngest child's departure, Mom wrote in her diary:

> It seems right in a way—almost as though everything is falling into place like a giant jigsaw puzzle. It sounds insane, but I feel "I am the chosen one" by God for some purpose. Because it's all too strange.

After all we've been through, suddenly everything is getting straightened out, after eight years.

Eight years earlier, in 1965, they had bought the North Keeler house and acquired the six-flat, more than doubling their workload. They had expended relentless effort and planning during that time to get it all done, so it was not sudden. And "the chosen one"? Mom had said of Dad, "He lives in his own little world of delusion," but Mom had her own delusions. Raised as a child to feel special, and now, living in an insular microcosm, with little time to read, she had neither witnessed firsthand nor learned of the extraordinary accomplishments of striving, hardworking people throughout the wider world. She viewed her determination and success in a riot-riven community as so exceptional, there was only one explanation: she must have been chosen by God.

Perhaps she had been "chosen" to spiral down into an ever-more bitter and frustrated mental state. The last buffer between her and Dad left with Billy. She had cultivated few real friends over the years, and her tedious bragging about her accomplishments drew scorn (or possibly envy) rather than praise. "Lil, you're nothing but a drudge," said one of her supposed friends after Mom expounded on her work.

The constant recipient of her ire, Dad tuned her out. "I'm an executive secretary," she cried at him in frustration, "and I'm scrubbing hallways on the West Side!"

"So what?" he retorted. "I'm a chemical engineer."

CHAPTER 42: Mom's World

By this time, Mom was fifty-seven, and her world was drawing down around her. Her repetitive diary diatribes focused not only on Dad but also on his cruel and overbearing mother. The unfounded praises she had heaped on her mother-in-law in the letter to me in Germany just a few years earlier ("she was always right and actually my best friend") were replaced by a vitriol that burst forth from feeling duped and manipulated. Mom had come to believe that the six-flat was not a gift from my grandparents when they left the West Side, but a form of vicious retribution to make her suffer.

"I can't stand myself for being so stupid!" she wrote, regarding her in-laws. "Here they have $250,000 in the bank, and the Gartzes have me mopping halls and scrubbing floors! I have to risk my life! Humiliate myself to survive!"

Mom's handwriting looks so agitated in this entry, it appears as if her brain were exploding on the page. She had other choice descriptives for Grandma Gartz:

> dreary, self-righteous bitch; that tyrant with no pity,
> no mercy; she could leave her daughter-in-law to
> fight for her life like an alley rat doing her son's work.

Mom wrote repeatedly of her desire for a loving relationship with Dad and with her children, but her only role model for dealing with frustration was her volatile, insane mother. Now an empty-nester, and surely menopausal to boot, Mom, though certainly not mentally ill, acted increasingly like Grandma K, ranting and accusing, viewing her children's busy, adult lives and long-distance jobs as a personal insult.

> *Linda can summarily walk out on me after coming home from Europe.*
> *Paul didn't visit me when he was on a business trip to Chicago.*
> *Billy doesn't write me letters. They're so important and so BUSY! I don't have the treatment I deserve!*

As the only child in the Chicago area, I hosted my parents for occasional dinners and celebrations, like their anniversary, Mom's birthday, and Mother's Day. After we invited Mom and Dad for another evening at the coach house, a few positive thoughts again slipped into her mind.

> *They made a lovely dinner and drinks, and I was treated nicely. I've adjusted my thinking and accept their living together and won't consider it a personal affront. Bill is really brilliant, and I hope someday they will be married. She would do well to marry him.*

Then she'd fall again into wailing self-pity, her self-imposed pain so palpable, it tears my heart:

> *From this point on, I have no children. Linda is lost to me, and I will have no more family gatherings. My heart is so very heavy, and tears are welling up in my eyes. I should do what orthodox Jews do if a girl marries outside the faith: hold a funeral for all my children, because to me and Fred, they no longer*

exist. I have a new prayer: God, please protect me
from my children.

———

A lot of what Mom wrote in her diary she also said aloud, but I hadn't heard or seen that last sad, misguided quote until after her death. By 1974, a combination of Mom's unrelenting anger and misery, and the past three years living with Bill, made me question our philosophy on marriage. We had loved, lived, and worked together harmoniously since 1971, and been a couple for nine years. With our similar upbringings, we seldom disagreed on work ethic (important) or money (spending little and saving were priorities), and we respected each other's space. When we did argue, we made up quickly. I believed strongly that I wouldn't bring children into our relationship without that "piece of paper," and I knew I wanted kids someday. I'd brought up the marriage and kids idea to Bill a couple times, but his iconoclastic nature avoided the subject. "Who cares?" and "It doesn't matter," were typical responses.

One evening, as we sat in our living room, throwing a dish towel for our Labrador retriever, LeRoi, to fetch, I was direct. "Look," I said, "you know we're going to stick together. We might as well get married so Mom isn't freaking out all the time." LeRoi grabbed the towel in his teeth and tossed it at us, barking, staring with eager eyes, until we threw it again—and again.

Bill tossed the towel up the stairs. LeRoi bounded after it and returned for more. "Do we really want to give in to her rants?"

"Bill," I said, with stern resolve, "we've been together nine years! What do you mean, 'give in'? I think we've pretty much proven to ourselves that we're meant to be a team. We're great together. Let's just take the anxiety out of my mother's life—and ours. I'm serious about this!"

He turned to me, his brow furrowed. "What worries me is that your mother might literally go insane one of these days," he said, throwing the towel for LeRoi one more time. He drew me toward him and gave me a long kiss. "I think I can put up with you for a few more years," he said, and smiled into my eyes.

"But can I put up with you?"

He rolled me onto the floor. "Do you know how much I love you?" he whispered in my ear. I pushed him back to see his face, those hazel eyes taking on a vulnerable tenderness that enveloped my heart. I held his gaze; my mouth moved toward his.

"Tell me again," I said, a tease and a choke in my voice.

LeRoi barked at us like he always did when Bill and I fooled around, ready for love.

The following week, we drove north to my parents' house to tell Mom about our decision. We didn't know that she'd been stewing all day about our "sinful living."

I rang the bell. Mom answered the door, scowling. Before we could even say hello, she lit into us. "So, it's you two. Listen, I can't take it anymore that you're not married."

I tried to stop her. "Wait, Mom. We have something to tell you."

Bill interrupted. "No, let her talk." He put his hand on his hip and cocked his head. *Uh-oh.* He was ready to engage. Mom turned on him.

"I was always nice to you and treated you like a son, and now you've done this to me! If I had to do it all over again, I would have sent all my kids out to work. Other girls with a high-school education treasure their mother, but mine— Northwestern and a trip to Europe to boot! And she's living with a man like a common whore!"

Before I could open my mouth, Bill jumped in. "I resent

that remark," he said, his eyes flickering with anger. He drew himself up and faced her directly.

"Tough!"

A visit that I had expected to bring Mom joy had turned on its head. I ignored her unfiltered epithet to get us back on track. "We really came over here to tell you we're getting married."

"In the meantime, Mr. Gartz can take the garden, the buildings, and the kids and shove the whole thing up his ass!" Now that she had an audience, she was covering all the built-up resentments that tortured her psyche.

"Mom. Mom!" I was yelling now. "Listen to me! I said we came over to tell you we're getting married."

She paused for a moment, looked from one of us to the other, as if she were emerging from a trance, and finally said, "Really?"

"Really."

Her eyes opened wide and her expression switched instantly from bitter to delighted surprise. "That's wonderful. That's great news!" She hugged me, then Bill. "Congratulations! You know, Bill, I always did like you."

"I like you too, Mrs. Gartz, but you're a manic depressive." He smiled ruefully at his nutty future mother-in-law. We said we had to get going and just wanted to tell her the good news.

As we left, Mom shouted after us, "Take good care of my little girl!"

CHAPTER 43: End of an Era

Bill and Linda's wedding, May 30, 1975.

Bill and I wanted low-key nuptials—no hall, no band, no wedding party—not even a new dress. I'd wear my mother's flowing, 1942 satin wedding gown, which Bill's mom, a superb seamstress, fitted for me. Bill and I stuck by our notion that it was our relationship—not the marriage—that was important, so we kept as much the same as possible: no rings, no name change for me, and no new anniversary date. We would get married on the tenth anniversary of the day we met: May 30, a Friday in 1975. The following day, our families and friends would celebrate in my parents' beautiful backyard.

On May 30, the yard was lovely with spring-green grass,

tall purple *Allium giganteum*, red roses, white-edged hosta, freshly unfurling ostrich ferns, and late-blooming multicolored tulips—a perfect setting for our garden wedding. But the day was chilly and overcast, rain spitting down intermittently, so we moved the flower-festooned arbor, under which Bill and I would take our vows, into the family music room.

I descended the winding front staircase, my mother's shimmery gown grazing the steps, my two closest friends holding the train. At the bottom, Dad smiled broadly, took my arm, and led me to the arbor. There he kissed my cheek, gave Bill a hug, and told us both, "Be happy." The judge read our simple vows; we each said, "I do," and kissed. Afterward, Mom, in a pretty flowered dress, smiled and shook our hands. Mission accomplished.

The December following our wedding, Bill sold the three-flat with its renovated coach house, and together we bought a home in Evanston. It was a sturdy, redbrick two-story in a quiet neighborhood, but the previous owners' slovenly habits presaged plenty of work.

With my summers free from teaching, I tackled the redecorating. When I pulled off the ugly green-flocked wallpaper in the front hallway and living room, I discovered why such a hideous choice looked brand-new: it had been installed solely to hide walls riddled with thousands of cracks. Following a rigid daily schedule of patching, sanding, and painting, I planned to finish the first floor by September. I may have been a little less compulsive than my parents, but not much. There was no way I was going to hire out what I could do myself.

A few months after Bill and I had moved into our new home, Grandma Gartz insisted Grandpa wait while she bent over to secure his shoelaces before he left to drive around Villa Park, still looking for cast-offs "too good to throw away." At nearly eighty-seven, with a lifetime of savings, he still couldn't escape his impecunious childhood.

After he left, Grandma lay down on her pink, bloom-covered couch. When Uncle Will came home, he called her name.

No response. He gently shook her shoulder. "Mom?" Silence. Surely consumed with dread, he called an ambulance to rush her to Elmhurst Hospital, where the whole family gathered to visit the next day. She lay in a stroke-induced coma, tubes up her nose and needles in her arms, her twisted, tiny figure all but dissolving into the white sheets.

I stared in disbelief. *Could this be the same strong, invincible woman who so intimidated our family and ran roughshod over Dad? Whom Mom hated with an outsize passion?* She had shrunk, it seemed, to one-fourth her size, her desiccated lips white and peeling. Having never seen Grandma look frail and small, I sobbed uncontrollably at her bedside— not because I loved her, this woman who seldom had a good word for her only grandchildren and who had been so unkind to Dad and Mom—but because death became real to me for the first time. I now viscerally understood mortality in its finality and inevitability, a shroud hovering to envelop strivers and slackers with equal dispassion.

Mom, her mouth set in an angry grimace, gazed down at her mother-in-law's withered form without a scintilla of compassion. After we returned home from the hospital, Mom said to me between clenched teeth, her voice venomous, "I wouldn't put a drop of water on those parched, dry lips. After all she's done to me, she can very well go to hell!"

Grandma died on May 22, 1976, and Dad drove up to Evanston to tell me. We had no first-floor furniture yet, so Dad sat next to me on the edge of my bed, his shoulders heaving, then settling. "You must feel free now, Dad," I said, my hand on his shoulder.

"Yes. Yes, I do." He took a deep, trembling breath, letting it out as a sigh. "She tried to be a good mother, but just didn't know how." I threw my arms around him, kissing and wiping away his tears. We hugged for a long time. She was, after all, his mom.

Despite our family's fraught relationship with Grandma G, one thing had been clear: in more than six decades of marriage, she and Grandpa had always been in love. Of course, they'd had their share of disputes, but when they posed for photos, Grandma laid her head against his shoulder or grasped his arm tightly, holding him close.

In my naive youth, I was stunned to see him weeping uncontrollably throughout her wake, regaling each visitor with the same account—over and over. "She bent down to tie my shoes," he cried out, his voice breaking, his eyes red and swollen. "She tried to help me, but *she* was dying."

Grandma had been the love of Grandpa's life, the woman whom he had exhorted in letters sixty-five years earlier to leave Transylvania and come to Chicago to marry him:

> If you love me, I hope that you also will come here. . . . I would greet you with greatest joy and thankfulness, and take you in my arms. . . . If you don't want to come, then I also know that you don't love me. Because if you loved me, you wouldn't do anything other than come here.

Grandpa didn't last long after the death of his beloved Lisi. The following March, after several hospitalizations, his heart just gave out, broken and battered, the will to live gone. He passed on to find his Lisi, wherever she might be.

CHAPTER 44: Dad's World

Mom plays cello for the family,
December 1977.

About the same time as Bill and I were planning our wedding, Mom welcomed her eighty-two-year-old uncle John, Grandma K's brother, to live with her and Dad. Ever loyal and duty bound, Mom took on the responsibility for not only his care (he was in failing health), but also for renting and maintaining his house in Elmwood Park, about a thirty-minute drive south and west of their home. I'm quite certain that Mom presented this situation to Dad as a fait accompli. He was probably happy to have another man in the house.

As if the three West Side buildings weren't burden enough, Mom and Dad now drove regularly to Elmwood Park to meet with tenants and handle maintenance. Dad's secretive nature kicked in when he spotted a small side door that led to an abandoned room in the basement, dim and cobwebby. He immediately saw its possibilities and began fixing it up as a hidden personal retreat. When Mom wasn't around, he cleaned it out and added a desk, a lamp, office supplies, a small rug, pictures on the wall—even a bed. Unobservant to subtle changes, Mom focused only on her to-do list and the task at hand. One Saturday, he noted on his calendar, "Worked at Uncle John's. Lil noticed nothing."

While Mom wrote compulsively and about little else other than her fury at Dad or me, Dad, too, had his own journal—his Fireman's Fund daily planner, in which he wrote notes on his inspection appointments and details about his clients. But he also included brief diary entries, like the one above, about his hideaway.

On November 8, 1975, my parents' thirty-third wedding anniversary, he made a comment which exposed the anger he, too, felt in the marriage, but which he seldom spoke aloud. Bill and I treated them to dinner at a cozy German restaurant, Zum Deutschen Eck, on Lincoln Avenue. Afterward, Dad wrote about the evening: "Lil started an argument about how she put the building inspector in his place. I told her, 'That's not how you handle a building inspector.' There was truce at dinner. No talk on way home. Happy anniversary. Humbug."

And a few months earlier: "Lil started her usual argument about her being overworked and me running around to all sorts of parties. She made supper for herself alone. I didn't eat."

Dad's personal entries throughout 1977 make one thing perfectly clear—he was spending lots of time with Lena, a secretary he'd become close friends with at Fireman's Fund. He took Lena to work several times a week (she lived about twenty minutes from my parents' house) and often drove her home at the end of the day. When Mom had the occasional play or concert for the evening, Dad picked up Lena. If he came home late from work, he had been either with Lena or with his other coworkers.

Dad didn't want to be alone with Mom, so he arranged to spend every holiday, every outing to German dances, every Fireman's Fund event with Lena and her family (Lena's mother, as well as her sister and brother-in-law), and often Lena's ex-husband, with whom she'd remained friendly. Dad made the plans and Mom went along because she enjoyed Lena and her family's company and had had few other options for making friends.

My parents took turns hosting holidays with Lena or her sister. Every New Year's Eve, they went out as a group. Mom felt Lena was *her* friend as well as Dad's. It seems Mom had no clue that the woman whom she entertained and socialized with was having an affair with her husband. Mom would have exploded, broken down in tears, or both, had she known.

It was Dad's diary entries that tipped me off. Some of them were cryptic, and I had to tease meaning out of his entries. I figured he was taking Lena to his secret hideaway at Uncle John's Elmwood Park house based on a symbol he had created: a circle with a cross inside. Lena and Dad saw each other multiple times during the week, sometimes for coffee before work, sometimes for supper. Because he had a more flexible schedule than she, he might spend a day dictating reports at Lena's house, waiting, as a favor to her, for a delivery she was expecting. If he just met her for coffee, he used her name in the diary. If it was something more, she was represented by the symbol.

One day during this time, I was chatting with Mom in her dining room. She leaned back against the long, perforated white radiator cover, her hands behind her back, a confessional, embarrassed look on her face. In a moment of rare and uncomfortable intimacy, she said, "You know, Dad and I haven't had sex in more than twenty years."

"Oh," was all I could muster. My face heated. She had never spoken to me about sex, unless it was to warn me against the premarital kind. But I knew one thing for sure: if Mom wasn't having sex with Dad, her sex life was over. Her moral compass precluded any affair. Not so for Dad. He was fulfilling his needs independently, secretly.

One of the few groups of friends Mom hung out with regularly was the Tri Psis, mothers of Tri Deltas, into which she was invited after I graduated from Northwestern. When Mom left town for a weekend with the Tri Psis, Dad spent the night in his Elmwood Park grotto with Lena, thrilled with reactivating his sex life. "Three times. Three times," he wrote. "Spring has come. Like a couple of teenagers!"

Should I be shocked? Furious at his betrayal of my mother? Or should I look at it as the consequence of Mom's out-of-control rants and unkind comments over the years?

Or, on the other hand, should I blame Dad for Mom's anger? He'd foisted the basement apartments on her, despite her vehement objections, and expected Mom to manage a rooming house with eleven tenants, several living in our own apartment, while he traveled half the year.

With each unable to empathize with the other's position, Mom and Dad couldn't find wholeness in one another. By the late sixties and into the seventies, what loving intimacy could possibly have existed between them? Mom often screeched at Dad, "You son of a bitch!" She nagged incessantly and called his parents and brother the "most disgusting family that ever lived!" Dad was dismissive of Mom and her legitimate complaints, retorting, "Aw, quit your complaining. It's all in your head."

Sometimes he tried to reach out. "What's the matter, kid?" he once asked, when she sat brooding and sobbing in the dining room.

She turned away, fed up and furious that it wasn't obvious to him. "This man is unbelievable," she wrote.

At a German event, Dad asked her to dance. Mom wrote later, "I fixed him with a cold stare, waving him away, and told him, 'Go ask someone else.'" Mom's face took on the look of a Diane Arbus photo subject in moments like these: her eyes glazed from drink, her features drooping with bitterness and cynical sadness.

Yet Mom and Dad still cared for one another. One Christmas, as we exchanged gifts, Dad handed Mom a string. "Follow it," he said mischievously, his eyes glinting. She rolled the line in her hand as it twisted around furniture and under throw rugs, ending in a hidden corner of the music room, where it was attached to a cello! She had played the instrument in high school, and for several years had been talking about starting up again. Now she had no more excuses. She clapped her hands in excitement, gave Dad a quick smack on the lips, and said, "Why, thank you, Fred! That's just wonderful." A few months later, she joined Wright Junior College's orchestra.

Mom looked after Dad's health. He had started becoming a little paunchy during the thirteen years of travel, when, for weeks at a time, he had eaten most meals in restaurants. By the 1970s, his active social life, including drinks and heavy eating, drove his weight up to thirty, forty, fifty pounds past ideal. Dad's mother had suffered several heart attacks, then died of a stroke, and he had inherited her cardiac disease. His doctor prescribed blood-pressure medication, but Dad forgot to take it. Mom clipped reminder notes into a large clothespin she set on the kitchen table, next to the bottle of medication. She later began taping reminders to the front door, too. He couldn't be bothered when there was so much fun awaiting him.

CHAPTER 45: A Convergence of Change

Bethel Evangelical Lutheran Church, West End and Keeler, Chicago's West Side.

In the spring of 1978, Bill's father spotted an ad in the *Chicago Tribune*. An immigration attorney in downtown Chicago was selling his law practice and retiring to Virginia. "It's worth investigating," his dad told Bill. The two of them met the lawyer in his office, discussed price, and by the end of the session, with money borrowed from his father, Bill owned an immigration law practice. He was thirty-two.

At the same time, Winnetka District 36 informed teachers that my middle school would close in June of 1978, due to lack of enrollment. Sixth grade would be incorporated into the existing seventh- and eighth-grade junior high, so my job was secure. But it was a transitional moment, spurring me to rethink my future.

Was it possible I could work in a field other than those the 1950s had assured me were the only viable options for women? Could I move beyond the "nurse, teacher, secretary" model, eight years after the women's movement had cracked open society's restrictive notions of acceptable women's roles? Bill's new law practice gave me a starting point. We decided it would be an investment in our future together if I worked as his office manager while simultaneously searching for a new career for myself. I took a year's leave of absence from teaching.

Bill dove into research to learn the nuances of immigration law. He set up accounting systems, and created efficient practices to deal with the complex bureaucratic details of the Immigration and Naturalization Service. I scheduled his appointments, ordered supplies and equipment, and spent every spare moment plotting a new career course by following the advice in the job-search book *What Color is Your Parachute*?

After several months of learning about careers as far afield as banking, computer-systems analysis, advertising, journalism, and public relations, and after setting up dozens of informational interviews, I still had no clear direction. I despaired of ever finding my way.

I thought of teaching in a business environment, where video was emerging as a new technology for training, so I signed up for a video-production class. It was a perfect fit! Producing a video incorporated everything I had loved about teaching: researching, relating to an audience, working with people, and being the creative person in charge. But at the end of a production, I would have a tangible product, not just the *hope* that I had made a difference. I began networking to find a start in the field of television.

At the same time as I was moving my career in a new direction, our former family church embarked on changing the history of West Garfield Park. By 1978, the neighborhood was the national poster child for urban decay. People arrived with wheelbarrows at the scores of homes that had been burned out or shuttered. They chipped away at the hulking remains, stealing vacant buildings brick by brick, carting away the pieces to sell. The area drew comparisons to Berlin after World War II, but there was no Marshall Plan.

Reverend Nelson and his sister, Mary, who had come to work at Bethel on the day of the August 1965 riots, were desperate to save the community they had embraced. Going door-to-door, encouraging folks to come to Sunday services and become part of the solution to poverty and crime, they had built up a vibrant church congregation. Mary told me several years later, "By 1979, we knew we had to do something about housing, or there wouldn't be a community to be church of."

She and David asked Bethel's members to each contribute $10 per week to raise $5,000 to purchase and rehab an abandoned three-flat at 367 North Karlov Avenue, just a few blocks from my parents' buildings. With that bold move, Bethel New Life was born. Mary Nelson was its first president, gaining national renown over the years for her creative approach to providing low-income housing, childcare, jobs, transitions from prison, and assisted living for the elderly. It became into one of the nation's most successful community-development organizations.

While Mary was getting Bethel New Life off the ground, I interviewed at Catholic Television Network (CTN) in Chicago. I'd learned through networking that it was a great place to get started because it wasn't a union shop, so I could try my hand at everything. I interviewed with the station director, Judy, a tiny, wiry fortysomething with an outsize personality. I told her my goal was to become a producer, but the only position open was as an intern on the minicam crew. "Get started with that," she said, "and something may open up in production. I want to see more women in this field, and I'll help you get started."

I worked with the camera and audio men and the different producers of CTN's varied religious programs that were broadcast on its own TV station. We called ourselves "The God Squad," rolling out of the garage in an equipment-laden van, heading to our shoot location, where I hauled gear, dragged cables, and set up lights.

After a couple months, Judy asked me to sit down across from her behind a desk stacked with crisscrossed papers and VHS videotapes. Removing her rings and rubbing in hand lotion, its sweet lavender scent filling the room, she asked, "How'd you like to be in charge of your own show?"

I answered instantly, "That would be excellent!"

"We need a producer for a thirty-minute video targeted at the parents and sponsors of adolescents preparing for Catholic confirmation. Are you willing to take that on?"

"Absolutely," I answered with complete confidence, but I had no idea how I was going to pull it off. Early the next morning, I awoke at three in a panic. *How the hell do you produce a show, start to finish?* Working the rest of the dark early-morning hours until dawn, I made a three-page list on a yellow legal pad of everything I didn't know how to do.

After production started, I sat down each day with one of the station's producers, trying to appear calm, to get answers to my questions, sometimes learning only the day before what the next day's step was. I conducted research and interviews, organized and scheduled the shoots, logged all the tapes, wrote the script, and supervised the rough edit.

Judy was pleased. "Very nice work," she said. "You should be proud." I was—not to mention relieved. I almost didn't know how I'd done it, the pressure, and fear of failure, had been so great. After the rough edit was approved, we recorded a professional narrator. I had all the pieces ready for the final edit.

During that last step, the director, usually brusque and cynical over the poorly conceived productions he supervised day after day, blurted out with astonishment, "This is really good!" His spontaneous compliment washed over me in a warm rush. When the video won a Silver Award at the Chicago International Film Festival, I knew I'd found my career sweet spot.

My first break came when my résumé arrived on the desk of WLS's production manager, the woman who had purchased our three-flat and coach house six years earlier! She interviewed and then hired me to produce a youth-sports documentary, which won an AP award for Best Sports that year. I moved on to more work at ABC, producing six-minute television-magazine segments and later researching and setting up daily live consumer reports for the Chicago 4:30 newscast. In April of 1983, I landed the associate-producer position with an award-winning documentarian at Chicago's CBS affiliate, producing documentaries from subjects as varied as Chicago's homeless women and children, to the Chicago Children's Choir and America's failing schools.

Dad was closing in on sixty-nine and Mom on nearly sixty-five when they finally agreed to unload two of their West Side properties. Mom felt our original home was easy to manage, but the troublesome six-flat and two-flat next door to it were to go.

I don't know if my parents consulted a real-estate agent or just went straight to Bethel New Life because they knew Pastor Nelson and his sister, but in June of 1983, Mom gathered the necessary figures to show to Mary. The six-flat was appraised at $30,000, which was $10,000 less than when my grandparents had given it to them in 1965. Bethel's model for acquiring property would pay my parents $15,000 cash for the building, and the remaining $15,000 would be taken as a tax deduction. A similar split was presented for the building next door. My parents' income was not great enough for the tax deduction to mean much of anything, but they agreed.

After eighteen years of an upslope battle, traveling ten miles round-trip to maintain the buildings against an onslaught of break-ins, rat and roach infestations, feral dogs, purse snatchings, and armed holdups, Mom and Dad finally were giving themselves a break. My parents signed the papers, and Bethel New Life brought in Habitat for Humanity to finish up whatever requirements were needed to meet federal housing standards.

Bethel Lutheran Church had been the social vortex of Dad's young life, its vibrancy in the 1920s emblematic of a community on the rise. Now, six decades later, the church was still a hub in West Garfield Park, but of a dramatically different community, one which Bethel New Life was striving to raise out of the ashes. Property had sustained the Gartz family on the West Side after my grandfather started in the janitorial business, providing financial security for his family. Now my parents' buildings, half the value of which they had donated, would create a future home for the newer residents. In a way, my father had been right; by believing for twenty years that WGP was still his community, he and Mom had nurtured a small part of it, passing on the product of their commitment to a new generation.

Meanwhile, Fireman's Fund insisted it was time for Dad to retire, and on February 2, 1984, the company threw a retirement party for him. Friends from Dad's youth, neighbors,

Dad at his retirement party; Mom and Linda looking on.

and all his buddies at FF gathered in a downtown Chicago hotel to roast and honor Dad. Smiling and grasping people's hands in both of his, greeting everyone with hearty hugs of happiness, Dad was in his glory. At an open mike, stories flowed, enveloping Dad in fond memories.

"This man came out at two in the morning to rescue me when my car died," said Esther, the woman who'd been at the dance where my parents met. "You could always call on him, night or day."

"Fred played Santa Claus every year at the Christmas party," said a thirty-something gal. "The girls sat on his lap, and he'd ask them mischievously if they'd been good. Then he always ended with, 'Good girls go to heaven. Bad girls go everywhere!'" The audience roared while Dad crunched up his shoulders, grinning in faux embarrassment.

A fortyish man, whom Dad had trained right out of college, recalled, "Fred could fit anything into his company car. He always had strands of rope, bungee cords, blankets stored in the trunk. Once he managed to fit five empty forty-gallon drums into that sedan: two in the trunk, one lashed to the roof, and two in the back seat, sticking out the windows."

Mom put aside her resentments and talked about Dad's warmth and friendliness to all, then added this romantic remembrance: "I remember one of our early dates," she reminisced, "when an older couple came up to us and said if they were young again, they would wish to be us for that night." She leaned over and kissed Dad on the cheek before sitting down.

That Christmas, my parents, Uncle Will, Bill, and I traveled to Seattle to spend the holiday with my brothers. In a family photo of the visit, the rest of us are beaming, while Mom manages a wan smile. Looking at the snapshot later at my parents' house, I was shocked by Dad's enormous girth. In person, his happy ebullience overshadowed his physical appearance. I said to him, "You know, Dad, you really need to lose some weight. I'm worried you're going to have a heart attack."

"I know, I know," he said, then grabbed his round belly, shook it, and laughed, "All bought and paid for!"

His doctor ordered him to shed thirty pounds. "Your cholesterol and blood pressure are sky-high," he told Dad, "and you have fat in your blood. You've already had an attack of angina. You've got to bring that weight down, or you're a ticking time bomb." Dad agreed, but changed nothing. Sure, he'd had to lie down when he'd felt some chest pain a few years earlier, but he wasn't a complainer. He carried on. There was work to be done (he still worked around the house) and fun to be had. Even after retirement, he kept to his previous routine, driving downtown to have coffee and sweet rolls or eggs and sausages with the same Fireman's Fund crowd he had joked and talked politics with for the previous fifteen years.

———

After two years of doing the work of a documentary producer at WBBM, but allowed only associate-producer credit, I quit my position there and pitched a production idea to Chicago's PBS station, WTTW, in anticipation of Vatican II's twentieth anniversary. The nuns with whom I'd worked at Catholic Television were among the smartest, most educated women I'd ever met, yet they were treated as second-class citizens by the all-male Roman Catholic hierarchy. My proposal stated that *Changing Habits* would be a documentary about the conflict between American nuns and the Vatican.

"This is fascinating," said the executive producer at WTTW, flipping through my treatment, which laid out the story line and issues. It was the same woman who had hired me to produce my first documentary at WLS-ABC.

She called me a couple days later. "We want you to do this show for us," she said. "The timing is perfect."

Thrilled at the opportunity, I dove into the research that September of 1985.

CHAPTER 46: Not of Our Choosing

I was planning my shooting schedule in my WTTW office, when the phone rang at five thirty on September 23, 1985. It was Mom. "Linda, something terrible has happened."

"What, Mom? What's happened?" My mind leaped from one family member to another.

"Dad collapsed outside of Fireman's Fund." Breathless, she ran her sentences together. "Lena found him on the sidewalk when she left work. She said he was incoherent but alert. An ambulance took him to Ravenswood Hospital. The nurse there said we should wait in the main lobby. Can you meet me there?"

"I'm coming right now." I left the research notes, calendars, and to-do lists strewn about my desk, grabbed my purse, and dashed through the station's now-empty hallways, bounding down the stairways into the still-light evening.

In the lobby of the hospital, I scanned the hunched forms and drawn faces of the sick and injured awaiting care, looking for my mother. Standing alone at converging hallways, her head bobbed left, then right, a go-to tic when stressed. I called out, "Mom!" and strode quickly to her side. I grabbed her hand, then hugged her. A babushka covered her flattened hair, and a grimace of concern darkened her face.

"Have you seen Dad yet? Is he okay?"

"I just checked at the desk. He's arriving soon."

"What happened?" I put my hand on her shoulder.

"Not sure." She shook her head. "Lena said she found him slumped against a light pole outside the Fund. She said his words were garbled." Mom shook her head again. "Oh, brother! Now what?" she exclaimed.

We scanned the hallways, too agitated to sit, watching, searching for Dad's arrival. The scene was familiar from movies: green-garbed figures carrying charts, pushing patients in wheelchairs and gurneys; doctors and nurses chatting urgently, power-walking and disappearing around the corners of shiny-floored hallways.

A gurney wheeled toward us, flanked by two doctors, an orderly, and a nurse. It took a moment for recognition to click in. It was Dad, an IV dripping into his arm. "Dad!" The gurney stopped, and I leaned over to kiss his forehead.

He was alert, looking from me to Mom, but when he opened his mouth to speak, only a strange series of moans and unintelligible sounds emerged. "Ah-oh, ah-oh, oh-oh-oh." He shook his head as if trying to dislodge an impediment, but the uncommon fear in his face distressed me most of all.

He reached out to touch my fingers with his left hand. Certain he had my attention, he lifted his right arm with his left, held it aloft a moment, then released it. The arm dropped heavily onto the bed—like a huge sausage. He repeated the movement two, three, four times, looking up at me or Mom after each fall with that question and terror in his eyes: *Why can't I control my arm?* But his voice said, "Oooh, ah, oh, oh, oh."

Holding his hand and stroking his thinning, gray-streaked hair, I kept repeating, "Don't worry, Dad. We're here now."

Leaning over him, Mom peered into his face, her brow pinched with worry. "Are you okay, Fred?" He shook his head.

A cold wave climbed from my contracted chest to my brain, where it sloshed around.

"We have to get him to X-ray and CAT scan," the gurney drivers said. "Then the doctors will call you in to discuss what they find."

Mom and I stood in a darkened room with the neurologist. The doctor flicked a switch, and a panel of flat screens lit up. *Ka-chunk. Ka-chunk. Ka-chunk.* One by one, he shoved X-rays of Dad's brain into place, then used a pointer to inscribe circles around part of the image. "The patient has suffered a cerebral infarction, a stroke, to his left brain. There was a blockage in one or more arteries supplying blood and oxygen to the brain, causing brain cells to die."

"Oh my God!" Mom yelled out, her fist raised to her mouth. Mom's face had taken on an eerie blue cast from the screen's glow.

"Will he get better?" I choked out.

"Well, we have him stabilized, and the odds for survival are good. He'll have to be hospitalized for several weeks. We'll feed him intravenously until he can learn to swallow again—that can take a while. The left side of the brain controls the right side of the body, so . . . his right side is paralyzed. He probably won't walk again, but with physical therapy, he may be able to stand with some help. Since language originates in the left side of the brain, it's unlikely he'll regain any speech—or even understand much of what others say."

"Will he be able to read or write?" I asked.

"I'm afraid not. Those are all language-based skills, and . . ." he paused and looked down for a beat, as if he hated to say more. "Basically, his left brain has been wiped out."

My heart went hollow. Not this. Not for my funny, storytelling, garrulous Dad, who lived for conversation and camaraderie! "How long before we know if he'll improve?"

"Whatever progress we see in six months is about the most you can expect." His eyes softened. "I'm sorry. I know this is bad news, but we'll just have to wait and see."

"I can't believe this!" Mom blurted out, shaking her head, her mouth turned down. Most people I knew used that phrase when anything bad happened—from a car accident to the phone company cutting off service by mistake. It was a first reactive response to the bitter reality of what had happened. Who could actually *believe* the truth of it, in all its horror! Paralyzed! Speechless! *No! No! No!* But it was true.

It's like when people get a cancer diagnosis. *What? I didn't think this would happen to ME!* Even if they lived a perfectly healthy life. Even if they smoked two packs a day and did everything wrong. "I can't believe this!"

Of course, Dad had received every possible warning sign—as if his future had been stalled on the tracks of a railroad crossing with flashing lights and clanging bells and the screeching, ever-louder whistle of the oncoming train, bearing down on him. He didn't get off the tracks.

We all had encouraged Dad to lose weight, Mom had set out his blood-pressure pills, but only *he* could have chosen to change his lifestyle. Still, did he "get what he deserved"? No. That's too harsh. His generation was simply not as attuned to taking the warning signs seriously. It wasn't lack of discipline. He had discipline in spades—when it came to work. Eating large amounts was ingrained in his childhood by parents who did heavy physical work twelve to fifteen hours a day: "Finish everything on your plate, or you don't leave the table. Have seconds—and finish those, too!" For more than twenty years, his day job had been sedentary.

Mom took my arm as we made our way to the elevator and rode up several floors to find Dad in the intensive-care unit.

Amid the hospital hum, the green blips, the tonal beeps, and the waves of medical technology, he lay under pale sheets and blankets, his head propped against two crisp, white pillows, his face drained of color. Plastic tubes snaked up his nose, and an IV bag hung from a metal frame next to his bed, dripping sustenance into his veins.

Without his smile and the sparkle in his eyes, Dad's face looked haggard, much older than seventy. His chest rose and fell rhythmically, the breathing of deep sleep. I stroked his head again and kissed his cheek. "Bye, Dad. I'll be back. You'll get better. You'll see." I still held some hope. Perhaps the doctors were too pessimistic. Surely *my* dad would be different. He might be the miracle patient.

"Bye, Fred." Mom pecked him on the cheek and took a glance back at him, shaking her head again before exiting.

Once in the lobby, I enfolded Mom in my arms, gave her a quick squeeze, and then released her. Emotional expression hadn't been the strong suit of our family, especially between Mom and me. "It doesn't sound good," I said. "Will you be all right tonight?"

"I'll be okay. But for heaven's sake! This is just terrible!"

"Horrible. I never even considered a stroke. I thought heart attack was the big risk." We stood silent a moment, both trying to hold ourselves together. I hugged her again and said, "I'll call you tomorrow then. Take care, Mom. Bye."

On my drive back to WTTW, tears flowed down my cheeks, and my knuckles blanched, clutching the steering wheel. "Not *my* dad! Not *my* dad," I howled into the void, but I knew—the universe just shrugged.

I thought about the future, about when Dad would go home. How would Mom treat Dad? Over the last few years, as they'd unloaded two stressful buildings, she'd lost some of her volatility, but she had been so angry with him for so long before that. Would she still be bitter and resentful? Would she dredge up the past, scream at him when he couldn't respond or escape? Would she dump him in a nursing home, saying, "I've had enough trouble with this man"?

I should have known better.

Loyalty. Responsibility. Duty. These values were carved deeply into Mom's character. With Dad's daily needs taken care of for now, she jumped right on the practical: following up on insurance and Medicare and making sure his expenses were covered. She and I talked often about a future strategy. Where would he sleep? He couldn't go up and down stairs, so he'd need a hospital bed. If he couldn't walk, he'd need a wheelchair. She'd look into all of that. We still hadn't met with the hospital social worker, who would have suggestions. We'd make an appointment with her.

In between frantic research, planning, and shooting my documentary, I visited Dad at the hospital several times a week, often meeting up with Mom there. For the first few days, he was asleep when we arrived, so we just sat next to him. I caressed his hand, spoke soothing nothings. "They're taking care of you, Dad. You'll be okay."

Mom smoothed his hair, saying "Poor, poor Fred"—her sentiment for sad outcomes.

After about a week, he was awake more often at our visits, able to sit up in bed. Both Mom and I tried to be cheery when entering his room, hoping to raise his spirits. "Hello, Fred," Mom would say, smiling.

"Hi, Dad!" His head reeled right, left, up—searching for the source of our greetings.

"Mom, Dad can't see us when we're on his paralyzed side. Let's sit on his left." After we moved, he gave us a tight-lipped semi-smile and a nod—about all he could muster—to let us know he approved of our seating choice.

Mom took his hand and spoke gently. "Are you comfortable, Fred?" We didn't know if he understood the actual words, but he nodded, probably hearing in her pleading tone that she wanted a positive response. Except for his resistance to Mom's demands, his nature was to be agreeable.

When we came during mealtime, we saw how Dad struggled to eat with his left hand, pushing the spoon into the food at awkward angles, dribbling applesauce across the tray and down his chin and chest. Mom wiped away the drips and adjusted a large napkin across his chest. We took turns spoon-feeding him, Mom saying, "You're swallowing better, Fred."

Sometimes after a meal, he worked to move his mouth, deliberately shaping his lips into an O. He strained with a mighty concentration to squeeze out whatever was on his mind, like someone trying to lift an impossibly heavy weight. Just insensible syllables emerged. Shaking his head, he closed his eyes and fell back against the pillow, tears trickling out the sides of his eyes. I blinked rapidly. "It'll be okay, Dad." I whispered this mantra over and over with false confidence. Mom shook her head, blotting Dad's tears with a napkin, her mouth in a set line. He forced out a weak smile, put on a brave face.

Dad's doctor arranged for his transfer to the Rehabilitation Institute of Chicago (RIC), one of the country's best at helping the brain-injured regain lost abilities—or learn to cope with the limitations that redefined their lives in an instant.

At RIC, if he wasn't in some kind of therapy when we came to visit, he was seated in his wheelchair in the large central waiting area. He was but one of dozens of wheelchair-bound patients scattered about, their faces washed in a sallow fluorescent glow. When Mom and I walked up to him, I put my face in front of his to be sure he saw me. Mom wasn't good at remembering this subtlety.

"Hi, Dad!" I smiled brightly and kissed him.

Mom patted his shoulder, but our attempts at cheer couldn't counter the horror of his disabilities, his severe losses apparent to him now that the initial insult to his brain was healing.

"Oh, ba-ba-ba-ba-ba," he cried out, sobs wracking his body, his shoulders heaving through unintelligible sounds.

I leaned over to embrace him, vainly trying not to cry at his despondency, muttering over and over, "It's okay. It's okay." I'd seldom seen Dad sad; he could always find a glint of silver within a gathering storm, but now he was bound in a gray shroud of despair. Rubbing his back, Mom stared into space, her inner thoughts visible in her scowl at the injustice of it all—just when she had begun to hope their lives would get easier.

Dad bit his knuckle to stop crying, but his loss was too great. Over and over, he shook his head, looking from Mom to me, repeating, "Ba-ba-ba-ba-ba?" in a tone of anguished questioning, as if to say, "How can this be?"

RIC's goal was to teach Dad strategies to help him function as well as possible, with the help of caregivers. But he would never again be *selbstständig*. Four weeks after his stroke, Mom and I went together to RIC to spend the day observing Dad's multiple therapy sessions. His physical therapist, an energetic and enthusiastic woman of about thirty dressed in green scrubs, introduced herself to us, then got right down to business. "Since he can't move his right side, we're going to work those muscles *for* him so they don't atrophy and curl up."

She looked Dad in the eye, telling him what she was about to do, then picked up Dad's right leg by the ankle, her other hand under his knee. She pressed his lower leg toward his chest. "Keep the knee in a straight line with the trunk," she instructed us, "and hold it here for thirty seconds while supporting his knee. Do this ten times on each leg."

Mom practiced, and then I took a turn. Dad's leg was heavier than I expected. Pushing, lifting, and supporting this dead weight would be a workout for sixty-eight-year-old Mom.

"These exercises should be done at least twice a day: in

Dad works with an occupational therapist, 1985.

the morning, in the evening, and, ideally, once more during the day," said the PT. That was ninety minutes a day *just* for the exercises. How would Mom handle all this alone?

Dad was assessed by a speech therapist. He suffered from aphasia, the inability to use or comprehend language in any form, even though his intellect and cognition were still intact. An occupational therapist worked with him daily to develop left-hand dexterity. Dad got the tooth-brushing down fairly well, but he missed his face with the razor and usually ran the comb through the air above his head.

On one of our visits, the physical therapist wheeled him to his session. Upon entering the cubicle where they would work, Dad caught his image in a full-length mirror, set up to help patients observe themselves doing the exercises. It was the first time he saw a full-body reflection of the new person he had become. He stared at himself with bitter recognition: an invalid in a wheelchair. His paralyzed right arm was strapped down with Velcro onto a flat board so it wouldn't flop at his side. A seat belt prevented him from falling out of the chair.

He was mute, dependent. He pressed his lips together and slowly shook his head back and forth.

After the first month in rehab, Dad was crying less and less frequently when Mom and I came to visit. His previously enthusiastic personality was beginning to show through after the dark days of sobbing and hopelessness. When we arrived, his eyes lit up, and he smiled broadly. "BA-BA-BA!" he exclaimed in greeting.

Heartened by Dad's efforts to be cheerful, Mom herself looked less haggard and glum. Her eyes shining, with a bright smile and tone as if she were springing a surprise, she said, "Would you like to come home soon, Fred?" gesturing out the door to indicate "away."

He picked up her cue. "Oh, ba-ba—BA-ba ba," he intoned with enthusiasm.

He took first Mom's hand and then mine, pressing one to each cheek. Mom said, "We want you home, *too*, Fred."

CHAPTER 47: Reconciliation

Dad hugs Mom, 1986.

Just before Christmas of 1985, a Medivan drove up to my parents' home, where Mom and I waited to greet Dad. As the automated lift lowered him to the sidewalk, he looked up at his house, dropped his chin to his chest, and shuddered with silent tears. Mom and I embraced him from both sides.

"Welcome home, Fred."

"Welcome home, Dad!"

Then I turned his chair around and *kalumpfed* it backward, step-by-step, up to the front door. Inside, just to the left of the entryway, a hospital bed and portable commode were awaiting him in the music room, where Dad used to feed rats to Lucifer. "Here's your new bedroom, Fred," said Mom, gesturing. He nodded, but his eyes registered a whisper of surprise—and resignation at his new space. Perhaps he'd wondered, without being able to use words, how he'd get up to his second-floor bedroom.

Shelley, Dad's home health-care worker, came every weekday from nine to two thirty. Wearing a turban and a friendly smile, he walked over to Dad's bed and touched my father's shoulder. "Hi, Fred. How are you today?"

"Oh, ba-ba-ba-ba-ba," Dad said, pressing his lips together, shrugging his one shoulder, his eyebrows raised slightly in an expression of "not bad." Whether he comprehended Shelley's exact words or not, he understood the rhythm of social interaction.

"Okay, let's get you going today." Shelley bantered as he worked with Dad. A sturdy metal triangle, called a "trapeze," hung from an L-shaped arm above the bed. Grasping the trapeze with his left hand, Dad pulled himself to a seated position with Shelley's help. Chattering away, Shelley washed and shaved Dad, and combed his hair. Dad joined the conversation with just the right "ba-ba-ba-ba" intonations and facial responses.

After he was dressed, we helped Dad transfer to his wheelchair. Starting from a seated position at the edge of his bed, Dad scooted himself, using his good left hand, across a long, polished board: from bed to wheelchair and back; from wheelchair to commode and back; and, for short trips, from wheelchair to car seat and back.

It took about an hour to prepare him for the day, after which Shelley wheeled him into the kitchen for breakfast. At every meal, Mom tucked a large dish towel into his shirt collar, draping it over his stomach, and placed another on his lap. He'd learned to feed himself with his left hand, but still, something usually spilled.

Shelley's help allowed Mom to run errands and get out for a bit. Before leaving, Shelley put Dad into bed for a nap, arranging the pillows to support Dad's paralyzed arm. After his nap, Mom took over with afternoon exercises, dinner, and getting Dad ready for bed.

On one weekend visit, I commented, "You know, Mom, you look quite a bit thinner."

"Really? I wonder why. I'm not dieting." It came to me. The forty-five or ninety minutes of exercises she performed for Dad each day (morning exercises were performed by the caregiver Monday through Friday) were getting her into shape, too.

Mom seemed oddly content. The perpetual scowl was gone, and she was no longer prone to angry outbursts. Bustling from room to room, she still managed our former West Side home, kept track of the finances, and arranged for workmen as needed; but an inner peace, rather than crackling resentment, now accompanied her efficiency. After arranging for power of attorney, she gained access to the stock portfolio Dad inherited after his parents' deaths eight years earlier. He hadn't wanted her involved with it out of misplaced pride, but he had neither the interest in nor the aptitude for boring financial details. Multiple uncashed dividend checks, some over a year old, were stashed in his desk drawer. Mom took charge of the stocks, studied the market, read *Kiplinger's* financial newsletter, and talked with Bill and me about investment strategies. "I'm getting everything in order," she told me, proudly showing off her impeccably neat financial records.

Every garbage day, Mom set out aside piles of Dad's collected junk, but she waited until just before pickup to bring it to the curb, so he wouldn't see it. Otherwise, he pointed out the window, wagging his finger up and down at the heap of boards, boxes, ropes, and rickety cabinets, exclaiming in an agitated cavil, "BA-BA-BA-BA!"

Mom mollified him. "Okay, Fred, I'll bring it back," she said, then made a big show of taking a few pieces from the curb to the side of the house, throwing it all out at her next chance when he wasn't looking. "We have more garbage out there every week than anyone else on the block," she often told me in satisfied tones during my weekend visits. "I'm finally getting ahead."

Mom had seamlessly incorporated Dad's care into her

other duties. She doled out his medication, arranged for doctor and physical therapist home visits, monitored his blood pressure and recorded it on a graph, which Dad could understand because it was an image (right brain), not words (left brain). Showing him the chart, Mom would clap him gently on the back when he had improved numbers, saying, "Look, Fred! Good job with your blood pressure!" He smiled, making appropriate sounds of approval, and she gave him a quick peck on the cheek.

I'm not sure Mom even recognized her change from whirling fury to doting caregiver, but it turned my mind to ponder the transformation. With Dad's freewheeling ways behind him, she was no longer sidelined by frustration and bitter grievances. She could make all the financial and household decisions without Dad stubbornly thwarting her plans. The man with whom she'd fallen so wildly in love more than four decades earlier was beside her again.

As with my grandmother's death eight years earlier, when my heart broke at Grandpa Gartz's sobbing grief, I was still learning about marriage's mysterious bargain—how two people, so seemingly at odds with one another, could reunite in the most unexpected circumstances. The embers of my parents' once-great love, long buried under a landslide of careless deeds and words, had reignited, not as the flame of early passion, but as the contented glow of devotion.

My parents' letters and diaries had come to me like messages in a bottle, bobbing across a sea of time, their words transporting me on a telepathic journey—into their minds and hearts. Despite their missteps, I learned how so much of what they did turned out right. Their example of perseverance, work ethic, commitment, responsibility, *selbstständigkeit*, and devotion to duty was passed on to their children, allowing us to thrive in a very different world. Their emphasis on education encouraged all three of us to earn graduate degrees and inspired us to love learning. Their good hearts overcame previous prejudices as they continued their work and committed their full devotion to the tenants in our riot-torn neighborhood, despite the dangers to themselves.

On weekends, I often visited as Mom took Dad through his morning routine, chattering away, finishing by patting and smoothing into place a few errant strands of his hair with her hand. "Do you want to see how nice you look?" she asked, as she reached for a nearby mirror to hold in front of his face.

Dad mugged at his reflection. "Ooh, aah," he intoned, lifting his chin, closing his eyes, and simultaneously raising his eyebrows, smiling in mock self-pride. We all cracked up. So much of Dad's humor still shone through his expressive face and tone.

Dad didn't cry anymore, except over a sentimental movie or a tragic event, like when the Space Shuttle Challenger blew up in 1986. He often took Mom's hand, and, closing his eyes, held it for a long time against his cheek. He turned it over and gave the back a tender kiss. She stroked his cheek and his hair, then kissed the top of his head and bent over to kiss his lips. She put an arm around his shoulder. He lifted his face to hers, and they smiled into each other's eyes.

Mom hugs Dad, 1987.

NOTES

Page xxiv
1. "The Cost of Segregation," *Metropolitan Planning Council,* https://www.metroplanning.org/costofsegregation/default.aspx.

Page 7
2. Amanda I. Seligman, *Block by Block: Neighborhoods and Public Policy on Chicago's West Side* (Chicago: University of Chicago Press, 2005), 23.

Page 8
3. "Janitor for Forty Years Retires," *Garfieldian*, Aug. 4, 1954. Note: $20,000 in 1929 had the same buying power as $282,376.61 in 2017. Annual inflation over this period was about 3.05 percent. http://www.dollartimes.com/inflation/inflation.php?amount=20000&year=1929

Page 19
4. $.45 in 1932 was the equivalent of about $7.44 in 2017. http://www.dollartimes.com/inflation/inflation.php?amount=1&year=1932

Page 23
5. To see an example of the code my father used, go to http://www.wikihow.com/Create-Secret-Codes-and-Ciphers, #5.

Page 39
6. Albert Q. Maisel, "Bedlam 1946," *Life*, May 6, 1946.

Page 45
7. Isabel Wilkerson, *The Warmth of Other Suns: The Epic Story of America's Great Migration* (New York: Vintage Books, 2011), 376.

8. *1960 Fact Book; 1980 Fact Book;* Department of Development and Planning, City of Chicago, *Chicago Statistical Abstract, Part I: 1970 Census, Community Area Summary Tables* (July 1973) (hereafter *Chicago Statistical Abstract*). Table created from data is in Amanda I. Seligman, *Block by Block: Neighborhoods and Public Policy on Chicago's West Side* (Chicago: University of Chicago Press, 2005), 31.

9. Stephen Grant Meyer, *As Long As They Don't Move Next Door: Segregation and Racial Conflict in American Neighborhoods* (Lanham, MD: Rowman & Littlefield, 2001), 120.

Page 46
10. Isabel Wilkerson, *The Warmth of Other Suns: The Epic Story of America's Great Migration* (New York: Vintage Books, 2011), 376.

11. Kenneth T. Jackson, *Crabgrass Frontier: The Suburbanization of the United States* (Oxford, UK: Oxford University Press, 1987), 196-218: "[B]lack neighborhoods were invariably rated as fourth grade. . . . " Note: Redlining is a much more complicated subject than can be entertained in a bio-memoir such as this. The bottom line, as expressed in several studies, is that when blacks moved into a community, the area was redlined, making it difficult—if not impossible—for whites or blacks to obtain mortgages in the redlined area. That in turn created economic incentives for whites to keep blacks out.

12. Beryl Satter, *Family Properties: Race, Real Estate, and the Exploitation of Black Urban America* (New York: Metropolitan Books, 2010), 42.

13. Ibid.

Page 47
14. Stephen Grant Meyer, *As Long As They Don't Move Next Door: Segregation and Racial Conflict in American Neighborhoods* (Lanham, MD: Rowman & Littlefield, 2001), 8.

15. Arnold R. Hirsch, *Making the Second Ghetto: Race and Housing in Chicago, 1940–1960* (Chicago: University of Chicago Press, 1983, 1998), Table 1: "The Black Population of Chicago, 1890–1960" (U.S. Census Reports), 17.

Page 51
16. Martin Luther King, Jr., "Letter from Birmingham Jail," April 16, 1963, http://okra.stanford.edu/transcription/document_images/undecided/630416-019.pdf.

Page 53
17. Amanda I. Seligman, *Block by Block: Neighborhoods and Public Policy on Chicago's West Side* (Chicago: University of Chicago Press, 2005), 170.

Page 54
18. Ibid., 35. Per the U.S. Census Bureau, Chicago had 320,372 more blacks in 1960 than in 1950.

19. Ibid., 39.

20. Ibid., 39–40.

Page 55
21. Ibid., 129.

22. Amanda I. Seligman, *Block by Block: Neighborhoods and Public Policy on Chicago's West Side* (Chicago: University of Chicago Press, 2005), Table 5: "U.S. Census, 1960," 35.

23. Ibid.

Page 57
24. Michael T. Maly and Heather M. Dalmage, *Vanishing Eden: White Construction of Memory, Meaning, and Identity in a Racially Changing City* (Philadelphia: Temple University Press, 2016), 14-15.

Page 63
25. Claude Sitton, "Alabama Admits Negro Students; Wallace Bows to Federal Force," in *Reporting Civil Rights, Part One: American Journalism 1941–1963* (London: Penguin, 2003), 827. First published in the *New York Times*, June 12, 1963.

26. "This Day in History: JFK Faces Down Defiant Governor," *History*, http://www.history.com/this-day-in-history/jfk-faces-down-defiant-governor.

27. Claude Sitton, "N.A.A.C.P. Leader Slain in Jackson; Protests Mount," in *Reporting Civil Rights, Part One: American Journalism 1941–1963* (London: Penguin, 2003), 835. First published in the *New York Times*, June 13, 1963.

Page 64
28. "Byron De La Beckwith," *Biography*, http://www.biography.com/people/byron-de-la-beckwith-21442573#conviction-and-death.

Page 65

29. "Homeowner," letter to the editor, *Garfieldian*, May 18, 1966. Quoted in Amanda I. Seligman, *Block by Block: Neighborhoods and Public Policy on Chicago's West Side* (Chicago: University of Chicago Press, 2005), 2.

Page 100

30. Amanda I. Seligman, *Block by Block: Neighborhoods and Public Policy on Chicago's West Side* (Chicago: University of Chicago Press, 2005), Table 3: "North Lawndale Population," 34.

31. "Mapping Inequality: Redlining in New Deal America," *Digital Scholarship Lab* (University of Richmond), https://dsl.richmond.edu/panorama/redlining/#loc=4/36.71/-96.93&opacity=0.8.

Page 101

32. Beryl Satter, *Family Properties: Race, Real Estate, and the Exploitation of Black Urban America* (New York: Metropolitan Books, 2010), 96.

33. Ibid., 97.

34. Michael T. Maly and Heather M. Dalmage, *Vanishing Eden: White Construction of Memory, Meaning, and Identity in a Racially Changing City* (Philadelphia: Temple University Press, 2016), 14.

Page 102

35. Laura Shin, "The Racial Wealth Gap: Why a Typical White Household Has 16 Times the Wealth of a Black One," *Forbes,* March 26, 2015, https://www.forbes.com/sites/laurashin/2015/03/26/the-racial-wealth-gap-why-a-typical-white-household-has-16-times-the-wealth-of-a-black-one/. Note: As Shin explains, "The typical black household now

has just 6% of the wealth of the typical white household; the typical Latino household has just 8%, according to a recent study called "The Racial Wealth Gap: Why Policy Matters," by Demos, a public policy organization. . . . The racial wealth gap means families of color may not be able to give young members of their households gifts to invest in their future, similar to what their white friends are likely to receive."

Page 131
36. Derek Gee and Ralph Lopez, *Laugh Your Troubles Away: The Complete History of Riverview Park, Chicago, Illinois* (Chicago: Sharpshooters Productions, 2000), 145.

Page 134
37. Stephen Grant Meyer, *As Long As They Don't Move Next Door: Segregation and Racial Conflict in American Neighborhoods* (Lanham, MD: Rowman & Littlefield, 2001), 117–18.

Page 138
38. Martin Luther King, Jr., "I Have a Dream" (speech, Washington, DC, August 28, 1963), *American Rhetoric*, http://www.americanrhetoric.com/speeches/mlkihaveadream.htm.

Page 166
39. The black population in Los Angeles increased from about 63,700 in 1940 to about 350,000 in 1965. See "The Great Migration: Creating a New Black Identity in Los Angeles," *KCET*, https://www.kcet.org/history-society/the-great-migration-creating-a-new-black-identity-in-los-angeles.

Page 167
40. Sheila Radford-Hill, phone conversation with author, April 22, 2015.

Page 168
41. "In Chicago, Scores Hurt in Riot," *Chicago Daily News,* August 14, 1965.

42. Ibid.

Page 169
43. Burleigh Hines, "Hysterical Hate on the West Side," *Chicago Daily News,* August 14, 1965.

Page 170
44. Edmond J. Rooney, "A Night of Shame on Pulaski Road," *Chicago Daily News,* August 14, 1965.

Page 204
45. Notes Amanda I. Seligman, "Everyone remembers this wrongly because Mike Royko [a *Chicago Daily News* newspaper columnist in 1968] narrated it falsely. The shoot-to-kill order was not made public until about a week after the riots. I looked through the microfilm and discovered the discrepancy." Amanda Seligman, electronic communication with author, December 27, 2016.

46. Quotes from Barbara Lilly are from a phone conversation with the author, January 24, 2006.

47. "West Madison Street, 1968," *Encyclopedia of Chicago,* http://www.encyclopedia.chicagohistory.org/pages/6354.html.

Page 206
48. Charla Wilson, Archivist for the Black Experience, Northwestern University Libraries, Northwestern University, Evanston, Il. Email September 21, 2017. "According to the 'Northwestern University Responses to the Black Student Petition, April 22, 1968,' 5 black students entered in 1965; 54 entered in 1966; and approximately 100 applicants in 1968."

Northwestern University Responses to the Black Student Petition, April 22, 1968, Box 1, folder 3, Records of the 1968 Black Student Sit-In, Series 31/6/155, Northwestern University Archives, Evanston Il.

49. Black Student Statement and Petition to Northwestern University Administrations, April 22, 1968, Box 1, folder 3, Records of the 1968 Black Student Sit-In, Series 31/6/155, Northwestern University Archives, Evanston, Il.

Page 207
50. Northwestern University Responses to the Black Student Petition, April 22, 1968, Box 1, folder 3, Records of the 1968 Black Student Sit-In, Series 31/6/155, Northwestern University Archives, Evanston Il.

Policy Statement, Box 1, folder 3, Records of the 1968 Black Student Sit-In, Series 31/6/155, Northwestern University Archives, Evanston, Il.

51. Barbara Lilly, phone conversation with author, January 24, 2006.

Page 209
52. Frank Kusch, *Battleground Chicago: The Police and the 1968 Democratic National Convention* (Chicago: University of Chicago Press, 2004), p 53.

Page 238
53. "Marriages and Divorces, 1900–2012," *Infoplease*, https://www.infoplease.com/us/marital-status/marriages-and-divorces-1900a2012. Note: Within five years (1975), the divorce rate increased to almost 50 percent.

Page 261
54. "Son of Sharecropper: Dope Dealer Reaps Riches," *Chicago Tribune*, February 25, 1974.

Photo Credits

"Fig. 1: Chicago community areas," "Fig. 2: West Side community areas," "Figs. 3a, 3b, 3c, 3d: Racial composition of the West Side 1940–1970," and "Fig. 4: West Side schools" produced by the University of Wisconsin–Milwaukee, Cartography & GIS Center. © The Board of Regents of the University of Wisconsin System. Reprinted by permission.

"A Negro Family Just Arrived in Chicago from the Rural South" is reprinted from Chicago Commission on Race Relations, *The Negro in Chicago: A Study of Race Relations and a Race Riot* (Chicago: University of Chicago Press, 1922), facing p. 92.

ACT leaflet is reprinted from *Chicago Daily News*, "In Chicago, Scores Hurt in Riot," August 14, 1965, p. 4. Best attempts were made to find the creator of this leaflet.

"Outside NU Bursar's office, May 3,1968, with white sympathizers." Photo by James Sweet. Reprinted from the James S. Sweet Collection, Northwestern University Archives.

"Dunk tank at Riverview Amusement Park, date unknown" is reprinted from Living History of Illinois and Chicago, "Removal of the 'African Dip' dunk tank game from Riverview Amusement Park in Chicago, Illinois," livinghistoryofillinois.com.

"Dunk Tank, Riverview Park, circa 1921" is supplied courtesy of Sharpshooters Productions, Inc., printed from the original negative for use in *Laugh Your Troubles Away: The Complete History of Riverview Park* by Derek Gee and Ralph Lopez (Chicago: Sharpshooters Productions, Inc. 2000).

"West Side destruction after riots, April 1968." Photograph by Jo Freeman, www.jofreeman.com. Reprinted by permission.

Acknowledgments

Thank you to my parents and grandparents for the precious gift of their lives and thoughts, recorded in letters, diaries, photos, slides, films, audio tape, notes—so much more than can be listed here. Incredibly, they lovingly saved, labeled, and organized these thousands of family-history treasures, creating an archival collection that spans the twentieth century. The clarity and honesty of their writing put me into their hearts and minds and made visceral for me their emotions, traumas, sorrows, and happiness–just as they experienced them–in real time.

Thank you, thank you to my husband, Bill. For fifteen years, he's listened patiently to my dismay or thrill over discoveries in the archives. He's cooked dinner for years and has tolerated twenty-five boxes of family history stored in our garage and spilling over into an entire room of our house. I was a mere sixteen when we met, and I've never doubted his total love and devotion to me. I'm one lucky gal.

Thank you to the many editors without whom *Redlined* would never have been published; to Sharon DeBartolo Carmack, family-history maven, author, and genealogist, who first helped me to see a bigger picture and delve into deeper meaning; to Anjali Sachdeva, my mentor at Creative Non-fiction, who read my 135,000-word tome and, with wise

314 REDLINED

counsel and a firm grasp of story, led me to cut the chaff and uncover the kernel of my story and fine-tune the writing. I also owe gratitude to authors, writing instructors, and my neighbors, Sharon and Steve Fiffer, whose valuable advice helped move my story forward. Thanks to my She Writes Press editor, Annie Tucker, who took my almost-final manuscript to the next level.

Thanks to my beta readers. A special shout-out to Adrienne Lieberman, a reader extraordinaire, who placed scores of sticky notes throughout an earlier manuscript draft, noting everything from word choice and grammar tweaks to suggested cuts. She then graciously reviewed yet another draft.

Thank you to Susan Beck, who read an early manuscript and shared not only her takeaway from the story but also brought her keen sense of persuasive language to bear on my core message, title, and website. Another thank you to Susan and to dedicated teacher, Vikki Proctor, for working together with me to create questions for book groups and book clubs. We hope they enrich all readers' experiences.

Mary Nelson, founder and first president of Bethel New Life, which grew out of the Gartz family's church in West Garfield Park, was generous with her memories of our community, where she has served the neighborhood since 1965. My thanks also for putting me in touch with many longtime West Side residents, who shared their experiences with me for the book.

Dr. Josh Akin spontaneously responded to my description of the book with, "Redlined! That would be a great title." Yes, it is. Thank you!

The most consistent supporters and readers of my manuscript as it stumbled along for more than ten years were the members of my writing critique group, The Writers of Glencoe, Il. Their combined talent is immense. A special mention to those moderators at The Writers who so improved my craft and whose relentless enthusiasm and encouragement kept me going. A thousand thanks to Fred Shafer for his years of detailed notes, and to Sharon Solwitz and Anne Calcagno for their wise insight.

A big thank-you to the extraordinary and indefatigable Brooke Warner, publisher and founder of She Writes Press, for recognizing my book as both an important personal as well as historical story that needed to be told. I appreciate the opportunity to be published with a dynamic press and work with team members at the highest level of professionalism.

I'm forever indebted to Amanda I. Seligman, chair of the Department of History at the University of Wisconsin–Milwaukee, for her book *Block by Block: Neighborhoods and Public Policy on Chicago's West Side.* Who could have dreamed that an urban historian would write her PhD thesis on my former neighborhood? She generously agreed to read my manuscript for accuracy and has continued to offer a historian's insights throughout the process of publication.

To the dozens of wonderful memoirists, too numerous to mention, whose books inspired me with their honesty and taught me about good and truthful writing, I am thankful.

Finally, I'm grateful to Chicago's Newberry Library for its enthusiastic acceptance of the Gartz Family Papers as a donation to its Midwest Manuscripts Collection, where future researchers will find a history of twentieth-century life in Chicago as experienced through the lives of ordinary people who did extraordinary things.

About the Author

Linda Gartz is an author, television documentary producer, and curator of the Gartz Family Papers, an extensive collection of letters, diaries, photos, and much more spanning the twentieth century. Born and raised on Chicago's West Side, she studied at both Northwestern University and the University of Munich. She earned her BA and MAT degrees from Northwestern. Her documentary work has been honored with six Emmys, multiple film festival awards, and other awards. Her productions have been featured on ABC, NBC, CBS, PBS, and Investigation Discovery, syndicated nationwide. Go to www.LindaGartz.com to learn more. She is married and is the proud mom of two wonderful young men.

Author photo © Brian McConkey

Selected Titles from She Writes Press

She Writes Press is an independent publishing company founded to serve women writers everywhere. Visit us at www.shewritespress.com.

The Outskirts of Hope: A Memoir by Jo Ivester. $16.95, 978-1-63152-964-1. A moving, inspirational memoir about how living and working in an all-black town during the height of the civil rights movement profoundly affected the author's entire family—and how they in turn impacted the community.

The Beauty of What Remains: Family Lost, Family Found by Susan Johnson Hadler. $16.95, 978-1-63152-007-5. Susan Johnson Hadler goes on a quest to find out who the missing people in her family were—and what happened to them—and succeeds in reuniting a family shattered for four generations.

The Butterfly Groove: A Mother's Mystery, A Daughter's Journey by Jessica Barraco. $16.95, 978-1-63152-800-2. In an attempt to solve the mystery of her deceased mother's life, Jessica Barraco retraces the older woman's steps nearly forty years earlier—and finds herself along the way.

Times They Were A-Changing: Women Remember the '60s & '70s edited by Kate Farrell, Amber Lea Starfire, and Linda Joy Myers. $16.95, 978-1-938314-04-9. Forty-eight powerful stories and poems detailing the breakthrough moments experienced by women during the '60s and '70s.

All the Ghosts Dance Free: A Memoir by Terry Cameron Baldwin. $16.95, 978-1-63152-822-4. A poetic memoir that explores the legacy of alcoholism and teen suicide in one woman's life—and her efforts to create an authentic existence in the face of that legacy.

Uncovered: How I Left Hassidic Life and Finally Came Home by Leah Lax. $16.95, 978-1-63152-995-5. Drawn in their offers of refuge from her troubled family and promises of eternal love, Leah Lax becomes a Hassidic Jew—but ultimately, as a forty-something woman, comes to reject everything she has lived for three decades in order to be who she truly is.